AIR ACES

CHRISTOPHER SHORES

PRESIDIO PRESS

Published in the United States by
Presidio Press
31 Pamaron Way
Novato, CA 94947

Produced by
Bison Books Corp.
17 Sherwood Place
Greenwich, CT 06830
U.S.A.

ISBN 0-89141-166-6

Printed in Hong Kong

Wir gratulieren
zum
250.
Luftsieg.

CONTENTS

INTRODUCTION

The term 'Fighter Ace' is well-known to a wide and general public, but precisely what it means is of much more limited knowledge. A fighter ace is a pilot who has shot down five or more opponents in aerial combat — the term originated in France quite early in World War I, and proved of immediate attraction to a public hungry for heroes in the faceless, gray mass war being waged in the trenches. To different nations it came to mean different things, and in different air forces the requirements for becoming an ace differed. The concept was taken up or not by officialdom, depending largely on the national attitudes of the force concerned.

The Germans were quick to seize upon the morale and publicity advantages of the high-scoring fighter pilot, having incorporated in their system a firm place for the outstanding individual. Thus in both wars the German authorities were to expend much time and effort in investigating and verifying each claim in detail — a task much easier during 1914–18, when nearly all fighting occurred over their own lines, than during 1939–45. To become an *Experte* in the German air forces a pilot had to achieve 10, rather than five victories — and there were no shared victories. If more than one pilot participated in the destruction of a hostile aircraft, it was either credited to the pilot mainly responsible, or — where all were equally responsible — credited to the unit only, no individual including it in his score.

During World War I the Allied nations adopted a system whereby each shared victory was credited to the unit as one, but each individual involved added one to his score — even in cases where five or six pilots jointly obtained the kill. Thus the individual scores of the pilots in a unit would almost certainly amalgamate to a substantially higher number than the unit total. The French, Americans, Belgians and Italians adopted the concept of the ace at least semiofficially, but the British — ever keen to extol the virtues of the team and to play down the individual (officially at least) — refused to do so. They were however ready enough to give details of scores in decoration citations, and to a large extent decorations were awarded for prowess in combat which was of course represented by substantial scores! The detail with which a pilot's score was recorded and monitored depended to a large extent on the attitude of the unit commanding officer — particularly during World War I. Thus in World War I the French paid a degree of attention comparable to the Germans in checking and verifying victory claims, and only those confirmed — by wreckage found, or by independent witnesses on the ground — were included in scores, although shares were treated as whole victories. Other claims — probables — were not included. British scores were also assessed with shares treated as whole numbers, but scores included two categories of victory — 'destroyed' and 'out of control.' The latter would have been treated as 'probables' at best in the French Air Service, and not included. Early in the days of air fighting, when the British media was desperate for heroes to set against the Immelmanns and Boelckes of the 'Fokker Scourge,' victories were included which were no more than moral ones — 'driven down' or 'forced to land.' Few aircraft were destroyed on the ground during World War I, but those that were usually included in the score — as were tanks destroyed! More common kills were static observations balloons, which made up a large proportion of many pilots' scores.

Americans flying with the British or French had their scores assessed on the basis of the air force with which they were flying. When their own USAS units arrived, the French system was adopted — except for the two squadrons which operated under British control! The Belgians, Italians and Russians generally adhered to the French system, the Austro-Hungarians to that employed by the Germans. Many victories were obtained by two-seater aircraft — reconnaissance aircraft, fighting scouts and bombers. In the cases where the gunner was responsible for the victory, one was also added to the pilot's score as well as the gunner's; where the pilot scored with the front guns, only the pilot received the credit.

Many changes occurred during World War II. The British — still officially denying the concept of the ace, and refusing even to confirm victories (only 'claims' were confirmed) — treated their 'out of control' category as 'probables,' and no longer included them in the score, while the French took the opposite route, and now frequently included probables in a pilot's total! The French continued to treat the shared victory as a whole — whether confirmed or probable. It has long been believed that the British adopted a system of fractions for shared victories, amalgamating these mathematically; consequently the scores of lesser-known pilots have for some time been assessed on this basis. However after much research it has become evident that many of the scores announced for well-known pilots included shared victories treated as whole numbers. Certainly on their entry into World War II the Americans adopted this system at first, but from 1944 onward they treated shares as fractions — later decimals — and amalgamated. Thus a pilot claiming one individual victory, four shared with one other pilot on each occasion, and two shared with three others would have a score of $3\frac{1}{2}$ — or 3.5. In the French Armée de l'Air his score would be 7; in the Luftwaffe, unless it could be shown that he was the pilot mainly responsible for each victory, his score could well be as low as one, while in the RAF it could be anywhere from $3\frac{1}{2}$ to 7 depending on who had worked it out!

Italy decided in World War II that individual scores were undesirable, and no official check was kept. Details of pilots responsible for victories were noted in the records however, and in personal logbooks, so that totals became available. A large number of Italian victories were participative efforts however, and many totals for Italian pilots are believed to include shares treated as full numbers, although in other cases shares are given as a separate total – for instance, 6 destroyed and 14 shared. The Russians used a similar system, but again the scores frequently include the shares as whole numbers. The Japanese were so determined not to glorify individuals that, when they discovered that totals were being seized upon by the press, the names of claiming pilots were deleted even from official unit records. Information on Japanese pilots comes mainly from private sources, diaries and memories, and the scores frequently include an amalgam of individual, shared and probable claims – particularly in the Pacific War of 1941–45.

In this book each country is dealt with using the yardstick adopted by it at the time, though in each case this yardstick is made clear. Thus it is by no means easy to compare the results achieved by the pilots of one air force with those of another. In both wars the Germans kept the most exact count, along with the Americans in World War II. What of accuracy? This varied enormously, but as a rule of thumb it may be assumed that the larger the numbers involved, the greater the degree of overclaiming. In general, two actual losses for three claims was a good average, but in big fighter versus fighter battles the ratio would rise to one loss to two claims, or even worse. Accuracy of claims must always rely to some extent on the character and nature of the pilot. A steady, experienced, professional pilot would usually claim more accurately than a mercurial, excitable one, who would tend to be more optimistic of the results he had achieved. Frequently a pilot would claim accurately until he had built up a fairly big score, then tend to overclaim due to a growing belief in his own infallibility – and because of his earlier record he would tend to be more readily believed. Of course there were some charlatans who deliberately inflated their claims to obtain decorations and glory, but they were usually found out, and are believed to be much in the minority, most pilots making their claims in the very best of good faith.

Experience has shown that in general terms the Germans, Finns, Hungarians and French (confirmed victories) tended to be very accurate. While the Americans tended to make wild claims on occasions early in the war, once the majority of their aircraft were fitted with camera guns, claims became very accurate – though it remained difficult to assess which victories were shared. British pilots in general showed a distinct inclination to overassess results, and this was not improved by the lack of official investigation into claims, which could have rendered confirmations much more accurate.

Japanese and Russian claims seem generally to have been somewhat less accurate than those of the British, while in the majority of cases it has to be said – with some sadness by one who is deeply fond of Italy and the Italians – that Regia Aeronautica claims bore very little resemblance to the reality of the situation.

There were some odd situations. It has always been difficult to decide how to treat the radar operators in night fighters, whose input was vital to each success. The Americans treated them as aces in their own right, crediting each with the same victories credited to the pilots. In the Vietnam War this policy was extended to the Weapons Systems Operators in the rear seats of the Phantoms. In this work however it has been decided to limit the concept of the fighter ace to the pilot only – with a single exception. In line with the gunners in the fighting scouts during World War I, some mention is made of the turret gunners in the ill-fated two-seat Defiant turret fighters used in 1940/41. The claims of bomber gunners, while made in good faith, have been shown since the war to be inflated by multiple claiming by dozens of gunners in a formation to such an extent as to be quite unrealistic; they are not considered here.

Finally, many will ask – as they always do – why the scores of the German (and Finnish) pilots were so very much higher than those of the Allies in World War II? This is a subject which the cognoscenti have thrashed to death for years, but the situations and circumstances which led to these huge victory totals are explained here in some detail. Let this author state categorically that, after some 20 years' research into fighter pilots and fighter aviation, he is totally convinced that the majority of German and Finnish claims were well-founded, and frequently were *more* accurate than those of the air forces they opposed.

A book of this length can be no more than an introduction to this vast subject. A small bibliography of recommended additional reading is given at the rear, but if the reader's interest is kindled to dig further into this fascinating subject, it will have achieved its purpose. To indicate the size and breadth of the field of study, during World War II over 1000 British Commonwealth pilots, more than 1200 Americans, probably 2000 Russians and at the very least 4000 Germans were credited with five or more victories in the air, and thus became aces as the term is understood here. These men probably claimed well over 50 percent of all the victories credited to their respective air forces – they were truly the cutting edge.

1. WORLD WAR 1
The Flying Circus

When war broke out in August 1914 some initial thought had already been given to the prospect of combat between aircraft, but the low performance of the machines available at the time made the carrying of a machine gun relatively pointless, since the additional weight rendered the aircraft incapable of climbing to the altitude of, or catching any likely opponent. This is not to say that experiments had not already taken place, but application would have to await the greater engine power that swift development, fuelled by the demands of war, would soon bring. At first most military authorities saw the job of the aircraft as being mainly reconnaissance. Any offensive action was considered of peripheral interest, and definitely secondary to the main role.

During the early days of the war pilots frequently passed their opponents with no more than a wave of the hand, but it was soon clear that to disrupt the opponent's reconnaissance activity was a need of war. Coupled with the high-spirited aggressiveness of young servicemen and their ingenuity – and that of their mechanics on the ground – it was not long before pilots and observers on both sides were attacking each other with rifles, revolvers, carbines and handfuls of small steel darts (flechettes), while the darts, grenades and locally-made small bombs were delivered by hand against any likely ground targets. As soon as more-powerful engines became available, flexible machine-gun mounts were fitted for use by observers both in defense and offense. Initially these could be carried only by two-seaters, as the problems of firing through the moving disk of the propeller required that they be fired only to the rear and sides of normal tractor aircraft (those with the propeller at the front).

Both sides had shot down opposing machines using these armed two-seaters by early 1915, but still they were not fighters in the accepted sense. However both French and British pilots were experimenting with ideas to allow the fitting of fixed, forward-firing machine guns to fast single-seat scout aircraft which could be employed primarily for offensive use against hostile reconnaissance and bombing machines. One of the most aggressive French units at this time was Escadrille MS 23, which was equipped with two seater Morane Type 'L' parasol monoplanes and single-seat, mid-wing Type 'N's. The former were armed with one or two Lewis

Above left: Roland Garros, the first true fighter pilot.
Left: One of the first two aces of the war was Sgt Eugene Gilbert of Esc MS 49, who was credited with five victories before having to force-land in Switzerland in June 1915.
Above: Maj Lanoe Hawker, VC, the first ace of the RFC.

machine-guns for the observer, and flying these one victory had been claimed by Sgt Eugene Gilbert and his observer on 10 January 1915, and one by Cpl Jean Navarre and his observer on 1 April. Efforts were being made to fit one of the Type 'L's with a forward-firing Hotchkiss gun; wedge-shaped metal deflector plates were fitted to the rear sides of the propeller blades to allow fire through the disk. This was a far from ideal solution, as it could easily damage the balance of the propeller, causing severe vibration or even the loss of the blades. However, flying the first armed Type 'L', Lt Roland Garros claimed the first true 'fighter' victory of the war on 1 April 1915. During the next two weeks he was to claim two more aircraft shot down, one out of control and two forced to land. While this would have given him six victories with the Royal Flying Corps, under the more stringent rules of the French Air Service, only the three shot down were confirmed. On 19 April he suffered an engine failure over German-held territory and was obliged to land. He attempted to destroy his aircraft by fire, but was captured.

The German authorities were most interested in the aircraft which had been shooting down their reconnaissance machines, and handed the wreckage to Anthony Fokker with a request that he copy the device. Fokker's chief engineer recalled a design for an interrupter gear that had been patented before the war, and working on this principle swiftly developed a mechanical gear which caused the gun to cease firing when a propeller blade was in the line of sight. Fokker's own E.I monoplane was a suitable single-seat scout to fit such a device on to, and thus was born the first *true* fighter. More E.Is were hastily ordered and available aircraft of the type were fitted with Spandau-Maxim guns for issue to the various Feldfliegerabteilungen (Flg Abt) to protect their two-seaters.

Meanwhile however the French continued to employ Type 'L's and 'N's in the fighting scout role and certainly by June 1915 the first pilots to achieve five aerial victories (confirmed) had appeared. MS 49 had been formed in April, and with this unit the first ace was Adj Adolph Pegoud who achieved his fifth victory shortly before Sgt Gilbert, who had also been transferred to this unit. Gilbert gained his fourth and fifth victories on 4 and 17 June, while Pegoud claimed his sixth on 11 July. Gilbert has in the past been recorded as the first ace, but Pegoud just pipped him. Gilbert was forced to land in Switzerland on

27 June and was interned, while Pegoud was shot down and killed over Alsace by a German aircraft on 31 August without having added further to his score.

Meanwhile the British too had their first ace in the person of Capt Lanoe G Hawker. A Royal Engineer before the war, Hawker had transferred to the RFC in 1914 and gone to France with 6 Squadron at the outbreak of war. He was awarded an early DSO for reconnaissance flights and a lone bombing attack on Zeppelin sheds in a BE 2C but, ever a keen inventor, he had devised the fitting of a Lewis gun to a Bristol Scout, angled outward to miss the propeller. Obviously it required considerable skill — and luck — to achieve accurate fire with this device. With this 'lash-up' fitting, he sent a German two-seater down out of control on 21 June, and drove down another on 23rd. A month later on 25 July he first drove down one aircraft, then attacked another (from Flg Abt 3) which he shot down in flames near Hooye. He then hit an Albatros C.I which crashed East of Zillebecke; the observer, Hauptmann Roser, fell out in mid-air. This combat brought him the award of a Victoria Cross. A few days later he claimed another Albatros forced down, but subsequent combats after this were to be undertaken in one of the new two-seat FE-2 'pushers,' where a gunner in the front nascelle did the actual shooting. On 2 August an Aviatik was forced down, while on the 11th he and Lt Clifton (gunner) drove down another Aviatik and shot down one of the new Fokker E.Is, which crashed in Lille. A further scout shot down on 15 September brought his score to nine — four destroyed, one out of control and five forced to land or driven down. He then returned to England on leave.

Now however it was the Germans who were to come to the fore as the small numbers of E.Is gradually reached the front. The first claim was made on 1 July 1915 by Lt Kurt Wintgens of Flg Abt 67, but this fell over French territory and was not confirmed. A month later on 1 August however, the first confirmed victory was gained by Lt Max Immelmann of Flg Abt 62, who — although experiencing some difficulty with his gun — successfully brought down a BE 2C. Gradually more E.Is arrived, and several pilots began to build up scores flying these aircraft. Immelmann was well to the front, indeed his score had reached 15 by 18 June 1916, on which date he was killed in combat with FE 2Bs of 25 Squadron, RFC. Already fellow-Saxon Lt Oswald

Boelcke had passed his total, reaching 18 during July, while Wintgens matched this score on 25 September, but was then shot down and killed by the French ace Alfred Hertaux. While initially used as escort for two-seaters of the same unit, the advantages to be gained by grouping the Fokkers together gradually became apparent – particularly as growing losses caused the RFC to send out their aircraft in mutually protective formations, instead of singly. On 16 June 1916 therefore Boelcke had been ordered to form an all-fighter Kampfeinsitzer Sivry to operate over the Verdun area, where a great German offensive was to take place.

By now the pendulum had swung the other way! The appearance of the Fokkers had caused great problems to the RFC and the French – the 'Fokker Scourge' had taken a serious toll of their two-seaters, and had gained the Germans a high degree of air superiority during late 1915 and early 1916. The British had developed a fighting aircraft – the Vickers FB-5 'Gunbus' – a two-seater 'pusher' with provision for a flexible machine-gun in the front fuselage nascelle, even before the outbreak of war. Several had already reached squadrons at the front during the early summer of 1915, and in late July the first full squadron of these (11 Squadron) reached France. These proved capable of combating the Fokker, which had at best an indifferent performance, but were too few in number to have much impact. The FE 2, of similar design but better performance, also began to appear later in the summer, but it was January 1916 before the first full unit – 20 Squadron – could arrive. This was followed next month by the RFC's first single-seater scout squadron, No 24, formed and led by Maj Hawker VC. This unit flew a smaller single-seat 'pusher,' the DH 2. More DH 2s followed, with 29 and 32 Squadrons, and 60 Squadron came out to use the various French Morane types. Certainly the DH 2 and FE 2 both had the measure of the Fokker, but the best of all was the new French Nieuport 11 'Bebe.' This little tractor biplane carried a Lewis gun above the top wing, firing over the propeller arc – an idea tried by the RFC during 1915 on Martinsyde S.Is and Bristol Scouts in small numbers. The first unit so equipped was Escadrille N.11, and it was soon followed by others. The Nieuport was also rapidly developed, the C.11 being followed by the C.16 and C.17 before the end of the year; both the latter types were purchased in some quantity by the British, the first Type 16s joining 11 Squadron in May 1916.

Like the Germans, the French had soon realized the advantage to be gained by concentrating their fighters and in June 1916, even as Boelcke formed his Kampfeinsitzer Sivry, Capt Brocard, previously commander of Esc N11, formed Groupe de Combat de la Somme which incorporated Escadrilles N 3, 26, 73 and 103 under a single command. This unit was later numbered GC 12, and took the name *Cicogne*

Germany's First Ace – Max Immelmann, the Eagle of Lille

Leutnant Max Immelmann was a career soldier who had transferred to the Air Service in November 1914. He served as a pilot with Fliegerabteilung 10 from February to April 1915, and then in Flg Abt 62. On several occasions he engaged in combat while flying the L.V.G. two-seaters with which his units were equipped, but never with any success. When two Fokker E.Is were delivered to the unit he and Oswald Boelcke flew these, and it was with one of these that he gained the first confirmed fighter victory of the war for the Germans on 1 August 1915. During September three more victories followed, and then in October he became solely responsible for the air defense of the city of Lille. He gained two further victories during September to become the first German ace. Late in 1915 he joined one of the first special single-seater detachments, and in January 1916 received the highest Prussian decorations, the Pour la Merite (known as the 'Blue Max'). His score stood at 14 by the end of March, but he had twice shot off the propeller of his E.I when the synchronization gear malfunctioned. No further victories came his way until 18 June, when he gained his 15th hit, but by then his friend and arch-rival, Boelcke, had already overtaken him. Later that day he engaged seven FE 2bs of 25 Squadron, RFC, but his aircraft was seen to break up and he was killed. The Germans believed that he had again shot off his own propeller, but the British credited his demise to Lt G R McCubbin and his gunner, Cpl J Waller. Immelmann had developed a turn at the top of a zoom climb to return to the attack on an enemy which has been known ever since as an 'Immelmann Turn'.

(Storks) from N3; for a time the Groupe was increased in size by the attachment of three more escadrilles, N37, 62 and 65. In the autumn a further such unit, GC 13, was formed under Capt d'Harcourt. Among the French pilots serving with these units Sous Lt Jean Navarre, a prewar military pilot, had gained his 12th victory by 19 May 1916, but was shot down and badly wounded on 17 June, while a young Caporal, Georges Guynemer, was close behind with 11 victories by July. The RFC was also producing new exponents of aerial fighting; Capt AM Wilkinson of 24 Squadron claimed seven victories in DH 2s by the end of August, while with 11 Squadron an ex-reconnaissance pilot, Lt Albert Ball, was achieving great success with the Nieuport Scout, having claimed 16 victories by this time to challenge the French top scorers. During September Guynemer was to claim three in a day on one occasion, and run his total up to 18, while Lt Charles Nungesser of Esc N65 was only one behind him, having shot down the German ace Otto Parshau (8 victories) for his own 10th success earlier in the summer.

After experience with Boelcke's unit, and faced by the new French and British fighter units which had wrested air superiority from them by mid-1916, the Germans now formed several Jagdstaffeln (Jasta), the first on 10 August, and by October 24 had been set up. This action coincided with the availability of the early examples

...airmen did not contribute materially to the final outcome, they had proved that the air weapon could be decisive if properly employed. They had also proved they were men of unique courage. With few exceptions they fought with unusual gallantry and without the savagery that marked the battle on the ground. They had managed to preserve human individuality in a war of mass attrition and waste. When they fell, their value was above that of the sparrows and their fall was noted. Their tragedy lay in their personal sacrifice, freely given, which their leaders wasted or did not understand until it was too late; nor were they aware of the fact that the "war to end all wars" had only been a prelude.

Edward Jablonski
"Warriors of the Air, A pictorial history of World War I in the air"

Above: Frank Luke, American ace, painted by Charles McVicker.
Right: French Ace, Sous Lt Jean Navarre (12 victories) with a Morane Parasol in 1915.
Far right: Eliot White Spring, painted by Walt Stewart.

11

Boelcke – 'father' of the German Fighter Force

Like Immelmann a native of Saxony, Oswald Boelcke had joined the army in 1911, but had transferred to the air service in June 1914, qualifying as a pilot on the day war broke out. Serving initially with Flg Abt 13, he

transferred to Flg Abt 62 in April 1915, on several occasions undertaking sorties in unarmed Fokker 'Eindekkers.' He gained his first victory on 4 July 1915 when his gunner shot down a Morane two-seater as he piloted an L.V.G. The armed E:Is arrived shortly afterward, but it was not until 19 August that he claimed his first victory with one of these. He was then sent to Metz to undertake bomber escort sorties, gaining three victories during September and two more in October. On 12 January 1916 he claimed his eighth victory, and on that date he and Immelmann both received the Pour le Mérite. He was then posted to Flg Abt 203, but had now clearly resolved his views on the need for concentration of fighting aircraft. He made representations along these lines, and was ordered to form Kampfeinsitzer Sivry for the Verdun Offensive. Ten further victories, including four in March and four in May, had raised his score to 18, but after Immelmann's death he gained only one more before he was grounded and sent on a tour of inspection of the Balkans and East.

He was recalled in August when the decision was taken to form the new Jagdstaffeln, and was given command of Jasta 2. He was allowed to hand-pick the pilots for this, his choice including several pilots then of note

and some promising new ones, including his friend Lt Erwin Boehme, and a young reconnaissance pilot, Lt Manfred von Richthofen. Equipped initially with Fokker D.IIIs and Albatros D.Is, Boelcke kept his new unit training while he continued to fly over the front. He claimed victory number 20 in a D.I on 2 September, and then six more by the time Albatros D.IIs arrived on 16 September. He had by now also prepared his *Dicta Boelcke* for his pilots, which was to become the bible of every German fighter pilot, making Boelcke the true 'father' of the German fighter force.

His leadership, as well as his example, was to prove inspiring, and with the new D.IIs he now led Jasta 2 fully into action. During their first combat his eight fighters engaged 20 British aircraft, claiming four without loss. Boelcke's own score now rose at an astronomical rate, reaching 30 by the end of September and 40 on 26 October – all his Jasta 2 claims being against the British. On 28 October he led his men to attack a force of DH-2 fighters, but his Albatros was seen to collide with that flown by Lt Boehme, and he crashed to his death. Ironically Boehme survived, hysterical with grief. He recovered to lead the unit, finally being shot down and killed over a year later at the head of Jasta 29 with his own score at 24.

of new fighting biplanes of several types – Fokker D.IIIs, Halberstadt D.Is and Albatross D.Is, IIs and IIIs. The Albatros and Halberstadt types were both armed with two machine-guns on the nose of the aircraft, with interrupter gears, and the Albatros particularly was superior in performance to all the Allied fighters then at the front, including the recently introduced FE 8 'pusher' of the RFC.

Fighting during the last quarter of 1916 was very fierce, with successes on both sides. At the head of his new Jasta 2, Boelcke pushed his total up to 40 by 26 October, but two days later was killed in a collision with another aircraft from his unit. On the Allied side Ball's score was close to this level, his 31st being claimed on 1 October (although this total included nine and one balloon destroyed – one of them shared – one out of control and 20 forced to land). Ball too then departed the front; he was sent back to England for rest and a period of training. New names were appearing however. Capt JO Andrews became 24 Squadron's top scorer on the DH 2 by the end of November with 14 victories. This unit had lost its famous commander during that month, Maj Hawker falling in an epic fight with a rising star in Boelcke's Jasta 2; he was the 11th victim of one Manfred Rittmeister von Richthofen.

The French were seeing much of the action at this time, mainly in the Verdun area, and indeed by the end of 1916 GC 12 would have claimed over 200 victories, 17 of these credited to René Dorme and 16 to Capt Alfred Hertaux, both of Esc SPA 3. Hertaux, commander of the unit, had introduced the new Spad S.VII fighter to action during September, to replace the Nieu-

Below left: Capt Alfred Hertaux (21 victories) commander of Esc SPA 3 with one of his Spads.
Bottom left: Sous Lt Rene Dorme (23 victories) of Esc SPA 3 in his Spad S VII 'Pere Dorme IV'.
Above: Capt Albert Deullin of Esc N 3 in 1916 with a Nieuport C 17.
Far right: Lt Heinrich Gontermann (39 victories) of Jasta 15, whose total included 17 observation balloons.

port – this changing the unit's designation from N 3 to SPA 3 at that time. 'Pere' Dorme was wounded on 20 December and hospitalized, but Hertaux continued to do well, reaching his 20th victory on 6 February 1917, while his most brilliant pilot, Guynemer, had gained his 30th by the end of January. The unit's fourth great ace at this time was Albert Duellin, who had 11 by early February, when he was posted to command SPA 73; he would increase this total to 14 by late April.

While the scouts fought for control of the air above, it was the reconnaissance machines, still far greater in numbers, which took the brunt of the casualties as they carried out their more mundane corps reconnaissance, photographic and artillery-spotting duties. In April 1917, as the British opened the Battle of Arras, they were to suffer disastrous casualties to the increasingly ascendent Jastas. The life expectancy of the average new pilot or observer out from England was reduced to a matter of hours in the air; 'Bloody April' it came to be called, as five RFC aircraft fell for every one lost by the Germans.

Now it was that Manfred von Richthofen, recently promoted to command Jasta 11, and clear successor to Boelcke with his score already at 31, really came into his own. In the one month Jasta 11 was to claim 89 victories – by far the highest total gained by any unit at the time – and of these 21 were credited to Richthofen; raising his total to 52 and making him the top scorer of the day. His other pilots did equally well; the tiny Kurt Wolff also claiming 21 during April; Karl Schaefer gained 15 to raise his personal total to 23; Lothar von Richthofen, Manfred's younger brother, also gained 15 during his second month at the front. In other units too, German pilots were doing well; Lt Werner Voss of Jasta 2 taking his total from 17 in mid-March to 28 by early April, while in Jasta 5 Heinrich Gontermann claimed 12 of the unit's 20 successes to raise his score to 18.

In an effort to regain their slipping superiority, the Allies rushed into service new types which had the advantage of the hydraulically operated Constantinescu interrupter gear which had recently been developed. However, although the Spad S.VII and Sopwith Pup, which both began to appear late in 1916, could equal the performance of the new German types, they suffered from the disadvantage of having only one gun each. The British two-seater Sopwith 1½ Strutter, with a fixed forward-firing Vickers and observer's flexible Lewis gun, also appeared as bomber and fighter-reconnaissance with considerable initial success. Hard-pressed over the front, the RFC gained the assistance of the Royal Naval Air Service, which dispatched further Pup squadrons to augment the RFC on the Western Front early in 1917, following these with their new Sopwith Triplanes – superb machines which could out-maneuver all German types facing them. Indeed 1917 was to be a year of tremendous growth and development. Steadily during the middle months of the year the British, on whose front most aerial combat was now taking place, wrested back the superiority, introducing further new types, notably the SE 5, which was the first Allied two-gun fighter, soon to be developed into the SE 5A, one of the classic fighters of the war. The SE 5 introduced one synchronized Vickers gun on the nose and one Lewis gun above the wing – an arrangement adopted by some of the later Nieuport types. Also introduced was the relatively unsuccessful single gun, back-stagger DH 5. RFC units also received some of the French Spad S.VIIs, and others the new Bristol F2A and F2B two-seaters – destined to become one of the most successful and famous British aircraft of the war. In September came the Sopwith Camel – the first

The Red Baron

Eldest son of a Silesian nobleman, Manfred Freiherr von Richthofen was a career soldier, serving in the cavalry on the outbreak of war. Service in Poland and in the West was followed by the characteristic loss of enthusiasm for the ground war felt by many cavalrymen as static trench warfare set in. Richthofen applied to transfer to the air service, and in May 1915 became an observer in Flg Abt 69. After first meeting Oswald Boelcke, he applied for pilot training, but found this difficult, lacking natural aptitude. He was however qualified in time to fly at Verdun, and was quick to fix a machine gun to the top wing of his two-seater, shooting down a French Nieuport which fell on the other side of the lines and was not confirmed as a result. Posted to the Eastern Front again, he was 'spotted' here by Boelcke as likely fighter pilot material, and in September 1916 was ordered to join the new Jasta 2. Boelcke's most promising protege, he shot down an FE 2b during the unit's first major combat on 17 September, and within a month had six victories, increasing this number to 10 by 23 November. On that day, in his longest, hardest combat to date, he shot down Maj Lanoe Hawker, VC, of 24 Squadron, the RFC's first ace. Late in December, with his total at 14, he first began painting areas of his aircraft scarlet to identify himself and strike fear into the hearts of his opponents. January 1917 saw him take command of Jasta 11, a unit so far unsuccessful, and on 16 January he received the Pour le Mérite.

At the start of April his total already stood at 31, and since Boelcke's death he was by far the most successful pilot. During the Battle of Arras no unit was more successful than his Jasta 11, which gained no less than 89 victories. Some 21 of these were claimed by von Richthofen, raising his score to 52, well past Boelcke's total of 40. In June 1917 the first Jagdgeschwader, JG I, was formed with him in command, but on 6 July in combat with FE 2Ds of 20 Squadron, RFC, he was wounded in the head. Always a careful and calculating pilot, who attacked when position and odds were right, he now became more cautious as his wound continued to trouble him, but still his score rose – 60 by September 1917, 70 by March 1918, and on 20 April 1918 two Sopwith Camels of 3 Squadron, RAF, brought his total to 80. Next day in a fight with Camels of 209 Squadron he was hit and crashed to his death. Claims were submitted by Capt A R Brown (13 victories) of 209 Squadron, and by machine gunners of the 53rd Battalion, Australian Field Artillery. Officially Brown was credited with shooting him down, but controversy regarding the conflicting claims continues to the present time. His loss was a great blow to the German nation; no other pilot would reach his score, and no better fighter leader would appear. It has frequently been claimed that von Richthofen preyed on relatively defenseless two-seaters, but his score included nearly 40 fighter aircraft of all types – DH 2s, FE 8s, Pups, Camels, Spads, Nieuports, Bristol Fighters and so on – while many of the others were relatively tough FE 2s. Certainly the red-painted aircraft of his 'Flying Circus' created a sense of inferiority in the RFC that took long to remove.

Werner Voss

One of the youngest German aces, Werner Voss served in the cavalry in 1914, transferring to the air service when his regiment was disbanded in September 1915. Initially an observer, he trained as a pilot in 1916, being posted to Jasta 'Boelcke' (ex Jasta 2) in November, where he flew with Manfred von Richthofen. His first two victories were gained on 27 November, and by 17 March 1917 his total had risen to 17. On 8 April he received the Pour le Mérite after 28 victories, and on 20 May was posted to command Jasta 5. Here he gained six further victories by early June, but at the start of July he was moved to Jasta 29. Invited to join JG I by Richthofen, he spent a few days with Jasta 14 before joining the Jagdgeschwader to lead Jasta 10. A brilliant pilot and aggressive fighter, he was considered the one pilot who might catch von Richthofen, but he found leadership a worrying burden, and his rate of scoring slowed during mid-1917. In August he tested one of the first Fokker Triplanes at the front, claiming 10 victories between 3 and 23 September to raise his total to 48 – second only to the 'Red Baron.' His last success was over a DH 4 bomber. Later that same day he was killed in the epic dogfight described in detail elsewhere.

true two-gun fighter for the Allies, incorporating two synchronized Vickers in the nose. On the German side of the lines, the Albatros D.III was followed by the D.V and Va, while the success of the Sopwith Triplane led the Germans to develop and press into service their Fokker Dr.I of similar configuration. Other German types, Pfalz D.III biplanes particularly, were also introduced. Many new aces appeared – and many fell – during 1917, a year which saw great advances in the tactical and strategic employment of air power. Properly co-ordinated and escorted bombing raids were now undertaken, and close-support of ground forces by strafing fighters and other types was developed during the year.

While the Germans were executing such efficient havoc with the RFC during the spring, the Allied scouts continued to do the best they could to support the hard-pressed Corps squadrons. Capt Alan Wilkinson, the DH 2 ace, was back in April as a flight commander in 48 Squadron, equipped with the first Bristol F2As, and with these he was to achieve considerable initial success, being credited with eight in 10 days, six of them in one day. By the end of the month his score was stated to be 19, although not all his claims have been accounted for. Flying the tried and tested Nieuport 17 with 60 Squadron, ex-Corps observer Canadian WA 'Billy' Bishop claimed 15 victories between 25 March and the end of April, followed by another eight during May. Back at the front during April with 56 Squadron, a new unit which introduced the first SE 5s to action, Albert Ball swiftly gained 12 more victories to become top Allied ace at the time, with a score of 44, but on 6 May he failed to return from a dogfight – he is believed to have been the victim of anti-aircraft fire. Also back in action after recovery from his wounds, Esc SPA 3's René Dorme raised his total to 23 during May, but was shot down and killed on the 25th by

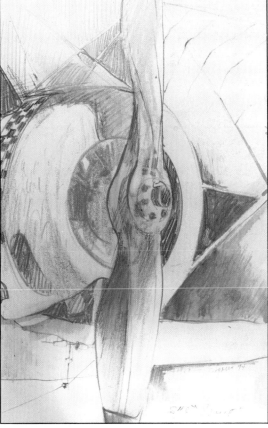

Left: The great Australian RNAS pilot Capt Robert Little (47 victories).
Far right: Escadrille Lafayette ace Raoul Lufbery and the propeller of his S 4C (right).
Above: A painting of Capt Eddie Rickenbacker by Bill Robies, the 'Hat in the Ring' emblem showing on the side of his Nieuport.

Heinrich Kroll of Jasta 9 (30 victories). An unusual Allied ace at this time was Capt FJH Thayre, most successful of all FE 2 pilots in combat. Flying in 20 Squadron with Capt RF Cubbon as gunner, the pair shot down 19 aircraft between 29 April and 7 June, bringing Thayre's personal score to 20. On 3 May they fought 26 Albatros scouts alone, claiming two shot down and driving off all the others, although reduced to using their automatic pistols when all their machine-gun ammunition was expended. Sadly this brave pair were killed a few days after their final victory, when shot down by anti-aircraft fire.

The RNAS pilots were also doing well, although several of their force's leading pilots had already gained early victories during 1916 over the Dunkirk-Ostend area, flying Nieuport Scouts, Sopwith Pups and 1½ Strutters. RA Little and RS Dallas, both Australians, already had nine victories apiece when they arrived on the Western Front in the spring of 1917. With the deadly Triplane they were rapidly to increase these totals, Little's score standing at 38 by July and Dallas's at about 34. They served with 8 (Naval) and 1 (N) Squadrons respectively. With 10 (N) Squadron, Canadian flight commander Raymond Collishaw claimed 29 victories on triplanes between late May and the end of July to add to nine earlier successes gained on all three Sopwith types. His flight claimed a total of 87 victories between May and July at the front.

During June the Germans followed the formation of the French GC 12 by forming the first Jagdgeschwader, JG I, incorporating Jastas 4, 6, 10 and 11, all under the command of Manfred von Richthofen. No further such units were to be formed until the following year, principally because of the lack of suitable leaders. The month saw the loss of several of Richthofen's pilots however. On 4 June Lt Karl Schaefer, recently posted from Jasta 11 to command Jasta 28, brought his score to 30, but next day fell in combat with FE 2Ds of 20 Squadron, RFC. Lt Karl Allmenröder, still a member of Jasta 11, gained his 30th victory on 26 June – all claimed since mid-February 1917 – his total including two Sopwith Triplanes of 10 (N) Squadron during late June. On the 27th he was shot down and killed by the Triplane leader, Flt Lt Ray Collishaw; Collishaw fired at great range and did not even realize he had hit Allmenröder and did not claim his Albatros as a victory.

A new French ace had now appeared with Esc N 26. Armand Pinsard claimed his 16th victory on 5 June, although he was then seriously injured in an accident. On 28 July Guynemer became the first Allied pilot to achieve 50 victories, but on 11 September he would disappear during a patrol with his score at 54. Charles Nungesser had raised his total to 30 during August, but a series of accidents in which he suffered considerable injuries, kept him away from the front for many weeks. It was the pilots of the British Empire who were now enjoying the greater chances to score, and during the later summer of 1917 many new aces appeared and existing leaders added to their totals. Capt JO Andrews, back in France with 66 Squadron, now flying Pups, raised his total to 24 by July. His claims including six destroyed, four out of control, two forced down and 12 driven down. By mid-August, Bishop had passed Ball's score with a total of 45 – the last 11 after 60 Squadron had converted to SE 5s – and he had received the Victoria Cross. However, then he left for Canada on a recruiting tour. In 1 Squadron, still Nieuport-equipped, Lt Tom Hazell had claimed a total of 20 victories by mid-August, while Capt Philip Fullard claimed 19 destroyed (including three balloons) and 23 out of control for a total of 42 between May and November. At that point he broke his leg playing football and was invalided home; he saw no further action.

This period was also marked by the appearance of the first two leading American aces. Adventurer Raoul Lufbery, an American of French parentage, had joined the French forces in 1914, becoming a pilot the following year. Gaining his first victory on 30 July 1916 with the new Esc N 124 'Lafayette,' a unit of American volunteers, his total reached 17 by September

1917. Much less well-known was Capt Clive Warman, a Philadelphian who served in 23 Squadron, RFC, flying Spad S.VIIs with this unit. Claiming his first victory on 6 July, he had four by the end of the month, but he added 11 more by 19 August, on which date he was wounded. His total included 10 aircraft destroyed (one of them shared), three more out of control and two balloons shot down.

With the tougher opposition they were now facing, the scores of the German aces were not rising so fast during the second half of 1917. Von Richthofen had been wounded in the head in combat during July, although on his return to action he was to raise his score to 60 during

Top: Manfred von Richthofen's famous Jasta 11 in March 1917. Von Richthofen himself is in the cockpit of the Albatros D III, while seated on the ground at the front is his brother Lothar (40 victories).
Above: Pilots of JG I. Left to right: Wüsthoff (27 victories); Reinhard (20); von Richthofen; Löwenhardt (53); Lothar von Richthofen (40).

Berthold – The 'Iron Knight'

Rudolf Berthold transferred to the air service in 1913, becoming a pilot two years later following meritorious service as an observer in the opening months of the war with Flg Abt 23. On return to this unit, now equipped with A.E.G. twin-engined 'battle planes,' he was slightly wounded on 15 September 1915, and was obliged to force land, Lt Hans Joachim Buddecke shooting a British scout off his tail as it attempted to administer the *coup de grace*. In January 1916 the unit formed a Kampfeinsitzerkommando Vaux, in which

Berthold served with Wintgens, Buddecke, von Althaus and Hohndorf – all distinguished pilots. His first two victories in February 1916 were followed by a minor wound on the 10th of that month. He gained three more successes by mid-April, but then crashed his Pfalz E.IV monoplane during a test flight and was off operations until August due to his injuries. His score had risen to 10 by the end of September, and in October came the award of the Pour le Mérite. The unit became the basis for Jasta 4 at this time, but on 16 October he was posted to command the new Jasta 14, flying Halberstad D.II biplanes. Operating on a quiet sector of the French front, he gained only three more victories before being posted to Jasta 18 in August 1917. now on the British front, he gained one victory on 21 August, and then 14 more during September alone. Early in October however he was severely wounded in the right arm, and was hospitalized for some months.

Although the wound refused to heal properly, he insisted on rejoining his unit at the start of March 1918, but before the month was out

was posted to lead the new Jagdgeschwader II, which had been formed a month earlier under von Tutschek. He tried to get new aircraft for this unit, first obtaining Siemens Schuckert D.IIIs, and then Fokker D.VIIs, with which he led the unit into action in May 1918. Although frequently in great pain from his arm, he gained three more victories that month and another eight in June. In August he added three more, and on the 10th shot down two DH 4 bombers to raise his score to 44. He was then badly shot-up by escorting Camels and crashed for the sixth time. Still the 'Iron Knight,' as he had become known, tried to return to combat, but was ordered not to fly by the Kaiser personally.

Following the war he led his own Freikorps unit against Communists in Bavaria and then against the Russian Bolsheviks. In March 1921 after his unit had demobilized, he found himself surrounded by a Communist mob in Harburg. The leader promised him freedom if he surrendered his arms, which he did, but he was then clubbed unconscious with rifle butts, strangled with his Pour le Mérite ribbon, and shot in the back seven times.

Top-scoring survivor of the German Air Service

Ernst Udet was an early transferee to the air service, but was slow in making his mark as a fighter pilot. As early as March 1916 he was serving with Kampfeinsitzerkommando Habsheim, and flying a Fokker E.I 'Eindekker.' With this unit he shot down a Farman F 40 bomber during a French air raid on Mülhausen on 18 March. He did not score again until he joined the new Jasta 15 in October 1916, then claiming five French aircraft shot down by the following May. Moving to Jasta 57, he began to find his form during the latter part of 1917, claiming 14 British aircraft between August 1917 and February 1918. He then joined von Richthofen's JG I in March, serving here with Jasta 11, and claiming three further RFC machines. At the end of May he was posted yet again, this time to Jasta 4 on the French

front, and with this unit during the summer he claimed 21 French aircraft. Early in August the British became the opponents again, and by 26 September he had added 18 more RAF aircraft to his total to reach a score of 62 – Germany's number two ace of the war, and the highest scoring to survive. His total included no less than 42 fighting scouts of almost every type employed by the Allied air forces.

After the war Udet became a world-famous stunt flier, appearing in films and at air shows all over the world. He also formed his own relatively successful aircraft manufacturing company. Seduced into the new Luftwaffe by his old commander, Hermann Goering, he was placed in charge of aircraft procurement – a job beyond his capabilities. A good-natured pleasure-loving playboy, Udet became increasingly depressed as the realities of World War II exposed his inadequacies, and in November 1941 he took his own life in despair.

September. Heinrich Gontermann, now commander of Jasta 15, had reached a total of 36 by the end of August. Some 11 of these were observation balloons, against which he was the most successful German pilot. It was at this time that the first of the new Fokker Dr I triplanes reached the front, most going to JG 1. One was given to Oblt Kurt Wolff, now commanding Jasta 11, but while leading a patrol of Albatros in this with his score at 33, he was shot down and killed on 15 September by Flt Sub Lt NM Mac-Gregor of 10 (N) Squadron (9 victories) in one of the new Sopwith Camels, which had also just reached the front. Another triplane had gone to Werner Voss, now recruited by Richthofen to JG I as commander of Jasta 10. Voss liked the new aircraft and claimed 10 victories between 3 and 23 September to raise his total to 48 – at the time second only to his commander. After shooting down a DH 4 bomber on the 23rd he went out again but was engaged by six SE 5s of 56 Squadron – the nearest thing to a 'crack' unit of aces the RFC was ever to field. He fought an epic single-handed dogfight against six aces: Capt JTB McCudden (57 victories), Lt CA Lewis (7 victories), Lt RA Mayberry (22), Lt GH Bowman (32), Lt APF Rhys-David (23) and LT RTC Hoidge (27). He fought them for 10 minutes, eluding them all and putting some bullets into every SE. Finally Rhys-Davis got below him and poured two drums of Lewis fire into the underside of the triplane, then attacked with both guns. The Fokker fell away, stalled and crashed into the British lines. His victor, an impetuous Old Etonian who always flew with a volume of Blake's poetry in his pocket in case he became a prisoner, was credited with three victories on this date to raise his total to 20; on 22 October he led a patrol over the front, but failed to return from a fierce dogfight.

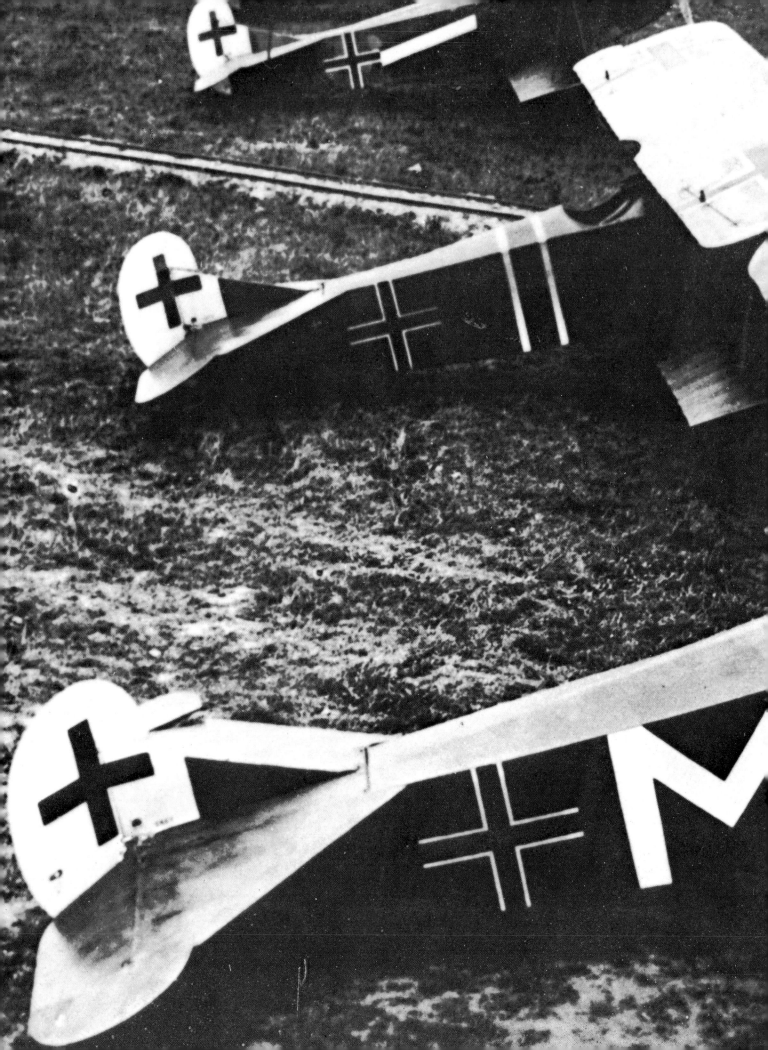

Georges Guynemer – the idol of France

One of the elite band of French pilots to gain a victory in 1915, Georges Guynemer had been turned down for the army in August 1914 due to his frail and delicate appearance and poor health. Attempting again in November, he was successful in getting into the Air Service and was trained as a pilot in 1915, joining Escadrille MS 3 as a Caporal. On 19 July, flying a Morane Type 'L' parasol, he and his observer shot down a German two-seater, but thereafter he flew single-seaters – initially the Type 'N,' and then the Nieuport as his unit became N 3 – the famous 'Cigogne' unit. He was shot down in September, the first of seven times, but survived unhurt. By July 1916 his score had already risen to 11. On 23 September of that year he claimed three in one day and during late 1916, as the new Jastas fought to regain control of the air, he claimed two in a day on four occasions, gaining his 30th but by the end of January 1917. He was now second highest scoring Allied ace and a national hero, only the RFC's Albert Ball being credited with a higher total at this time – and Guynemer's were all confirmed crashed.

During 1917 his escadrille was re-equipped with Spad S.VIIs, and in February he was promoted to the rank of capitaine at the age of 22 (having been commissioned earlier). He twice claimed three in a day during March, and on 25 May gained four victories. Throughout June and July he scored repeatedly, gaining his 50th on 28 July and reaching 53 by 20 August. He was then requested to retire from active service as his health was poor, and his death would have an adverse morale effect on the French nation. Flying a new Spad S.XIII named Le Vieux Charles, as had been his earlier aircraft, he gained his 54th and last victory on 6 September. Five days later on a patrol with another pilot, he failed to return after engaging a German aircraft. No initial German claim was made, but later it was stated that he had been shot down by Leutnant Kurt Wissemann (5 victories). His body and the wreckage of his aircraft were not recovered, being obliterated by shells in no man's land during an artillery barrage. Although his score was later exceeded by René Fonck, he remained in French hearts as *the* great ace of the war. His total confirmed victory tally was 54, but he had made in total 89 claims, and this would have been his score had he been a member of the RFC.

On return from leave late in October, Gontermann added three more victories to his total, but then on the 30th he took a new triplane up to test fly. The top wing collapsed and he crashed to his death. The aircraft was then grounded until the wings had been strengthened. The triplane, good as it was, had taken three of Germany's greatest aces to their deaths inside two months, and its reputation had become tainted. Not all was gloom for the German fighters however. During September Jasta 21, a previously undistinguished Prussian unit led by Bavarian Eduard Schleich, gained 41 victories; Schleich personally was credited with 17 of them. Following an illness, he took over the Bavarian Jasta 32 later in the year, and was created a Knight. He increased his personal score to 25 by the end of the year. Another name which was beginning to be noted was later to become one of infamy. Oblt Hermann Goering, despite wounds and illness, was scoring steadily, and by 21 October had 15 victories to his credit. Rudolf Berthold, one of the original 'Eindekker' pilots of 1916, at the head of Jasta 18 had claimed 14 victories during September to reach a total of at least 28, but he was then badly wounded for the second time, and was hospitalized.

Another great ace of this period was Canadian JST Fall, one of the RNAS pilots on the Western Front. First flying here during the spring with 3 (N) Squadron on Pups, he claimed seven during April and his total reached 11 by August. Posted to 9 (N) Squadron to fly the new Camel, he claimed 14 more during September alone (nine of them shared). By the end of the year his

Two famous commanders and good friends in World War I became Luftwaffe top brass in World War II: Bruno Lörzer (left), commander of JG III, and Hermann Goering, commander of JG I.

Nungesser – man of steel

Having gone to South America in search of his fortune as a young man, Charles E J M Nungesser returned to France on the outbreak of war, serving initially with the cavalry. He joined the Air Service in January 1915, at first flying Voisin 'pushers' in which he was soon engaged in a number of combats, he and his gunner being credited with one victory. Posted to Escadrille N 65 as a fighter pilot, he gained a further victory but was then injured in a crash in January 1916. On recovery in March he returned to action, and by late September had 17 victories – at the time only one behind the leader, Guynemer. This total included one of the early German aces, Otto Parshau (8 victories) whose demise was Nungesser's 10th victory. From December 1916 to May 1917 Nungesser was back in hospital, having earlier fractures reset, but then returned to action, achieving his 30th victory on 17 August 1917 over a Gotha bomber. His health was now so bad due to his multiple injuries that he was taken off operations for a spell on training, but while so engaged he was involved in a car accident, and was further hurt. He was able to return to the front in early 1918, at which time he was the surviving top scorer, and although he was frequently obliged to walk with a stick, and required help in getting into and out of his aircraft, he continued to gain successes – still

flying Nieuport types, culminating in the Type 27. Now his score was closely followed by a rising star, René Fonck, and by July 1918 Fonck had overtaken him. With 40 victories Nungesser again spent a spell in hospital, but on 14 August he was to shoot down four observation balloons in two flights. Next day came his 45th and last victory of the war.

With many decorations from all the Allied nations, he became a barn-storming and stunt pilot after the war. In 1927 he and Capt Coli took off in a specially built Levasseur monoplane – Oiseau Blanc – on 8 May to attempt an East to West crossing of the Atlantic. They were never seen or heard of again.

total had reached 34 — 18 destroyed (six shared), 15 out of control (three shared) and one shared driven down.

During these early years of air combat fighter pilots had come from several classes of serviceman in the air services of all the combatants. Firstly there were the career soldiers who had transferred to the air service before or at the start of the war out of interest, or because of a belief in the future of air power; these men were generally engineers. Secondly there were the cavalrymen who, after the initial weeks of war, found themselves with little prospect of action in the stalemate of the trenches, and saw the air service as offering more adventure than the life of the infantry in the mud. As the air services grew and casualties multiplied there came many who had been wounded or sick, and who had been classified as unfit for further service in the trenches, or were otherwise classed as unfit for

Bristol Fighter crews of 20 Squadron, RAF. Left to right: Lt D Latimer (21 victories) and his gunner Lt TC Noel; Lt Paul Iaccaci (11) one of a pair of American brothers in the unit; unknown; Capt TP Middleton (21).

military service; this group of 'invalids' achieved remarkable results, considering their disabilities. Finally, particularly from late 1917 onward, there would be the men recruited directly into the air services from civilian life.

A relatively quiet winter preceded a year of violent action in 1918 — a year which was to see a further substantial development in the size and scale of the air war, and the introduction of further new aircraft and of tactics whose sophistication were not to be matched again until well into World War II. While many new pilots of note were to appear during the 10 months which followed, many of those who had gained success during the earlier fighting were to add to their laurels, numbers of British Empire aces returning to the front for a further tour of duty.

The turn of the year saw the departure of two leading RFC pilots, one of whom had just become the new Allied top scorer with a total of 57. This was Capt James McCudden, originally a DH 2 pilot, and subsequently a 56 Squadron flight commander on SE 5s. A great hunter of high-flying German reconnaissance aircraft, his score

included no less than 40 such two-seaters; his total was made up of 43 destroyed (one shared), 13 out of control and one forced down and captured. Another departure was that of Capt Andrew McKeever of 11 Squadron, who had emerged as the most successful exponent of the Bristol Fighter. Between late June and the end of November 1917 he had been credited with victories over 29 aircraft and one balloon, eight of these being gained by the rear gun, manned on seven of these occasions by Sgt (later Lt) LF Powell. On two occasions this team claimed four in a single fight. Numerous other pilots were credited with substantial scores on the F2B, but nine were to equal McKeever's total. He was not to remain the highest scoring two-seater pilot however. During May 1918 fellow-Canadian AT Atkey was posted to 22 Squadron to fly F2Bs after gaining four victories by aggressive use of the DH 4 bomber while with 18 Squadron earlier in the year. With Lt CG Gass as gunner, Atkey was to claim 29 victories in a single month! Among other remarkable 'Brisfit' men was the future Air Vice-Marshal Sir Keith Park, later commander of 11 Group, Fighter Command, during the Battle of Britain, and of Malta in 1942. As a flight commander with 48 Squadron in 1917, this New Zealander claimed 20 victories, including four Albatros scouts on 17 August.

While British scores had been rising so fast, a new French ace had also appeared. After a relatively slow start, serving with a variety of units, Esc SPA 103's Lt René Fonck had pushed his score up to 21 by January 1918, at a time when most French pilots could find few opponents other than observation balloons on their fronts. Albert Duellin, one of the leaders of early 1917, had risen to command GC 19 by the start of 1918, but even a pilot of this caliber was only able to push his total from 14 in April 1917 to 20 by the end of the war. Among the other newer names, Ernst Udet of Jasta 37 had claimed 14 British aircraft between August 1917 and February 1918 to add to six victories against the French that he had gained between March 1916 and May 1917, while with the RFC Canadian AD 'Nick' Carter claimed 18 between October 1917 and February 1918 flying Spad S.VIIs with 19 Squadron.

By early 1918 Russia was out of the war and America was in. The Germans were preparing for a war-winning offensive fueled by reinforcements from the East before the forces from the New World could arrive in strength. In February two more Jagdgeschwadern were at last formed, JG II (Jastas 12, 13, 15 and 19) and JG III (Jastas 2 'Boelke', 26, 27 and 36). JG II was initially commanded by Bavarian nobleman Hpt Adolf Ritter von Tutschek, an outstanding pilot who had claimed 20 victories during 1917, but on 15 March 1918 he was shot down and killed with his score at 27. His place was taken by the gallant Berthold, whose wounds were still far from fully healed. JG III was in the hands of another fighter veteran, Bruno Loerzer, who was to lead it to great success during the year.

Among new fighter types appearing at this time was the Spad S.XIII, which was developed into the best French fighter of the war. A few Spad types with a shell-firing cannon mounted between the cylinder banks of the engine were also built, but were employed only in small numbers. Spad S.XIIIs were also supplied to the British, and later in the year to the squadrons of the newly arrived US Air Service after the Americans had suffered heavy losses with their initial equipment of obsolescent Nieuport 28s. With the British forces, the Sopwith Dolphin, an aircraft with a good altitude performance, capable of carrying up to four guns, gradually replaced the Spad S.VIIs in RFC squadrons. In the spring the Germans introduced the excellent new Fokker D.VII biplane, followed by small numbers of Siemens Schuckert D.IIIs and IVs.

In March 1918 the great German offensive began, aimed mainly at the British section of the line. It gained much ground, and indeed nearly succeeded in breaking through completely. British squadrons were thrown in to strafe and bomb the advancing foe, and some very heavy air fighting developed as the German scouts preyed on these low-flying formations. On 1 April, in the midst of the fighting, the RFC and RNAS were amalgamated to form the Royal Air Force, although the only initial change was some cross-posting of ex-RNAS and RFC pilots between squadrons.

Von Richthofen's score had reached 70 during March and on 20 April he shot down two Sopwith Camels of 3 Squadron, RAF, to raise his total to 80 – the highest score any pilot of any nation was to achieve throughout the war. The very next day he was shot down and killed in combat with Camels of 209 Squadron (ex 9 (N) Squadron), though whether by fire from Camel ace A Roy Brown, or from Australian machine-gunners on the ground has never been finally resolved.

After gaining 18 victories in a short period to raise his total to 28; Capt George McElroy, an Irish flight commander in 24 Squadron, crashed his SE 5A on 7 April. Injured he would not be fit to fly again for nearly three months. After a full year's service at the front with 60 and 29 Squadrons, Capt WE Molesworth had reached 20 victories, all claimed while flying various models of the Nieuport Scout. In 43 Squadron, Capt Henry Woollett, an ex-DH 2 and DH 5 ace on his second tour, twice claimed three scouts shot down during two patrols on 12 April to become the third British pilot – and second member of 43 Squadron – to claim six in a day. With the French, René Fonck's score reached 35 during April, while the first elements of the US Air Service entered action, and produced their first ace. Lt Paul F Baer had been trained by the French as a member of the 'Lafayette' Escadrille, but first claimed on 11 March 1918 after this unit

René Fonck – Allied Top Scorer

René Paul Fonck left the engineers in February 1915 to attend the officer cadet school at St Cyr, then joining Escadrille C 47 to fly Caudrons. On 1 March 1916 he gained his first (unconfirmed) victory over a Fokker, and on 6 August forced a Rumpler to land and be captured. One more confirmed and one unconfirmed victories followed – actually shot down of course, by his gunner in the lumbering two-seater. In April 1917 he at last transferred to fighters, joining Esc SPA 103 in GC 12 – 'Cigognes.' After a fourth unconfirmed claim on 3 May, he gained an official victory on the 5th and another on the 11th. On 12 June he brought down two Albatros Scouts, and further victories followed. By January 1918 his official score reached 21, and on 12 April it rose to 35. On 9 May he set a French record, bringing down four two-seaters and two scouts during two patrols to gain six in a day. Many double and triple victories were included in his score, and by 1 August he had passed Guynemer's total and had 57 victories. He shot down three in a single head-on pass on 14 August to raise his total to 60, while on 26 September he again shot down six in two sorties – four Fokker D.VIIs, an Albatros D.V and a two-seater. Another two-seater on 1 November raised his score to 75 – top Allied ace of the war – but by his own reckoning his unconfirmed successes raised his total to 120. It was believed that, while many of his victories were examples of great virtuosity, others were flights of the imagination. Considered something of a braggart, he was never held in as high esteem as Guynemer. After the war he became a demonstration pilot and attempted a trans-Atlantic flight in a Sikorsky S.35 in August 1926; the aircraft crashed, killing two of the crew, but he survived. In the late 1930s he rejoined the Armeé de l'Air, becoming Inspecteur de l'Aviation de Chasse until 1939, when he retired. He died in June 1953.

Georges Madon – the unknown ace

Georges F Madon, France's number four ace, remained a much lesser-known personality than the famous top trio. Born in Tunisia, he was attached to the Aeronautique Militaire at the start of the war, but during a flight on 5 January 1915 he force landed in Switzerland and was interned. Finally escaping, he got back to France where he joined Esc MF 218, but was then transferred to Esc N 38 to become a fighter pilot. He claimed his seventh victory on 15 February 1917, by which time the unit had converted to Spads, and by October had increased this total to 16. During the next year he claimed 25 more, his 40th on 11 August 1918. Many of his combats took place far in German territory, and it was believed that he had many more victories here that could not be confirmed due to lack of witnesses. He remained in the service after the war, but was killed on 11 November 1924 when he crashed during a display flight.

had been transferred to the USAS as the 103rd Aero Squadron. His fifth claim was made on 23 April, and by 22 May his score had risen to nine. It was not until May that the first US-trained pilot was to score; this was Capt Douglas Campbell, who claimed the first victory for the 94th Aero Squadron on 14 April, gaining his fifth on 31 May. In the same unit Capt Eddie Rickenbacker became the first US-trained ace, gaining his fifth on 30 May, but he was then hospitalized for some weeks due to an ear infection.

A new star was appearing with the German forces at this time – Oblt Erich Löwenhardt. He took command of Jasta 10 in April, and by the end of May reached a score of 24. In JG I he was

Right: At a 1918 contest between new fighter prototypes a group of leading German aces and unit commanders, every one with the coveted Pour le Merite at his throat, gather for a photograph. Left to right: Walter Blume (28 victories) Jasta 9; Josef Veltjens (34) Jasta 18; Josef Jacobs (41) Jasta 7; Oscar von Bönigk (26) Jasta 2; Eduard von Schleich (35) Jasta 32; Ernst Udet (62) Jasta 4; Brune Lörzer (41) JG III; Paul Baumer (43) Jasta 5; Hermann Goering (22) JG I; Heinrich Bongartz (33) Jasta 36. Above: Germany's No 3 ace, Oblt Erich Löwenhardt (53 victories) of Jasta 10, who died in a mid-air collision with another German fighter on 10 August 1918.

to vie for the lead with Ernst Udet, who had joined this Jagdgeschwader in March, serving with Jasta 11 – Richthofen's old unit. For the British, May was to prove an expensive month, and among those lost was the great naval ace, Robert Little, who was killed while trying to intercept a Gotha bomber at night on 27 May; his final score was 47. Also lost was Nick Carter of 19 Squadron, who had added 13 more victories with the new Dolphin since March; he was shot down on 19 May and became a prisoner. His victor was Lt Paul Billik of Jasta 52, Carter being the 16th of his 31 successes; Billik himself was to suffer a similar fate on 10 August. However late in May 'Billy' Bishop returned to France as commander of the new 85 Squadron, and although ordered to do little flying he went up at every opportunity. He claimed 27 more victories between 27 May and 19 June, including four Pfalz D.III scouts and a two-seater on his last engagement. With his score at 72, he was then ordered back to England at the request of the Canadian government, as the new leading Allied ace.

As the German offensive was at last held and Allied counter attacks were launched, severe fighting continued throughout the summer and autumn of 1918. The level of losses suffered by the greatly-strengthened British, French and American forces rose very considerably. Once again German scores mushroomed and many new aces appeared, while old ones pushed up their totals; Kurt Wüsthoff, the youngest Jasta commander at the age of 19, had brought his

score to 27 with Jasta 15 by June, but on the 17th was forced down in Allied lines after being wounded by SE 5As of 24 Squadron, RAF, and became a prisoner. Lt Karl Menckhoff had led Jasta 72 to 60 victories in six months on the US sector of the front, and had brought his own total to 39 when on 28 July he became the unit's only loss. He was seen to shoot down three US Spads – not confirmed because they fell in Allied lines – but was then hit by another and came down, like Wüsthoff to become a prisoner.

Lothar von Richthofen had been wounded several times since spring 1917, frequently being absent from the front for long periods as a result. Now however, as commander of Jasta 11 he claimed 11 victories between 25 July and 12 August to bring his total to 40, but was then seriously wounded in the leg and saw no further action. A third von Richthofen, Wolfram, a cousin of Manfred and Lothar, who flew in Jasta 11 also at this time, achieved a score of eight. During July JG I passed into the command of Hermann Goering, who now had 20 victories. He was to prove a strict disciplinarian as commander. He was mainly an administrator, as he flew rarely and added only two further victories to his score by the end of the war. Among the other old guard of pilots, Eduard Ritter von Schleich added 10 further victories to raise his score to 35 by the beginning of October, flying at the head of Jagdgruppe 8. Rudolf Berthold, though frequently in great pain from his unhealed wounds, con-

23

Albert Ball, VC

Albert Ball joined the army on the outbreak of war but was an early applicant for transfer to the RFC, qualifying as a pilot in October 1915. After brief service with 22 Squadron in England, he joined 13 Squadron in France to fly Be 2s, also flying the unit's Morane 'N' Bullets, and Bristol Scout. When a few of the precious new Nieuports were supplied to the RFC by the French, Ball was posted to 11 Squadron to fly one of these. On 29 April 1916 he drove down one two-seater and forced another to land for his first two victories. Three more 'forced to land' successes followed, two on 1 June, and on 25 June he destroyed a balloon. On 1 July he shot down a Roland two-seater, but then, so intensive had been his flying of late, he requested a rest. He was transferred instead to 8 Squadron to fly the BEs again for a few weeks, and was then posted back to 11 Squadron in mid-August. At once he was back in the thick of the fighting, forcing two Rolands to land on 17 August and shooting down three more, all of which crashed, on the 21st. All available Nieuports from all squadrons were then concentrated in 60 Squadron, where Ball continued to develop his own tactics of hunting alone, attacking from below and firing upward with the upper-wing-mounted Lewis gun pulled down into the cockpit to allow him to fire at an acute angle. On 28 August he forced two Rolands and another aircraft to land, and shot down a fourth. A DSO and Bar to this were both gazetted during September, and by 1 October his score had risen to 31. Of these, nine aircraft and one balloon were claimed destroyed (one shared with another pilot), one out of control and 20 forced to land. Sent back to England for a rest and a period of training, he received a second Bar to his DSO in November.

Early in 1917 he was posted to the newly formed 56 Squadron which was receiving the first early Se 5s. At first Ball did not like the new aircraft, and when a move to France was

made in April 1917, he took along his own Nieuport 23, gaining his first victory with the unit over an Albatros two-seater on 23 April while flying this. Thereafter he flew an Se for his next 10 victories, all gained by 5 May. On 6 May he flew his Nieuport again to bring down an Albatros scout for his last victory. Next evening he was involved in a dogfight with some red Albatros D.IIIs, accompanied by a Sopwith Triplane and a Spad. He disappeared into cloud and was not seen again, later being claimed by German sources to have been shot down by Lothar von Richthofen, brother of the famed 'Red Baron.' However, research has shown that von Richthofen had in fact claimed the triplane, and had then been wounded himself – almost certainly by Ball; it is believed that Ball then spun into the ground in bad visibility. He was subsequently awarded a posthumous Victoria Cross, his final score standing at 44. At the time of his death he was leading Allied ace, ahead even of Guynemer, but it must be said that his total included many victories which would not have been included under the French system, and that in total claims, confirmed and unconfirmed, the Frenchman was still undoubtedly ahead. The breakdown of the 44 was 21 aircraft destroyed (one shared), one balloon, two out of control and 20 forced to land.

McCudden – a true professional

'Mick' Mannock – ace with one eye

Often listed as British top scorer, Major Edward Corringham 'Mick' Mannock was a telephone company employee before the war, and was interned by the Turks in 1914 as he was working in that country when hostilities commenced. He was later released as a likely noncombatant due to a faulty right eye. Joining the RFC despite this disability, he was posted to 40 Squadron in France late in 1916 to fly Nieuports, gaining his first victory on 7 January 1917. By July he had claimed only one further success – over a balloon in May – but then in three months he enjoyed much success, claiming at least 17 victories; one of these, an Albatros D.III shot down on 12 August, was flown by Lt Joachim von Bertrab (5 victories). The unit then converted to SE 5As, with which he gained one victory on new year's day 1918. On return to England his score was recorded to be six destroyed and 17 out of control, although only 20 of these victories have been found. Posted to the newly formed 74 Squadron as a flight commander, he returned to France in Spring 1918. Involved in very

heavy fighting during the next two months, he appears to have made a total of 36 claims between 12 April and 17 June, including three Pfalz D.IIIs on 12 May, three more and a Hannoveraner on 21 May, and yet another three on 1 June. Several of the claims appear not to have been accepted however, and some were shared with his whole flight. Posted to command 85 Squadron when Bishop returned to England, he had made eight more claims by 26 July. On that date he and another pilot shot down a Junkers CL 1, but his own SE was hit and burst into flames, and he was killed. After the war he was awarded a Victoria Cross, the citation indicating that he had some 50 victories, but subsequently his biography, written by the 74 Squadron ace, J I T Jones, quoted his score as 73 – one above Bishop, whom Jones obviously disliked and disapproved of. Looked at most generously the highest total that could be placed upon Mannock's score is 71, although even 68 seems optimistic. Undoubtedly he was a great leader and pilot, idealized by his subordinates, but probably not in fact the British Empire Number one.

Some 40 destroyed (2 shared), one balloon and 17 out of control (one shared) have been identified, with four to seven more (two to five shared) possible claims of unknown category.

Major James Thomas Byford McCudden had joined the RFC before the war as a mechanic, and after service as an observer and gunner in Farmans and Morane Parasols, trained as a pilot in early 1916 – one of the RFC's relatively small number of NCO pilots. Flying DH 2 'pushers' with 29 Squadron, he gained his first five victories with this unit in late 1916 and early 1917. Commissioned, he returned to England as an instructor, but returned to France in July 1917, joining 66 Squadron on Pups, but managed to get a posting to 56 Squadron with the first SE 5s, as a flight commander. While leading patrols over the front frequently, he also specialized in intercepting high-flying two-seaters, one of which he forced to land in Allied lines on 30 November 1917. By the time he left 56 Squadron in early 1918 his score had risen by 52, of which 40 were two-seaters; his total of 57 included 43 destroyed (one shared), 13 out of control and one captured. His most successful day was 16 February 1918, with three Rumplers and a D.F.W. shot down. On return to England he received the Victoria Cross, DSO and Bar and a Bar to his MC. In July he again set off for France to take command of 60 Squadron, but crashed while taking off from a French air-field, and was killed.

Raymond Collishaw – the greatest naval pilot

Among a number of outstanding fighter pilots of the RNAS, Lt Col Raymond Collishaw was undoubtedly the greatest. An ex-merchant seaman who had crewed on Scott's Antarctic expedition, this Canadian flew in 3 Wing, RNAS in early 1916 on Sopwith 1½ Strutters, claiming three victories during October. Early in 1916 he joined 3(N) Squadron, claiming one victory with this unit flying a Pup. Posted to lead a flight in the new Triplane-equipped 10(N) Squadron, he claimed five, including two seaplanes on 12 May, before moving to the Western Front. Here he then claimed 29 victories between 30 May and 27 July, his flight gaining 87 altogether during this period. On leave from late July until November 1917, he returned to command 13(N) Squadron on Camels in the Channel area, claiming three more victories, including another two seaplanes. January 1918 saw him posted to lead 3(N) Squadron, which became 203 Squadron, RAF, in April. From June to September 1918 he claimed a further 19 victories to raise his total to 60, 43 destroyed (one shared) and 18 out of control, he also had 100 indecisive fights, during which at least 15 more were driven down. Despite his high score, he received only DSO and Bar, DSC and Bar, but no Victoria Cross – indeed none of the pilots of the RNAS were to receive this award. In 1919 he commanded 47 Squadron in South Russia, shooting down one Bolshevik Albatros Scout, and claiming a second out of control. He remained in the RAF, becoming an air vice-marshal, and commanding the Western Desert Air Force during 1940 to 1941, before retiring.

'Billy' Bishop – British Empire No 1

William A Bishop arrived in France with the Canadian Mounted Rifles soon after the outbreak of war. Like many others, his German counterparts included, he transferred to the RFC in 1915, training as an observer. After service with 21 Squadron he was injured in a bad landing; on recovery he sought pilot training and on completion was posted to 60 Squadron in March 1917 to fly Nieuport Scouts. He claimed his first victory over an Albatros D.III on 25 March, and a second six days later. Some 13 more victories followed during 'Bloody April,' one of these a balloon on the ground, while May brought another eight, one of them shared. This virtuosity brought a DSO, and then on 2 June he took off early alone to attack a German airfield at dawn; here he claimed three Albatros D.IIIs shot down as they took off to intercept him. He was subsequently awarded a Victoria Cross for this particular combat, and this has given rise in more recent years to much controversy regarding his score. It was virtually unknown for a Victoria Cross to be awarded for an action without any corroborating witnesses, and research into German records undertaken by enthusiasts since does not appear to indicate losses commensurate with his claims. Checking of other claims frequently produced the same result, and in consequence much doubt had been cast on the veracity of his claims and his total. Certainly he was by no means the only pilot to come into question in this manner, and no judgement or opinion is offered here.

Constant combats with Albatros Scouts through the summer raised his total to 45 by mid-August, the first to pass Ball's score. From late July his last 11 victories had been claimed flying SE 5s, to which 60 Squadron had by then converted. Now a major with a Bar to his DSO and an MC, he returned to Canada in September on a recruiting tour. He came back to England early in 1918, becoming chief instructor at the Aerial Gunnery School. He was then made commanding officer of 85 Squadron flying SE 5As, and on 22 May returned to France with orders to do little flying. Frequently operating alone, he flew on every opportunity, and in the period 27 May to 19 June claimed 27 more victories; four Pfalz D.III scouts and one two-seater were claimed during his final combat. With a DFC added to his earlier decorations, he was ordered back to England to a post at the Air Ministry, and then in August returned to Canada to help form the new Canadian Air force. With an official score of 72 (sometimes quoted as 75) he was the RAF's top scorer. At least 58 of his victories were classified as destroyed, only one of these being shared. After the war he formed a commercial aviation company with fellow ace W G Barker, VC. Later he served in the RCAF during World War II as an air marshal in charge of training; he died on 11 September 1956.

tinued to fly at the head of JG II until ordered by the Kaiser personally to stop following his sixth crash on 10 August; by this time his score stood at 44.

Meanwhile in JG I Erich Löwenhardt had seen much action, and had passed Voss's score to reach 53 — second only to von Richthofen. On 10 August he too was brought down when he collided with another Fokker D.VII. Both pilots took to the parachutes with which the Germans were now issued, but Löwenhardt's failed to open, and he was killed. His old rival, Udet, was to claim 21 French aircraft shot down by 4 August, and then 18 British by 26 September to pass Löwenhardt's total and become the new number two, and surviving top scorer with 62 victories — 42 of which were fighting scouts.

Among the German units, Jasta 11 was to emerge as top scorer with 350 victories, followed by Jasta 2 'Boelcke' with 336. Third was Jasta 5 with nearly 300; this unit produced several high scorers, two of whom spent most of the war as NCOs. Fritz Rumey claimed 45 victories between July 1917 and September 1918, but on 6 October collided with a 32 Squadron SE 5A and was killed, while Josef Mai was credited with 30 between March 1917 and September 1918. Paul Baumer served with Jasta 2 and 5, claiming 43 by 9 October 1918, and Josef Jacobs became top ace of Jasta 7 with 48. Josef Veltjens, a close friend of Berthold who flew in most of the latter's units with him, commanded Jasta 15 in JG II, his 18 pilots claiming 157 victories during the last five months of the war, Veltjens accounting for 23 to bring his total to 35. In October a fourth Jagdgeschwader, JG IV was formed with Bavarian units under von Schleich, commander of Jasta 34b. In this new formation was another Bavarian knight, Oblt Robert Ritter von Greim, whose 25 victories included a British tank destroyed by him on 23 August.

Like the British, the Germans had a number of Naval Air Service fighter pilots, and employed many of these on the Belgian sector of the Western Front later in the war. Their first ace was Oblt Friedrich Christiansen, who claimed 21 victories over the coastal area between Dunkirk and Ostend while flying a lumbering two-seater Hansa-Brandenberg seaplane. His total included a coastal dirigible airship, a Felixstowe F2A flyingboat and the British submarine C-25 (which was in fact only damaged). Later the corps' two most successful pilots were Gotthard Sachsenberg and Theo Osterkamp, who flew with the Marine Jastas at the front during 1918. By August Sachsenburg had 31 victories, but who was then seriously wounded, while Osterkamp, who had claimed four victories in a single engagement to bring his score to 16, led 22 D.VIIs to attack 22 RAF DH 9s on 12 August 1918, 19 of the bombers being shot down without loss. In the last weeks of the war he received one of the first new Fokker D.VIII monoplanes, and in a dogfight with USAS Camels caused two to collide

and crash for his 25th and 26th victories. Following his 32nd victory he suffered an attack of influenza in the deadly 1918 epidemic, and did not leave hospital until the war ended.

What then of the Allies while the Germans were engaged in this final plethora of scoring? The French once again began to produce a number of high-scorers during the heavy fighting of the spring and summer, although most gained the majority of their successes over the greatly increased number of German observation balloons now to be seen. Capt Georges Madon of Esc SPA 38 had claimed 16 victories by the end of 1917 after some two years of service, but now he had added 25 more, reaching his 40th victory on 11 August 1918. The great Nungesser — France's Rudolf Berthold — was back in action early in the year, reaching his 40th in July, but in that same month his score was overtaken by Fonck, whose score was now rising rapidly. Nungesser, still flying his beloved Nieuports, returned from another stay in hospital in mid-August, to claim four balloons on the 14th, and then a single aircraft next day for his 45th and final victory. During the month however, Fonck at last passed Guynemer's score and by the end of August had a total of 60. In September he would, for the second time, claim six in a day. Finally, on 1 November, he made his last claim, to reach a score of 75 as top Allied ace of the war.

Among the other French pilots Lt Maurice Boyau, French International Rugby captain before the war, served in Esc N 77 (later SPA 77) — the 'Escadrille des Sportifs' — which included a number of leading sportsmen among its pilots. He had reached his 20th victory by early June 1918, and on 15 September got two balloons to bring his score to 34. Next day he shot down another — his 18th balloon — but as he dived to aid a fellow pilot in trouble he was hit and shot down by ground fire. The extent to which the balloons had become the main prey of the French pilots at this time can be judged by the totals of some of the other leaders. Lt Michel Coiffard of Esc SPA 154

Above left: The RAF's top balloon buster, Capt Anthony Beauchamp-Proctor, South Africa's top scorer of World War I with 54 victories.
Above: Maj Tom Hazell (43 victories) gained his successes flying Nieuport Scouts, SE 5As and Camels.
Below: Belgium's great balloon buster, 2nd Lt Willy Coppens by the tail of his Hanriot HD 1 fighter.

had become France's greatest 'balloon strafer,' claiming 28 of these among his score of 34 before his death on 27 October. Pinsard, recovered from his 1917 accident, returned to add 11 balloons to his score during the summer to reach a total of 27 victories. Among other aces of this period, Lt Jean Bourjade of Esc N 152 included 24 balloons among his total of 28 victories, Sous Lt Claude Haegelen of Esc SPA 100 included 12 in a score of 23, and Lt 'Marc' Ambrogi included 11 in a score of 14.

All however were overshadowed by the greatest 'balloon buster' of the war — Belgium's top ace, Willy Coppens. Belgium's tiny air force had played an active part alongside the other Allies, its fighter unit (later expanded to three escadrilles) flying first Nieuports, and then Spads, Camels and Hanriot HD 1s. Two leading aces had appeared with scores in double figures. However the first — Edmond Thieffrey (10 victories) — became a prisoner of war when shot down in February 1918. Coppens had flown Sopwith 1½ Strutters in 1916, and then Nieuports during the second half of 1917, but with no success. Flying a Hanriot; he shot down a German fighter on 25 April 1918 for his first victory, but soon afterward attacked and destroyed two balloons. Thereafter he hunted these exclusively, and when he shot down his last on 14 October, had destroyed 36 of them for a final total of 37 victories.

The RAF and USAS also produced their own 'balloon busters' at this time. Tom Hazell had returned for a second tour with 24 Squadron in July 1918, and by October would add 23 more victories to raise his total to 43; 10 of these were balloons. The RAF's top scorer against the gasbags was a South African, Anthony Beauchamp-Proctor, who flew SE 5As with 84 Squadron. During early 1918 he claimed 24 victories over aircraft, but on 1 June shot down his first balloon. By early October he had become one of the most successful pilots of the war with a score of 54, which included 15 balloons; of his 39 claims against aircraft, 21 were destroyed (only one shared) and 18 out of control. Another great 'balloon buster' at this time was an American, Lt Louis J Bennett Jr, who was attached to the RAF, flying SE 5As with 40 Squadron. During August he shot down nine balloons, four of them in one day, plus three aircraft, but was then shot down by ground fire on the 24th after getting his last two balloons. He leapt from his burning aircraft at 25 meters, but died of his injuries a few minutes later.

Bennett's meteoric success escaped publicity completely in the US and was eclipsed by another American balloon expert during the following month. 2nd Lt Frank Luke Jr shot down his first balloon on 12 September, and over the next 16 days raised his total to 18, 13 of them balloons, before being shot down and then killed on the ground while resisting capture.

A greatly increased number of Americans were becoming aces now. Lufbery had been killed in May 1918, while two other aces who flew with the French soon followed. 2nd Lt Frank Baylies gained 12 victories with Esc SPA 3 before

Below center: Lt Eliot White Springs (15 victories) with a Camel of the US 148th Aero Squadron.
Below right: Capt Field E Kindley (12 victories) of the US 17th Aero Squadron with his Camel late in 1918.

Far left: Capt Eddie
Rickenbacker (26 victories)
in his Spad XIII.
Above: Hpt Herrmann
Goering (22 victories)
Commander of JG I in 1918.
Left: Capt WE 'Bull'
Staton (26–27 victories)
and his gunner, Lt JR
Gordon with their Bristol
F2B of 62 Squadron RAF, at
Planques, France, in
May 1918.

being killed in combat on 17 June, while Lt David Putnam died on 12 September after gaining nine victories with the French and four with the USAS. In the 94th Aero Squadron Eddie Rickenbacker returned from hospital late in July to fly one of the new Spad S.XIIIs, and by the end of October had become unquestionably the top American ace with a score of 26. During this same period Capt Jacques Swaab, another Spad pilot with the 22nd Aero Squadron, claimed 10 victories, but most other US high scorers gained the bulk of their victories with, or attached to the RAF. USAS pilots on attachment included Maj Reed G Landis who, like Louis Bennett, flew with 40 Squadron on SE 5As and claimed 12 victories, including two of the nimble Fokker Triplanes. Other SE 5A pilots were Elliot Springs who gained four with 84 Squadron and then 11 with the US 148th Aero Squadron, a Camel unit which operated under RAF command. George Vaughan claimed seven with 84 Squadron, then also flew Camels with the 17th Aero Squadron, where he added six more. Field Kindley flew Camels from the start with 65 Squadron, RAF, and then with the 148th, claiming a total of 12.

Serving as full members of the RAF however, other Americans gained higher totals. With 24 Squadron on SE 5As Capt William Lambert was credited with 22, while brothers August and Paul Iaccaci flew Bristol Fighters with 20 Squadron, being credited with 18 and 11 victories respectively. Camel pilot Kenneth Unger flew in 210 Squadron after being rejected by the USAS, gaining 14 victories between June and November 1918. On SE 5As with 92 Squadron flight commander Capt Oren J Rose was credited with 16 aircraft — 14 destroyed and two out of control, claiming two in a day on three occasions. In 1 Squadron, now also an SE 5A unit, Howard Kullberg claimed 16 between May and September, and flying the rarer Dolphins with 79

Squadron Frederick Gillet claimed 14 aircraft and three balloons for a total of 17.

Generally it was the RAF that produced the bulk of the Allied high scorers during 1918, but not without heavy cost. On 19 June Roderic Dallas, now leading an ex-RFC squadron on SE 5As (No 40) was attacked and killed by three Fokker Triplanes as he returned from a fighter-bomber raid on the Cambrai area. He had claimed 12 more with the SE, taking his total to 51 at least (27 destroyed, 12 out of control, 1 driven down, 1 balloon, and several category unknown); the great ex-Naval ace fell to Lt Hans Werber (7 victories), commander of Jasta 14. During July McCudden returned to France to take command of 60 Squadron, but was killed in an accident on his way out' His brother John, an ex-DH 4 bomber pilot, had become an ace with nine victories, but was shot down and killed with 84 Squadron on 18 March. George McElroy was back with 40 Squadron, recovered from his crash, and by the end of July had raised

Top: Maj Roderic Dallas (51 victories) of 40 Squadron, RAF, in his SE 5A in spring 1918.
Above: Canadian members of 41 Squadron, RAF, in summer 1918. Left to right: Lt SA Puffer (6 victories); Lt Gadd; Lt WC Shields (20); Lt WG Claxton (36); Capt FR McCall (37); Lt EHF Davis (5).

Barker – RAF ace in Italy

One of no less than four Canadians among the top-scoring nine British Empire pilots, William George Barker transferred to the RFC late in 1915, serving first as a BE 2 observer in 9, 4 and then 15 Squadrons. With 9 Squadron he shot down a Roland attacking his aircraft on 29 July 1916. Commissioned and trained as a pilot, he rejoined 15 Squadron to fly RE 8s, and in one of these got his second victory on 25 March 1917. After a period in England as an instructor, he joined the new 28 Squadron to fly Camels, leaving for France in October 1918. Here he shot down two Albatros D.Vs on 16 October, and by the end of the month had claimed five of these scouts shot down. The squadron then moved to Italy where by late March 1918 he claimed a further nine aircraft destroyed and one out of control, plus four balloons. Also, on 12 February with one other pilot he destroyed five small spherical tethered balloons, which have since been included in his score. He applied to return to France, but was posted instead to 66 Squadron with which unit he claimed a further 16 victories by mid-July. Posted again to command the new 139 Squadron, he took his Camel, B6313, with him, and over the next two months claimed a

further six victories, two of them out of control. When he returned to England in September his decorations included a DSO and an MC and two Bars. Posted as commanding officer of the School of Air Fighting at Hounslow, he requested a short spell in France to become reacquainted with the latest combat conditions. Attached to 201 Squadron, with a brand new Sopwith Snipe and a roving commission, he became engaged in an epic single-handed dogfight on 27 October, when after shooting down a two-seater, he was

engaged by a large formation of Fokker D.VIIs, and while he claimed three shot down in flames, he was hit three times and shot down, crashing in British lines. He survived his multiple wounds to receive a Victoria Cross in November 1918. His final score of 52 included 37 aircraft destroyed, one forced to land and crash, five out of control, and nine balloons, five of them shared. In partnership with 'Billy' Bishop in commercial aviation in Canada after the war, he was killed in a flying accident at Ottawa on 12 March 1930.

his score to at least 46 and possibly 49. On the last day of the month he failed to return, believed shot down by ground fire. Another pilot – often heralded as British top scorer – died on 26 July. Maj 'Mick' Mannock went down in flames during a combat with a German two-seater. He had claimed 17 victories with the Nieuport Scout in 1917 but during 1918, as a flight commander in 74 Squadron, had brought his total to about 54 by mid-June. Posted to command 85 Squadron after Billy Bishop's departure, he made eight further claims before his death; many of his claims appear to be questionable and may not have been confirmed. His VC citation, published after the war, mentioned 50 victories, but his biographer, ace 'Taffy' Jones, claimed that he had gained 73 – one more than Bishop. Research shows this to be unlikely.

Not all the great men fell however. John Gilmore had increased his total to 44 by mid-July, before being posted to command a unit in Italy. In August Henry Woollett brought his total to 36, including nine balloons. Ex-RNAS pilot Sam Kinkaid of 201 Squadron had 30, some 17 of them 'out of control' claims (this South African was to add at least five more in South Russia in 1919), while Welshman Ira 'Taffy' Jones of 74 Squadron had claimed at least 34 victories since April with 74 Squadron. His final score was listed as 40 – though claims for six of these have not been found. In 41 Squadron Canadians Frederick McCall and William Claxton brought their totals to 37 and 36 respectively. McCall had been credited with his first six as an RE 8 pilot in 13 Squadron, becoming a fighter pilot in the spring of 1918. Some 13 victories during June alone raised his total to 23; this included a

Halberstadt destroyed and two scouts out of control on 28 June and five victories on the 30th – three Albatros scouts destroyed, one more and one Fokker D.VII out of control. A total of 14 more victories over the next seven weeks included eight of the new D.VIIs, one of which he forced down in Allied territory, where it was captured, and four Albatros two-seaters – three of these shared. He was then taken ill, and was still home in Canada on sick leave when the war ended. His total included 17 destroyed (four shared), one forced down and captured, and 13 out of control (one shared) with 41 Squadron, plus six category unknown with 13 Squadron. Claxton's period of success with the squadron coincided with McCall's. He has been credited with 39 victories – 37 aircraft and two balloons – in the past, but an assessment of his claims makes it clear that he claimed 37 *including* two balloons and one aircraft driven down – the latter not qualifying as a victory in 1918. First claiming a Fokker Triplane out of control on 27 May, he was credited with 19 more victories in June alone. On the 28th he claimed two Pfalz D.IIIs and a Fokker D.VII out of control, while on 30 June – also McCall's big day – he claimed six in two flights – three Pfalz destroyed and one out of control, one Albatros scout destroyed and one DFW two-seater in flames. By 13 August his score had risen to 36, but on the 17th he was shot down in German lines with a severe head wound, only cranial surgery by a German surgeon saving his life. His score included 20 destroyed (two shared), two balloons and 14 out of control.

Unlike the other Dominions, whose personnel served in ordinary RFC, RNAS or RAF

Raoul Lufbery – America's great ace of the Escadrille 'Lafayette'

Major Raoul Lufbery was born in France, but his parents emigrated to the United States when he was still an infant. An adventurer, he served in the US army in the Philippines, from 1908 to 1910, and in 1912 joined the French pioneer pilot, Marc Pourpe in the Far East as his mechanic. In 1914 both went to France, and Lufbery joined the Foreign Legion so that he could transfer to the air service and follow Pourpe to Esc N 23. When Pourpe was killed in December 1914, Lufbery applied for pilot training, and in October 1915 joined Esc VB 106 as a bomber pilot. Transferring to fighters, he joined the Esc N 124 'Lafayette' which had been set up with American volunteers, gaining his first victory on 30 July 1916, and his fifth on 12 October of that year. When the US entered the war his score stood at 17 but, while transferring to the USAS, he remained with the Escadrille until January 1918. After brief service with the 95th Aero Squadron, he then joined the 94th as commander. On 19 May 1918 he took off after a two-seater, but as he attacked, his aircraft was seen to burst into flames. He leapt out to avoid the flames, and fell to his death – the greatest ace of the 'Lafayette.'

America's No 1 – Eddie Rickenbacker

Edward V Rickenbacker was a racing driver before the war, enlisting as driver to General Pershing, and being obliged to change the spelling of his Germanic named to an Anglicized form when his country went to war. He transferred to the Aviation Section in August 1917, joining the 94th Aero Squadron in March 1918. At once in action, flying the Nieuport 28 fighter, he claimed his first victory over an Albatros on 29 April, adding four more in May to become the first US-trained pilot to become an ace on 30 May. He was then forced to stop flying due to an ear infection, not returning to action until the end of July, when the unit had re-equipped with Spad S.XIIIs. During September 1918, now a flight commander, he claimed six victories, including one balloon. In October he added 14 more, including two shared and three balloons. This gave him a score of 26, making him the American top scorer of the war. Promoted to command the squadron, he was

Frank Luke – the maverick balloon- buster

Much has been made of the USAS Number two ace, 2nd Lieutenant Frank Luke Jr. Luke, one of nine children of a family of German ancestry, was undoubtedly an aggressive, shy, yet braggardly individual, and a fine shot. Joining the signal corps in September 1917, he transferred to the aviation section, reaching France newly commissioned in January 1918. He finally reached the 27th Aero Squadron of the 1st Pursuit Group in July, after further training and other duties. He was not popular because of his attitude; on 16 August he broke away alone to attack an aircraft, claiming a victory which apparently was not confirmed. On 12 September he shot down a balloon and shared a second, three successes giving him a taste for such prey. On 15 September, covered by another German-American, 1st Lt Joseph F Wehner, he shot down three balloons while Wehner shot down a Fokker D.VII which tried to attack Luke. Next day they were out again, each shooting down one balloon, Reportedly, Wehner shot another D.VII off Luke's tail, but this does not seem to have been confirmed. Some sources indicate that they brought down three more balloons that evening, but US records indicate that their score for the day was three – one each and one shared, so that probably it was only the latter gained in the evening. On the 18th the two pilots shared two more balloons, but then became involved with German scouts, Luke shooting down two D.VIIs, and then a Halberstadt on his way back to base. Wehner however was shot down and killed, his score at five (three of them shared), not eight as has previously been stated.

Upset by Wehner's death, Luke was sent on leave to Paris, but returned early and went up on 26 September with another pilot – who was shot down and killed. Depressed, he went absent for a day, but returned on the 28th and again shot down a balloon and an aircraft. He landed at the 'Cigogne's' base and remained away overnight, unauthorized. On return to his own base next day he was grounded for indiscipline, but took off in anger; his arrest on landing was ordered. He dropped a note to troops on the ground asking them to watch three German balloons, and then shot down each in turn. Wounded during the attack on the second, after the third he strafed German troops, but then came down in enemy lines. Drawing his .45-in automatic, he tried to make a fight of it, but fell dead, shot in the chest. After the war, when eyewitnesses reported the facts of his last flight, he was awarded a posthumous Congressional Medal of Honor. He had obtained 18 victories in 17 days; 13 of these were balloons, four of them shared.

also awarded the Congressional Medal of Honor, the supreme American award. After the war he became much involved in the automobile and aviation industries, although during World War II he undertook much traveling and special assignments for the air force. On one of these his aircraft came down in the Pacific, he and his crew surviving for 21 days until rescued.

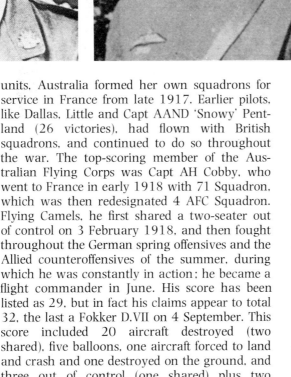

Above: Top scorer of the Australian Flying Corps was Camel ace Capt Arthur Cobby (30 victories).
Center: The only known night fighter ace of World War I, Maj CJQ 'Flossie' Brand, claimed five of his 11 victories during the hours of darkness.
Far right: A little-known but high-scoring Australian-born ace with the RFC/RAF was Capt AAND 'Snowy' Pentland (26 victories) who flew Spads and Dolphins with 19 and 87 Squadrons.

units. Australia formed her own squadrons for service in France from late 1917. Earlier pilots, like Dallas, Little and Capt AAND 'Snowy' Pentland (26 victories), had flown with British squadrons, and continued to do so throughout the war. The top-scoring member of the Australian Flying Corps was Capt AH Cobby, who went to France in early 1918 with 71 Squadron, which was then redesignated 4 AFC Squadron. Flying Camels, he first shared a two-seater out of control on 3 February 1918, and then fought throughout the German spring offensives and the Allied counteroffensives of the summer, during which he was constantly in action; he became a flight commander in June. His score has been listed as 29, but in fact his claims appear to total 32, the last a Fokker D.VII on 4 September. This score included 20 aircraft destroyed (two shared), five balloons, one aircraft forced to land and crash and one destroyed on the ground, and three out of control (one shared) plus two Albatros scouts apparently claimed in early May, date and category unknown. On 28 June he claimed two two-seaters — an LVG and a Halberstadt — and a Pfalz D.III destroyed, while on 7 August he shared two Pfalz in flames and shot down a two-seater. After the war he served in the RAAF, and in World War II commanded an operational Group in the Southwest Pacific as an air commodore. He was killed in a flying accident on 11 November 1955.

Another successful Australian in 4 AFC Squadron was Capt R 'Bow' King, who transferred to the AFC from the cavalry. His first victory over a two-seater occurred on 14 May 1918, and by 2 October he had claimed 20 victories including at least 11 two-seaters and four balloons; his last balloon victory on 2 October was achieved by dropping a bomb on it. The unit then became one of the first to convert to the new Sopwith Snipe fighter which was to replace the aging and increasingly out-classed Camel. Although the Snipe's time at the front was brief in the extreme, King was to be its greatest exponent, and in eight days, from 28

October to 4 November, he claimed seven more victories — six of them Fokker D.VIIs. This total included three on 30 October and two on 4 November. His total of 28 included 14 destroyed (one shared), eight out of control, four balloons and one unclassified, plus one Albatros two-seater shared with five other pilots.

Night fighting was an art developed only late in the war, and was still in its infancy when hostilities ceased. The most successful night fighter was an RAF pilot, Maj CJQ 'Flossie' Brand. A South African, Brand initially flew by day as a flight commander with 1 Squadron in early 1917 on Nieuport Scouts; he claimed three destroyed (one shared), one balloon and two out of control between 4 March and 1 May. Early in 1918 with 112 Squadron on home defense, now flying Camels, he shot down a Gotha bomber at night on 19 May. Later in the year he commanded 151 Squadron, the first RAF night-fighter unit to serve in France. Here he brought down another Gotha during the night of 17/18 September, while three nights later he shot down a DFW and shared an AEG, both two-seaters. Finally on 30 October he claimed a Frederiskshafen 'Gigant' for his fifth night victory, to bring his score to 11. During 1940 as Air Vice-Marshal Sir Christopher Quintin Brand, he commanded 13 Group of Fighter Command during the Battle of Britain.

The RAF also saw the emergence of the only Indian fighter ace yet to appear. Flying SE 5As with 40 Squadron, 2nd Lt Indra Lal Roy claimed eight victories, three destroyed and five (one shared) out of control. Apart from the fighter pilots of the RFC, RNAS and RAF, at least 65 other pilots qualified as aces flying with bomber or Corps units, the top-scoring bomber pilot being Capt DA Stewart of 18 Squadron (DH 4s) with 20 victories and the top corps pilot was Lt CR Pithy of 12 Squadron (RE 8s) with eight. Among at least 50 gunner aces, the top men were FR Cubbon of 20 Squadron (Thayre's gunner) with 18, and CG Gass of 22 Squadron (Atkey's gunner) with 16.

Other Fronts

While the Western Front clearly was the focus of the main fighting during the war, other fronts also saw aerial combat of a relatively sustained nature, and these areas also had their aces. German aid to their Turkish ally over the Dardanelles, Palestine and the Aegean brought clashes between German, Turkish, French and British aircraft, while in the Balkans a little-publicized campaign continued throughout the war, involving the Germans, Turks, and Bulgarians against Russians, Serbs, British, French, Rumanians, and, later, Greeks and Italians. The greatest ace here was a German, Lt Rudolph von Eschwege. This 21-year-old ex-Jäger had joined Flg Abt 36 in France in 1915, and had flown 'Eindekkers' in early 1916, claiming one unconfirmed victory. In August he arrived in Macedonia to fly the only fighter aircraft available to the air forces of the Central Powers in the area – a Halberstadt. After a further unconfirmed victory over the Aegean, he shot down a Nieuport of the RFC for his first official victory, then forced a Serbian Farman to land and be captured. A Sopwith 1½ Strutter on 30 March 1917 brought his total to six confirmed, when he was provided with an Albatros D.III sent from Germany specially for him. With this, although wounded in combat with two RFC BEs, he had 16 victories confirmed by the end of October. On 28 October he shot down his first observation balloon over the Struma front, evading escorting fighters on 9 November to destroy a second. On 19 November an observation aircraft fell as his 20th victory, but he failed to catch a third balloon over the Struma. Two days later it was there again, but much higher. As he attacked, it blew up violently; he flew into the mass of flames and crashed to his death. The basket had contained no observer but had been full of explosives, which had been fired electrically from the ground, so desperate had been the Allies to destroy the 'Eagle of the Aegean Sea.' Other German aces who served later in Macedonia included Vizefeldwebel Gerhard Fieseler (19 victories) and Offizierstellvertreter Reinhard Trepow (6 victories).

Von Eschwege's opposite number was Maj GW Murlis-Green, previously of the Suffolk Regiment, who had first flown in France as an observer late in 1915. As a pilot he joined 17 Squadron on the Macedonian Front, where he flew a BE 12 – a very poor fighter conversion of the obsolescent BE 2. Despite this second-rate equipment, he managed to shoot down a D.F.W. two-seater on 13 December 1916, and caused an Albatros two-seater to force land and crash next day. After three more victories came his greatest combat on 18 March 1917, when he brought down two twin-engined Friedrikschafens in a single combat. Another Albatros fell next day.

His last victory on this front occurred on 13 July 1917, when he dispatched his sixth Albatros two-seater while flying a two-gun Spad borrowed from the French. Awarded a DSO, MC and two Bars for his outstanding efforts, he returned to England to command a new night-fighter squadron with Camels on home defense. With this unit – 44 Squadron – he shot down a Gotha bomber at night on 18 December 1917 to raise his score to 10 (one shared), and received a Bar to his DSO. In June 1918 he commanded 151 Squadron in France.

After Murlis-Green's departure, the RAF, as it became in April 1918, strengthened its fighter force in Macedonia, and a new ace appeared. Canadian Lt AE de M Jarvis also served with 17 Squadron, and during 1918 flew a Bristol M.1C monoplane with this unit. He claimed a D.F.W. out of control and a second which fell on fire, both on 25 April – the latter shared with another pilot. Next day he shared in the destruction of another. The following month the fighter flight of 17 Squadron was detached to form 150 Squadron, and on 20 May, flying a

Top right: Maj GW Murlis-Green, RFC, top scorer on the Macedonian Front in Greece and later a night fighter pilot, gained a total of 10 victories.
Top left: Russian top scorer, Staff Captain Alexander Kazakov had 17 victories and possibly many more.
Above: Lt Ivan W Smirnoff (12 victories) front right with a Morane 'N' of the XIX Squadron of the Imperial Russian Air Force.

Camel, Jarvis sent down an L.V.G. out of control. SE 5As then became available, and during July, flying one of these, he gained four more victories, three destroyed and one out of control (all shared) to raise his score to nine (the identity of the ninth is not known, but this score was confirmed for him in records).

At least one Greek pilot, Commander A Moraitinius of the Naval Air Service, became an ace, engaging in 20 fights and claiming nine shot down. He also undertook a number of bombing raids and antisubmarine patrols, but was killed in a flying accident on 12 December 1918. The Greeks operated Nieuport Scouts, Spads and Camels with their fighter units.

In the East from 1914 to 1917 there was aerial combat over the battles fought between the Russians, and the German and Austro-Hungarian armies. Although a number of future aces of both Central Powers served here, opportunities for them to build up scores of any sort against the few Russian units did not offer themselves. Against the more numerous aircraft of the Central Powers however, several Russians were to become aces, and at least 18 have been identified – although several gained some or all of their successes serving with French units on the Western Front.

Staff Captain Alexander A Kazakov was, like so many other early fighter pilots, previously a cavalryman. He transferred to the air service in 1914, and at an early date developed a steel cable attachment with an anchor and weight on one end. Trailing this below his Morane on 18 March 1915, he 'hooked' a German aircraft and caused it to crash, although he was also obliged to come down as a result. Made commander of the XIX Corps Air Squadron in August 1915, he was to shoot down two Fokker 'Eindekkers' during the following year. In 1917 he was given command of the No 1 Fighter Group of four squadrons which was formed at that time, and continued to achieve success against German and Austrian aircraft, gaining his 17th confirmed victory over a Brandenberg two-seater on 29 August 1917 (his unofficial score has been quoted as 32). At the end of 1917, after the Bolshevik Revolution, he joined the White forces, and was attached to the RAF contingent in North Russia, commanding the Slavo-British Squadron. It is not known if he achieved further victories against the 'Bolos,' as he was generally flying two-seater

types now. On 3 August 1919, when the British decision to withdraw was announced, he took up a Camel and deliberately crashed to his death.

Lieutenant Commander Alexander P de Seversky was already serving as an aviator in the Naval Air Service on the outbreak of war. On an early mission over the Baltic his seaplane was shot down and as it crashed; the bomb it was carrying blew up and de Seversky lost his right leg. Returning to action, he later became chief of fighter aviation, and in a short spell was credited with 13 victories in 57 sorties. In September 1917 he led a mission to the USA, remaining there when the Russian Revolution occurred. In 1922 he set up Seversky Aero Corporation and became a US citizen. His company prospered, becoming one of the most successful in the US during the 1930s, and subsequently became the famous Republic Aviation.

Lieutenant Ivan W Smirnoff, an ex-infantryman, joined Kazakov's XIX Squadron in 1915 as a Sergeant, his first victory being gained by the gunner in a Morane Parasol he was piloting. Commissioned, he gained 11 more victories during the next two years, the last a German aircraft on 10 November 1917. Warned that the Bolsheviks intended to shoot him, he fled the country and later served for a time with the RAF. In 1922 he joined KLM, the Dutch airline, serving with distinction until 1949. In 1942 he was the pilot of a DC 2 airliner shot down by Japanese fighters over the East Indies, but survived. He died in October 1956.

An ace of the Russian Naval Air Service was Lt Mikhail Safonov who was credited with shooting down 11 German seaplanes over the Estonian Islands along the South Baltic coast during 1916 to 1917. Capt Paul V d'Argueeff (or Argeyev), although born in Russia, lived in France before the war, joining the French army in 1914. After being wounded, he transferred to the Air service, and in 1917 was posted to Russia with Escadrille SPA 124; here he gained six victories. After the Revolution the unit returned to the West where he added nine more. He died in France in 1922, the second highest scoring Russian-born ace. Several French escadrilles served in Russia. French aces who gained victories here include Lt Georges M Lachmann, who claimed five of his seven victories on this front, and Lt Louis F Coudouret, who claimed three of six. Lachmann later flew against the Bolsheviks in North Russia and Poland.

The Italian Front

Italy entered the war in May 1915 with a declaration against Austria-Hungary. The North Italian Alpine Front became the most important for air combat outside the Western Front, and many aces of several nations were to serve here. While three German Jastas briefly flew here until

March 1918, the main brunt of the fighting was borne by the units of the Austro-Hungarian Empire, which produced some very notable aces, flying Brandenberg D.I. 'Star-Strutters,' Berg and Phönix D.Is, and Albatros D.IIIs and D.Vs. They were faced by Italian-flown Nieuports, Spads and Hanriot HD 1s, and from December 1917 onward by three Camel squadrons and one squadron of Bristol Fighters of the RFC/RAF.

Virtually all of Italy's 43 aces flew in the same six squadrons, and all five of these with scores of 20 or more were in just two – the 76ᵃ and the 91ᵃ. Italy's top ace, Maggiore Francesco Baracca, became a pilot in 1912 and served first with the 70ᵃ Squadriglia on Nieuports in 1915–17. He then flew in the 91ᵃ Squadriglia when this was formed from a flight of the former unit with the first Spad S.VIIs in the spring of 1917. He had become leading ace by September 1917 with 19 victories, and by the time of his death in action on 19 June 1918 his score had risen to 34. Tenente-Colonello Pier Ruggiero Piccio was 34 years old when war broke out, and like Baracca was already a pilot. Initially he commanded the 70ᵃ Squadriglia, and later as a Ten Col commanded a fighter gruppo, but flew as a supernumary with the 91ᵃ. By late September 1917 he had 12 victories, and on 25 October – a big day for the Italian fighters – claimed two more. Awarded the Medaglia d'Oro in March 1918, he had 24 victories when the war ended. Also in the 91ᵃ was Capitano Fulco Ruffo di Calabria, who had been another of the original 70ᵃ Squadriglia members, and who flew often with Baracca. By the end of September 1917 he was number two ace with 13 victories, and on 25 October he added two more. Another holder of the Medaglia d'Oro, he had 20 victories by the war's end, while Tenente Ferruccio Ranza of the same unit had 17. Tenente Luigi Olivari had 12 and Tenente Giovanni Ancillotto 11 – not for nothing was the 91ᵃ known as the 'Squadron of Aces'!

The leading ace of the 76ᵃ Squadriglia, and Italy's number two was a late starter. Previously an observation pilot, Tenente Silvio Scaroni flew HD 1s from mid-1917 until he was seriously wounded in action in July 1918, being credited with 26 victories. The 76ᵃ Squadriglia's second most successful pilot was Tenente Flavio Torello Baracchini, who gained most of his victories in 1917 before Scaroni joined the unit. He was killed in action during 1918 with his score at 20.

On the other side of the lines, the leading Austro-Hungarian pilot was Hauptmann Godwin Brumowski, a professional soldier who had joined the air service in 1915, becoming commanding officer of Fliegerkompagnie (Flik) 12 in the East. Late in 1916 he visited the Western Front to study German fighter organization, and on return formed the first Austro-Hungarian fighter unit, Flik 41J, with Brandenberg D.Is. By late 1917 Austrian-built Albatros D.IIIs were received in time for the Caporetto fighting, in which Brumowski played a leading part. His final score has been quoted variously as 35–40. He served with the Austrian Air Force after the war, but was killed in a flying accident in 1937.

One of his most successful pilots was half-

Above: Tenente Flavio Torello Baracchini (20 victories), one of the two most successful pilots of the Italian 76ᵃ Squadriglia, with his Spad.

English ex-cavalryman Oberleutnant Frank Linke-Crawford, who joined the flying service in 1916, first flying on the Italian Front with Flik 12. He later transferred to Brumowski's Flik 41J, and late in 1917 was given command of Flik 60J. His aircraft went down in flames on 31 July 1918 when five aircraft from his unit were lost in combat with Italian and British fighters. It was originally believed that Capt Jack Cottle of 45 Squadron (11 victories) had shot down the 27 to 30 victory Austro-Hungarian number three ace, although recent research indicates that it is more likely that he fell to an Italian Hanriot.

Oblt Benno Fiala, Ritter von Fernbrugg, joined the air service in 1914, initially as a technical officer, and then as an observer on the Russian Front. He then moved to the Italian Front with Flik 10, and on 4 May 1916 was observer in a Brandenberg C.I which intercepted the Italian airship M.4 which had bombed Lubiana by night, but had suffered an engine failure. He shot this dirigible down with his

Italian Farman in Albania. Converting to single-seaters early in 1917, he moved to the Italian Front and later in the year served in Flik 60J. The most highly decorated NCO with 26–32 victories, he became a test pilot after the war. After 1938 he served in the Luftwaffe as an instructor, his two most brilliant pupils being the World War II aces Marseille and Nowotny. He lived to a ripe old age, dying on 1 August 1981. Another leading NCO ace was Josef Kiss, who became a pilot in April 1916. On the Italian front with Flik 55J he was wounded in combat with the Italian ace Scaroni on 25 January 1918, but on 24 May was shot down and killed by an RAF Camel – probably that flown by Capt WG Barker of 66 Squadron. With 19 victories to his credit, this NCO did get his commission – posthumously!

Linienschiffsleutnant Gottfried Banfield became an ace in rather different circumstances. A Naval Air Service pilot who flew Brandenberg K.D.W. fighter flyingboats over the northern Adriatic coast, his first four victories were all against balloons. Intercepting French and Italian air raids on Trieste, he then brought down three F.B.A. flyingboats and a Caproni trimotor by September 1916, his final score reaching nine.

German fighter units, Jasta 1, 31 and 39, served on the Italian Front from December 1917 to February 1918, but jointly claimed only some 22 victories. However, following the Italian collapse at Caporetto, French and British help was sent, the latter including an air contingent which initially included two squadrons of Camel fighters, later increased to three. These squadrons, 28, 45 and 66, remained in Italy for the rest of the war (45 Squadron was brought back to the West shortly before the end of hostilities to join the new Independent Air Force for bomber escort duties), and were later joined by 139 Squadron with Bristol Fighters, which was formed there. A number of experienced pilots went out with 28 and 45 Squadrons in the first instance, and a considerable number of RFC/RAF pilots either added to their scores, or became aces there.

Lt CM McEwen, MC, DFC and Bar, a Canadian with 28 Squadron, was credited with 27 victories between 30 December 1917 and 4 October 1918. This total included 23 destroyed (two shared), and four out of control. Capt PC Carpenter, DSO, MC, after getting two and two shared in France, added three more in Italy before being posted from 45 to 66 Squadron; with this latter unit he added 14 more for a final score of 21, five of which were claimed out of control. Capt CE Howell of 45 Squadron gained 19 victories in Italy, 17 destroyed and two out of control, while Lt HK Goode of 66 Squadron was one of the two top 'balloon busters' here. He claimed six aircraft destroyed and three out of control, plus three more destroyed on the ground, and also accounted for seven balloons, one of them shared. Most successful of all however was one of the RAF's greatest aces of the war,

Top left: The leading Austro-Hungarian ace was Hpt Godwin Brumowski with 40 victories.
Above left: Oblt Frank Linke-Crawford of Flik 60J with a Phöenix D I Scout in the background.
Top right: Austro-Hungary's most highly-decorated NCO, Offizierstellvertreter Julius Arigi, the Empire's second highest scoring ace with 32 victories.
Above right: One of the RAF aces in Italy was Capt MB 'Bunty' Frew of 45 Squadron who claimed seven here to add to 20 previously gained with the unit over France.

flexible machine-gun for his first victory. Training as a pilot, he flew two-seaters in which he is reported to have gained five victories, but finally in 1917 transferred to single-seater Brandenberg D.Is. He later became commander of Flik 51J, and on 3 March 1918 shot down Lt A Jerrard of 66 Squadron, RAF, who was later awarded the Victoria Cross. Fiala survived the war with a score of 27–29, joining Junkers aircraft as an engineer.

In the class-conscious and conservative Austro-Hungarian forces it was virtually impossible for an NCO to be commissioned, however splendid his service, and there is no better example of this than the number two ace, Offizierstellvertreter Julius Arigi. Becoming a pilot in November 1914 at the age of 19, Arigi served on the Russian and Balkan fronts, achieving an astonishing success on 22 August 1916 when in a single flight in a two-seater he and his gunner claimed five aircraft shot down! On 4 September they gained a further success over an

The classic German fighter aircraft of late 1917/early 1918 – the Albatros DVa.

Canadian-born Maj William Barker. After seven victories in France, Barker served in Italy with 28 and 66 Squadrons, and then as commander of the new 139 Squadron. He flew the same Camel with all three units, claiming 41 victories on this front from his total of 52.

By November 1918 When the war ended, 363 German pilots had gained five or more victories by the exacting standards of their service; 12 of them had claimed 40 or more, 21 had 30 to 39, and 38 had between 20 and 29. The somewhat less stringent French system had produced at least 158 aces, of whom 14 had 20 or more credited to them and 39 had 10 to 19. The scoring system employed unofficially for the British Empire produced nearly 800 aces, 37 of whom had 30 or more successes; 57 had 20 to 29, and 226 had between 10 and 19. Additionally 65 pilots of bomber or Corps observation aircraft were credited with five or more victories and some 50 gunners were also credited with at least five each. The Italians had 43 aces, 10 of them with 10 or more victories. The Americans had 22 aces who served only with the British forces, six who flew only with the French, and 82 who gained at least some of their successes with the units of the USAS, plus one naval pilot.

As has been seen, many of the aces subsequently saw service at command level with the air forces of their nations during World War II. Numerous Germans would see further action – initially in the months immediately after the war in the internal conflict with the Communists at home and on the Eastern Frontiers. Among those joining the Freikorps were Berthold, Jacobs, Veltjens, Baumer and the naval pilots, Sachsenberg and Osterkamp. Several managed to fly while so engaged, but Franz Büchner was shot down and killed by ground fire while on a reconnaissance flight over Silesia, his body being robbed and mutilated. Berthold was also killed in 1921. Sachsenberg and Osterkamp flew Junkers monoplanes with the Iron Division in the Baltic area, where they saw considerable action.

Several of the aces later supported Adolf Hitler. Most notable is Hermann Goering, who became the Fuehrer's deputy, and whose formation of the Luftwaffe in 1935 did much to reconsolidate German power. Goering's story is well-known but he recruited to the new Luftwaffe many of the surviving old aces. Ritter von Greim, Lörzer and Kurt Student (5 victories) were all generals commanding air divisions by early 1939, while von Schleich and Osterkamp were leading fighter Gruppen – I/JG 234 and IV/JG 132 'Richthofen' respectively. Udet had been seduced from stunt flying and running his own aircraft-manufacturing business, to be in charge of aircraft procurement for the Luftwaffe. Von Schleich soon left the operational scene, but in 1941 commanded all air units in Denmark, retiring soon afterward as a General due to ill health.

During 1940 and 1941, throughout the Battles of France and Britain, and the invasion of Russia, von Greim led Fliegerkorps V, Lörzer led Fliegerkorps II and Wolfram von Richthofen, a young cousin of the 'Red Baron,' who had commanded the Legion Condor in Spain, commanded the Stuka dive-bombers of Fliegerkorps VIII. All remained in senior positions for the rest of the war, and on 24 April 1945 von Greim, by then commander of Luftflotte 4, was called to Hitler's bunker in Berlin and ordered to take over command of the Luftwaffe from Goering, who was then in disgrace. Von Greim committed suicide by poison on 24 May after becoming a prisoner of the Allies. Oskar Freiherr von Boenigk (26 victories) also became a general, while Kurt Student had become commander of the Luftwaffe's paratroop force during the war.

The naval ace Christiansen had headed the Nazi Flying Corps in the 1930s, and was in charge of the military government of the Netherlands from 1940 onward. He was tried and convicted of the war crimes of the SS and other units against the Dutch after the war, but was later released. Veltjens had joined the SA as a stormtrooper in 1930, joining the Luftwaffe when it was re-formed; he died in October 1943 as an Oberst. Josef Jacobs served as a Major, but the only ace to see further action was Osterkamp. After a spell as head of Jagdfliegerschule 1, he formed Jagdgeschwader 51 in November 1939, flying as Kommodore. Between May and July 1940 he gained six victories, including a Dutch Fokker G.I, two Hurricanes and a Spitfire. He then became Jagdfliegerführer on the Channel during the Battle of Britain, and later in Italy. On 22 August 1940 he received the coveted Ritterkreuze (Knights' Cross) as a Generalmajor, later receiving promotion to Generalleutnant.

Among the Allies, some French aces also

Baracca – ace of Italy

A career cavalryman, Francesco Baracca had become a pilot in 1912, and when fighting started between Itlay and the Central Powers, was flying a Nieuport two-seater. After several indecisive combats, he was given a Nieuport 11 'Bebe' to fly during the latter part of 1915 with the 70ª Squadriglia, and on 7 April 1916 gained his first victory over an Aviatik two-seater. More soon followed, and by early May his score already stood at 10, three of which were shared. A flight from the unit then formed the new 91ª Squadriglia, which received the new Spad S.VII, and Baracca became a flight commander in the new unit, gaining his next victory on 13 May – again shared. During June he became unit commander, and by the end of September 1917 was leading Italian ace with 19 victories. Five more followed in October, including two in a day twice, the last two on the 26th being German Aviatiks. As the Austro-Hungarians, reinforced now by German forces including three Jastas, launched their great offensive at Caporetto, the 91ª Squadriglia was re-equipped with Spad S.XIIIs during the Italian retreat. With these by the end of November Baracca's score had risen to 30, but he was then rested. Awarded the Medaglia d'Oro – Italy's highest award – in March 1918, he returned to action in May, raising his score to 34 on 15 June when he shot down two more two-seaters. On 19 June he failed to return, and was later found dead with a bullet through his forehead; it was assumed that he had been killed by ground fire while strafing, but recent research in Austro-Hungarian records indicates that he was killed by the gunner of an Austrian two-seater while attacking from above and behind.

Italy's No 2 – Silvio Scaroni

Tenente Silvio Scaroni flew Caudron G IVs on observation duties until mid-1917, when he at last converted to single-seaters, joining the 76ª Squadriglia which flew Nieuport 17s and Belgian-designed Hanriot HD 1s. His first victory came on 15 November 1917 over an Albatros two-seater during the fighting late in the Austro-Hungarian Caporetto offensive. Two more victories followed during November, and then three Albatros C.IIIs during December. On 26 December his unit's base at Istrana was attacked by a strong force of bombers; intercepting, he shot down two Knollers and a Gotha – a new Italian record. His 11th victory, a Brandenberg, fell on 10 January 1918, and on 3 April he claimed his only balloon. He again claimed three – two Brandenberg scouts and a Phönix – on 7 July. On 12 July, in a big fight, he shot down an Albatros D.III and a Phönix scout, but was then shot down himself, surviving the crash, but with severe wounds. Awarded the Medaglia d'Oro, his final score was 26. In 1927 he commanded a fighter gruppo, and later went to Washington as air attaché. He served in World War II as a generale with the Regia Aeronautica.

saw further action in World War II. The most remarkable was Marc Ambrogi, who in 1940 was deputy commander of GC I/8, flying Bloch MB 152 fighters. With this unit he shot down a Junkers Ju 52/3m transport aircraft in May 1940. Two others who scored in both wars were Colonels Edouard Corniglion-Molinier and Lionel de Marmier. Corniglion-Molinier, with eight victories in World War I, claimed four or five more in the later war with GC III/2. He then led the Lorraine bomber squadron of the Free French in North Africa in 1941, and during 1942–1943 flew as a supernumerary with 341 (Free French) Spitfire Squadron from England De Marmier claimed six–nine with Esc SPA 81 and SPA 176, then three more in June 1940 as commander of I Escadrille Polonais (a Free Polish fighter unit). In 1941 he led Esc de Bombardment 2 in North Africa with the Free French attached to the RAF, operating Martin Maryland aircraft.

The only British pilot to gain victories in both wars was Air Vice-Marshal Stanley F Vincent. Flying Nieuports with 60 Squadron in 1916–1917, he was credited with three victories, adding two more in September 1940 flying Hurricanes with 229 Squadron when a Group Captain in command of Northolt and North Weald airfields. He later served with distinction in command positions in the Far East.

1919

As has already been noted, a number of British, German, Russian and other pilots fought on various fronts against Bolshevic forces in 1919, and several aces gained further victories in these conflicts. The newly independent state of Poland fought a full-scale war with Russia during 1919–1920, during which Polish pilots claimed several victories. One of these was credited to Porucznik (Lieutenant) Stefan Stec, who flew a Fokker D.VIII monoplane, and claimed a Nieuport Scout shot down on 29 April 1919; he had previously gained seven victories with the Austro-Hungarian air force.

In South Russia the White forces received considerable support from 47 Squadron, RAF, a composite unit with one flight equipped with Sopwith Camels. Against a variety of ex-German and Russian Air Service machines, including Albatros Scouts, Fokker Triplanes and Nieuports, the flight gained a number of victories. As already mentioned, the most successful pilot was South African Sam Kinkead (later a Schneider Trophy pilot), who claimed between five and 10 more victories here, while the squadron commander, Ray Collishaw, added two more. A third pilot, an American Lt Marion Aten, became the only new ace of 1919, gaining five victories and being awarded a DFC.

TOP-SCORING GERMAN FIGHTER PILOTS OF WORLD WAR I

Pilot	Score	Unit
Rittmeister Manfred Freiherr von Richthofen*	80	Jasta 2, 11, JG I
Oblt Ernst Udet	62	Jasta 15, 37, 11, 4
Oblt Erich Löwenhardt*	53	Jasta 10
Lt Josef Jacobs	48	Jasta 22, 7
Lt Werner Voss*	48	Jasta 2, 29, 14, 10
Lt Fritz Rumey*	45	Jasta 2, 5
Hpt Rudolph Berthold	44	Jasta 4, 14, 18, JG II
Lt Paul Bäumer	43	Jasta 5, 2
Hpt Bruno Lörzer	41	Jasta 26, JG III
Hpt Oswald Boelcke*	40	Jasta 2
Lt Franz Buchner	40	Jasta 9, 19, 13
Oblt Lothar Freiherr von Richthofen	40	Jasta 11
Lt Karl Menckhoff	39	Jasta 3, 72
Lt Heinrich Gontermann*	39	Jasta 5, 15
Lt Max Müller*	36	Jasta 22, 2, 28
Lt Julius Buckler	35	Jasta 17
Lt Gustav Dörr	35	Jasta 45
Lt Otto Könnecke	35	Jasta 25, 5
Hpt Eduard Ritter von Schliech	35	Jasta 21, 32b, JG IV
Lt Josef Veltjens	34	Jasta 14, 18, 15
Oblt Kurt Wolff*	33	Jasta 11
Lt Heinrich Bongartz	33	Jasta 36
Lt Theo Osterkamp	32 (+ 6WW II)	MarineJasta 2
Lt Emil Thuy	32	Jasta 21, 28
Lt Paul Billik	31	Jasta 12, 7, 52
Rittmeister Karl Bolle	31	Jasta 28, 2
Oblt Gotthard Sachsenberg	31	MarineJasta 1
Lt Karl Allmenröder*	30	Jasta 11
Lt Karl Degelow	30	Jasta 40
Lt Heinrich Kroll	30	Jasta 9, 24
Lt Josef Mai	30	Jasta 5
Lt Ulrich Neckel	30	Jasta 12, 6
Lt Karl Schäfer*	30	Jasta 11, 28
Lt Hermann Frommerz	29	
Lt Walter von Bülow*	28	Jasta 36, 2
Lt Walter Blume	28	Jasta 9
Oblt Fritz Ritter von Roth	28	Jasta 23, 16b
Oblt Fritz Bernert*	27	Jasta 2, 6
Vizefeldwebel Otto Fruhner	27	Jasta 26
Lt Hans Kirschstein*	27	Jasta 6
Lt Karl Thom	27	Jasta 21
Hpt Adolf Ritter von Tutschek*	27	Jasta 2, 12, JG II
Lt Kurt Wüsthoff	27	Jasta 4, 15
Oblt Harald Auffahrt	26	Jasta 18, 9
Oblt Oscar Freiherr von Boenigk	26	Jasta 4, 21, JG II
Oblt Eduard Dostler*	26	Jasta 6
Lt Arthur Laumann	26	Jasta 66, 10
Lt Oliver Freiherr von Beaulieú-Marconnay*	25	Jasta 15, 19
Oblt Robert Ritter von Greim	25	Jasta 28w, 34b, JGr 9
Lt Georg von Hantelmann	25	Jasta 15
Lt Max Näther	25	Jasta 62
Lt Fritz Pütter*	25	Jasta 68

*Indicates killed during the war.

Left: Maj Donald MacLaren (59 victories) the Canadian Camel ace of 46 Squadron is less well-known than most leading Commonwealth aces. His score included a high percentage of shared victories.
Top: The Bavarian ace Hpt Eduard Ritter von Schleich (left) of Jasta 32 (35 victories) converses with Oblt Ernst Udet, Germany's No 2 ace with 62 victories.
Center: The von Richthofen brothers Lothar (left) and Manfred.

TOP-SCORING FRENCH FIGHTER PILOTS OF WORLD WAR I

Capt René Fonck	75	Esc C 47, SPA 103
Capt Georges Guynemer*	54	Esc N, SPA 3
Lt Charles Nungesser	45	Esc VB 106, N 65, SPA 65
Capt Georges Madon	41	Esc MF 218, SPA 38
Lt Maurice Boyau*	35	Esc N 77, SPA 77
Lt Michel Coiffard*	34	Esc SPA 154
Lt Jean Bourjade	28	Esc N 152
Capt Armand Pinsard	27	Esc MS 23, N 26, N 78, SPA 23, SPA 23
Sous Lt René Dorme*	23	Esc C 94, C 95, N 3
Lt Gabriel Guérin*	23	Esc N 15, N 88
Sous Lt Claude Haegelen	23	Esc N 103, SPA 100
Sous Lt Pierre Marinovitch	22	Esc N 38, SPA 44
Capt Alfred Hertaux	21	Esc MS 26, MS 38, N 3
Capt Albert Deullin	20	Esc MF 62, N 3, SPA 73
Capt Henri De Slade	19	Esc SPA 159
Lt Jacques Ehrlich	19	Esc SPA 15
Lt Bernard de Romanet	18	Esc SPA 37, SPA 167
Lt Jean Chaput	16	
Capt Armande de Turenne	15	Esc SPA 48
Lt Gilbert Sardier	15	Esc N 77, SPA 77
Lt Marius Ambrogi	14 (+ 1WW II)	Esc N 507, SPA 90

TOP-SCORING FIGHTER PILOTS OF THE BRITISH EMPIRE IN WORLD WAR I

Maj William A Bishop	72	Canadian	21, 60, 86 Squadrons
Maj Edward C Mannock*	68 approx.	British	40, 74, 85 Squadrons
Maj Raymond Collishaw	62	Canadian	3 (N), 10 (N), 13 (N), 203, 47 Squadrons
(score includes two in South Russia, 1919)			
Maj James TB McCudden*	57	British	3, 20, 29, 66, 56, 60 Squadrons
Capt Anthony W Beauchamp-Proctor	54	South African	84 Squadron
Capt Donald M MacLaren	54	Canadian	46 Squadron
Maj William G Barker	52	Canadian	9, 4, 15, 28, 66, 139, 201 Squadrons
Maj Roderic S Dallas*	51	Australian	1 (N), 201, 40 Squadrons
Capt George EH McElroy*	49	Irish	24, 40 Squadrons
Capt Albert Ball*	47	British	13, 11, 8, 60, 56 Squadrons
Capt Robert A Little*	47	Australian	8 (N), 3 (N), 203 Squadrons
Maj Thomas F Hazell	43	Irish	1, 24, 203 Squadrons
Capt Philip F Fullard	42	British	1 Squadron
Maj John Gilmour	40	British	27, 65, 28 Squadrons
Capt J Ira T Jones	40	British	10, 74 Squadrons
Capt Frederick R McCall	37	Canadian	13, 41 Squadrons
Capt William G Claxton	36	Canadian	41 Squadron
Capt Henry W Woollett	36	British	24, 43 Squadrons
Capt Samuel M Kinkead	35–40	South African	1 (N), 201, 47 Squadrons
(score includes 5–10 in South Russia in 1919)			
Capt J Stuart T Fall	34	Canadian	3 (N), 4 (N), 9 (N) Squadrons
Capt William L Jordan	34	British	11 (N), 8 (N), 208 Squadrons
Capt Alfred C Atkey	33	Canadian	18, 22 Squadrons
Maj Geoffrey H Bowman	32	British	29, 56, 41 Squadrons
Maj Albert D Carter	31	Canadian	19 Squadron
Capt Andrew E McKeever	30	Canadian	11 Squadron
Capt Arthur H Cobby	30	Australian	71, 4 AFC Squadrons
Capt R King	28	Australian	4 AFC Squadron
Capt Leonard H Rochford	28	British	3 (N), 203 Squadrons
Capt Matthew B Frew	27	British	45 Squadron
Capt Reginald TC Hoidge	27	British	56, 1 Squadrons
Lt Christopher M MacEwen	27	Canadian	28 Squadron
Maj Gerald JC Maxwell	27	British	56 Squadron
Flt Lt AT Whealy	27	Canadian	3 (N), 9 (N), 203 Squadrons

Capt William C Campbell	26	British	1 Squadron
Capt John E Gurdon	26	British	22 Squadron
Capt Alexander AND Pentland	26	Australian	16, 19, 87 Squadrons
CaptWilliam E Staton	26	British	62 Squadron
Lt SFH Thompson*	26	British	22 Squadron
Maj Keith L Caldwell	25	New Zealander	8, 60, 74 Squadrons
Maj Robert JO Compston	25	British	8 (N), 40 Squadrons
Capt WFJ Harvey	25	British	22 Squadron
Capt Henry GE Luchford	25	British	20 Squadron
Capt Francis G Quigley	25	Canadian	70 Squadron
Maj John O Andrews	24	British	5, 24, 66, 209, 221 Squadrons
Capt Percy J Clayson	24	British	1 Squadron
Capt George E Thomson	24	British	46 Squadron
Capt Louis F Jenkin*	23	British	1 Squadron
Capt Edgar JK McCloughry	23	Australian	23, 4 AFC Squadrons
Lt Arthur PF Rhys Davids*	23	British	56 Squadron
Capt Stanley W Rosevear*	23	Canadian	1 (N), 201 Squadrons

*Indicates killed during the war.

TOP-SCORING AMERICAN FIGHTER PILOTS OF WORLD WAR I

Capt Edward V Rickenbacker	26	94th Aero Squadron, USAS
Capt William C Lambert	22	24 Squadron, RAF
Capt August T Iaccaci	18	20 Squadron, RAF
2nd Lt Frank Luke Jr*	18	27th Aero Squadron, USAS
Capt Frederick W Gillett	17	79 Squadron, RAF
Maj Raoul Lufbery*	17	Esc VB 106, N 124, French Air Service; 95th, 94th Aero Squadrons, USAS
Capt Howard A Kuhlberg	16	1 Squadron, RAF
Capt Oren J Rose	16	92 Squadron, RAF
Capt Clive W Warman	15	23 Squadron, RFC
Capt Elliott W Springs	15	85 Squadron, RAF; 148th Aero Squadron, USAS
1st Lt David E Putnam*	13	Esc MS 156, SPA 38, French Air Service; 139th Aero Squadron, USAS
1st Lt George A Vaughan Jr	13	84 Squadron, RAF; 17th Aero Squadron, USAS
2nd Lt Frank L Baylies*	12	Esc SPA 73, SPA 3, French Air Service
Lt Louis Bennett Jr*	12	40 Squadron, RAF
Capt Field E Kindley	12	65 Squadron, RAF; 148th Aero Squadron, USAS
Maj Reed G Landis	12	40 Squadron, RAF; 25th Aero Squadron, USAS
Lt Paul T Iaccaci	11	20 Squadron, RAF
Lt Kenneth R Unger	11	210 Squadron, RAF
Capt Jacques M Swaab	10	25th Aero Squadron, USAS

Below: Belgian ace 2nd Lt Edmond Thieffry (10 victories) in his 5eme Escadrille Nieuport 17.

TOP-SCORING ITALIAN FIGHTER PILOTS OF WORLD WAR I

Maggiore Francesco Baracca*	34	5ª, 70ª, 91ª Squadriglia
Tenente Silvio Scaroni	26	4ª, 44ª, 76ª Squadriglia
Tenente-Colonnello Pier Ruggiero Piccio	24	5ª, 91ª Squadriglia
Tenente Flavio Baracchini*	21	76ª Squadriglia
Capitano Fulco Ruffo di Calabria	20	70ª, 91ª Squadriglia
Sergente Marziale Cerutti	17	79ª Squadriglia
Tenente Ferruccio Ranza	17	70ª, 91ª Squadriglia
Tenente Luigi Olivari*	12	70ª, 91ª Squadriglia
Tenente Giovanni Ancillotto	11	77ª, 91ª Squadriglia
Sergente Antonio Reali	11	78ª Squadriglia

Right: A group of American pilots pose near Toul, France, in July 1918.

TOP-SCORING BELGIAN FIGHTER PILOTS OF WORLD WAR I

2nd Lt Willy Coppens de Houthulst	37	Esc 6eme, 1ere
Adj Andrew de Meulemeester	11	Esc 1ere, 9me
2nd Lt Edmond Thieffry	10	Esc 5 e
Capt Fernand Jacquet	7	Esc 2 eme, 1ere
Lt Jan Olieslagers	6	Esc 5me, 1ere

TOP-SCORING RUSSIAN FIGHTER PILOTS OF WORLD WAR I

Staff-Capt Alexander A Kazakov*	17 (unofficial 32)	XIX Squadron
Capt Paul V d'Arguéef (or Argeyev)	15 (9 in France)	Esc SPA 124
Lt Cdr Alexander P de Seversky	13	Fighter Chief, Baltic Navy
Lt Ivan W Smirnoff	12	XIX Squadron
Lt Mikhail Safonov	11	Naval pilot, Baltic
Capt Boris Sergievsky	11	2nd Fighter Squadron
Ens Eduard M Thomson*	11	

TOP-SCORING FIGHTER PILOTS OF THE AUSTRO-HUNGARIAN EMPIRE IN WORLD WAR I

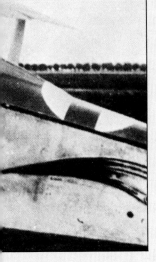

Hpt Godwin Brumowski	40	Flik 12, Flik 41
Offstelvtr Julius Arigi	32	Flik 60
Oblt Frank Linke-Crawford*	30	Flik 22, 8, 14, 12, 41, 60
Oblt Benno Fiala, Ritter von Fernbrugg	29	Flik 1, 10, 51J
Lt Josef Kiss	19	
Lt Franz Gräser	16	
Stabsfw Stefan Fejes	15	
Fw Eugen Bönsch	15	
Offstelvtr Kurt Gruber	14	
Oblt Ernst Strohschneider	14	
Hpt Raoul Stojsavlejevic	12	
Lt Franz Rudorfer	10	
Hpt Adolf Heyrowsky	10	
Oblt Friedrich Navratil	10	
Hpt Josef von Meier	10	
Linienschiffslt Gottfried Banfield	9	Naval pilot

When the residual conflicts which followed immediately on the heels of World War I had died down, a period of relative peace descended. Only in South America was this broken in a serious way, when a long-standing border dispute between Paraguay and Bolivia flared into the Gran Chaco War in 1932. The war was long and fierce, not ending until both countries were in a state of economic exhaustion in 1935. Paraguayan Potez 25 reconnaissance-bombers and Fiat CR 20 fighters were pitted against Bolivia's more numerous Curtiss Hawk, Osprey and Falcon types, and Junkers W.34 bombers. Each side suffered combat losses, but aerial fighting was relatively limited. Major Rafael Pavon emerged as top scorer with three victories, heralded as Bolivia's 'Ace of Aces.'

A more serious outbreak of fighting, involving substantial air forces on both sides, occurred on 18 July 1936 when a right-wing army-led insurrection began in Spain against the leftist Republican government and the growing anarchy surrounding it. Initially the greater part of the air force remained loyal to the government, although most officer pilots joined the Nationalist insurgents, much of whose true 'muscle' lay across the narrow neck of the Mediterranean, in Spanish Morocco. During August initial aid came from the dictators of Germany and Italy for the Nationalists, both nations sending transport aircraft to help fly across the African Army, and small fighter contingents, equipped with Heinkel He 51 and Fiat CR 32 biplanes — superior to the main Spanish service fighter, the Nieuport-Delage NiD 52.

Volunteers from many nations flocked to join the Republican forces in the spirit of a crusade against international fascism, while material aid came initially from the leftist Blum government of France. This consisted mainly of fighter aircraft — largely Dewoitine 371 high-wing monoplanes — and of Potez 540 bombers. A Nationalist drive from the South on Madrid brought heavy fighting in which German and Italian pilots joined the Spaniards in action against other Spaniards and a heterogeneous collection of Frenchmen, Americans, British, Czechs, Yugoslavians and others. An early edge was gained by the Nationalists with their superior aircraft and better trained pilots, but in October 1936 substantial Russian help began reaching the Republic, and in November Polikarpov I-15 biplane fighters, followed by I-16

monoplanes, started to appear over Madrid in the hands of Russian pilots. These proved superior to the He 51s, and an equal match for the CR 32s. More aid came from the European dictators, Mussolini forming an Aviazione Legionaria, and Hitler sending a similar force, the Legion Condor.

Greatly reinforced, the Republican forces opened an offensive on the Jarama River in February 1937 to lift the pressure from Madrid. This led to violent fighting, although it ended in stalemate. The following month the Nationalists attacked in the north, their Vizcaya offensive gradually crumbling away the industrial cities of the Basque region. Another Republican offensive at Brunete in March failed to make headway, or to remove the pressure in the north. Steadily larger numbers of aircraft, tanks and other material of the latest types were fed in by the totalitarian states, the Brunete fighting seeing the first appearance of the early models of Germany's famous Messerschmitt Bf 109 fighter. Aid from France ended before 1936 was out, and for the rest of the war the Western democracies maintained an attitude of strict neutrality. While the Nationalist leadership was soon firmly in the hands of Franco, the government forces remained split by conflicting groups, but increasingly under the dominance of the Communists. Gradually the foreign volunteers and mercenaries drifted away until by the end of 1937 most had gone.

Offensives followed one upon the other, but gradually the balance swung inexorably to the Nationalists' advantage, and from early 1938 onward it was only a matter of time. The Legion Condor gained its 100th aerial victory over Teruel during January 1938, while on 6 March its bombers played an active part in the war's greatest naval battle. Early in the summer of 1938 the Russians withdrew, Josef Stalin considering Spain to be a lost cause by then. Still the Republicans fought on, launching their last great offensive on the Ebro River in July. With all the Biscayan coast and its industrial resources in Franco's hands and with the remaining Republican territory split in two by a Nationalist drive to the sea in the East, the remaining months of the war saw a desperate defensive battle fought, as the Republic gradually shrank away to nothing. Right to the end Russian fighter planes — some built in Spain, and all now manned by Spaniards — appeared to fight the ever-growing numbers of Spanish-,

Above: The first successful fighter pilot of the Civil War was Spanish Nationalist Capt Miguel Guerrero Garcia (right) who claimed four victories flying Nieuport NiD 52 fighters. Seated next to him is Capt (later Cdt) Joaquin Garcia Morato who became top-scorer of the war, and Capt Narciso Bermudez de Castro who was killed in action after four victories.
Above right: No 2 Nationalist ace was Cdt Julio Diaz Benzumea with 25 victories.

German- and Italian-flown CR 32s, Bf 109s, He 112s and miscellaneous other types. The last victory of the war was claimed over an I-15 by Oberleutnant Hubertus von Bonin of the Legion Condor's J/88 in a new Bf 109E on 5 March 1939, and before the month was out, the war ended with the fall of Madrid.

The Nationalists own fighter forces claimed 294 victories and produced some 20 aces, 10 of them with scores of 10 or more. The Legion Condor also produced 20 aces in gaining 314 victories, although the greater number of pilots available kept individual totals somewhat lower. The Italians too claimed many victories, but were less specific about keeping personal scores, although at least 15 of their pilots are believed to have accounted for five or more. Of the Republican side less is known for certain, but numbers of Russians and Spaniards built up respectable scores, as did a handful of the foreign volunteers.

Capitano Miguel Guerrero Garcia claimed the second victory in the air for the Nationalists on 25 July 1936 when he shot down a Dornier Wal flying boat over the Straits between Africa and Spain. On 29 July he brought down a Vickers Vildebeeste over Granada, claiming another of these on 31st, and a Breguet XIX on 1 August. These four victories were the most victories claimed while flying a NiD 52 by any Nationalist pilot, and for a short time he was top scorer. He later flew CR 32s with Grupo 2-G-3, adding a further nine victories — four I-15s, three 'Papagayos' (assault bombers — R-5s and R-Zs) and two I-16s.

However no other pilot in Spain was to approach the success of Comandante Joaquin Garcia-Morato, who flew throughout the war, claiming a total of 40 victories. Most Nationalist Spaniards who became aces did so under Garcia Morato's command. One of the most successful was Comandante Julio Salvador Diaz Benzumea, who served with Morato in his original three-man 'Patrulla Azul' (Blue Patrol) in 1936. Claiming two victories while flying an He 51, plus 22 and a balloon in a CR 32, he was shot down on 30 October 1938, spending the last months of the war as a prisoner. Comandante Angel Salas Larrazabal claimed one light aircraft over Teruel while flying a NiD 52, and then flew CR 32s. On 29 October 1936 he shot down the first of the fast monoplane Tupolev SB-2 bombers to fall to a Nationalist fighter. With his score at five he moved to an He 51 unit, but after two further victories, joined the new 2-G-3 on CR 32s again, and by late September 1938 had raised his total to 16, including three SB-2s and an I-16 in a single sortie on 2 September.

Other stars of the 3 Escuadra later in the war were Captain Manuel Vazquez Sagaztizabal, who claimed $21\frac{1}{3}$ victories with 2-G-3 in CR 32s, but he was shot down and killed on 23 January 1939. The unit's only non-Spanish pilot of note was a Belgian nobleman, Count Rodolphe de Hemricourt de Grunne, who claimed 10 victories with 2-G-3. In 1940 he joined RAF Fighter Command in England, claiming three and three probables with 32 Squadron in Hurricanes. He was killed in action in May 1941.

One of the first Italian fighter pilots to reach Spain, Adriano Mantelli, served as a Sergente under the *nom de guerre* of 'Arrighi.' The first Italian pilot to shine, Magistrini (who claimed at least three victories), was killed on 14 November 1936, Mantelli taking his place as the leading light of the Aviazione Legionaria. On 3 November he became the first Italian to shoot down one of the fast SB-2s – only the second to be brought down in Spain – and he subsequently emerged as the Legionaria's top scorer with 15 victories. Another Italian to do well early in the war was Giuseppe Cenni – known as Tenente 'Stella.' He gained victories over six aircraft and a dirigible balloon, including three in one day in December 1936, before baling out during a storm and becoming a prisoner. In World War II he operated as a dive-bomber pilot, flying German-made Ju 87 'Stukas' over Greece, Malta and the North African desert. In summer 1943 he commanded the 5° Stormo Tuffator in Southern Italy, flying Reggiane Re 2002 fighter-bombers. He was shot down and killed by RAF Spitfires over Calabria on 3 September with five others of his unit, survivors reporting that he and his wingman had shot down two Spitfires before they fell. He was posthumously awarded Italy's highest medal for bravery, the Medaglia d'Oro. Capt. Enrico Degl'Incerti claimed six Russian-built fighters shot down and five more shared during 1937, but was killed in a flying accident soon after his return to Italy. One of the Italian Legion's 'characters' was Ten Col Ernesto Botto, who flew in the 32ª Squadriglia; he claimed two I-16s on 6 August for his first victories. On 12 October he claimed an I-15, but was hit and his right leg was shattered. He had by then claimed five victories, with shares in 15 others. He managed to land in a semiconscious state, but subsequently lost his leg. Returning to action with an artificial leg, his unit became known as 'Gamba di Ferro' (Iron Leg), carrying a stylized emblem showing an armored leg. He later commanded the 9° Gruppo CT in World War II, which also carried this emblem, and with this unit claimed the first Italian fighter victory over Malta – a Hurricane on 3 July 1940 – before serving in the Western Desert. His final score is uncertain.

Mario Bonzano, a career airman, saw service

Top left: Capt Angel Salas Larrazabal (right) with Cdt Joaquin Garcia Morato. He gained 16 victories in Spain and later seven more in Russia in 1941.
Center left: The highest-scoring fighter pilot to be killed in action in Spain was Nationalist ace Capt Manuel Vazquez Sagaztizabal (21½ victories) of Grupo 2-G-3.
Above: Ten Col Mario Bonzano, one of Italy's two top scorers in Spain with 15 victories, later added to his total over the Libyan desert in North Africa.
Top right: The other top scorer of the Aviacione Legionaria in Spain was Serg Adriano Mantelli.

in Ethiopia before going to Spain. Here he flew first as a squadriglia commander in the 'Asso di Bastoni' (Ace of Clubs) Gruppo, and later in 1939 commanded an experimental unit of Fiat G-50 monoplanes. He is reported to have equalled Mantelli's score of 15 in Spain. Subsequently he commanded the 20° Gruppo CT in the Western Desert in 1941–42, again flying G-50 fighters, gaining at least two more victories in the later conflict – two Hurricanes on 3 September 1941.

Among the initial batch of German fighter pilots in Spain, Eberhardt and Henrici gained initial notice as the most promising, but both were killed before achieving five victories. Hannes Trautloft later gained great fame in the Luftwaffe, but less was heard of Herwig Knüppel, who actually became the first German ace of the war. Claiming a Breguet XIX on 26 August 1936, a Nieuport LN 46 on the 27th and a Potez 540 on the 30th, he added three more French aircraft during September before the more effective Russian types arrived. Although the He 51s he was flying were hard-pressed by the new I-15s, he managed to shoot down one of these on 13 November, and on 12 December gained his last victory over an SB-2 – an almost unheard-of achievement for the slow Heinkel. Returning to Germany, he later became Kommandeur of II Gruppe, Jagdgeschwader 26, but was killed on 19 May 1940 over France after adding three more victories to his score to raise his total to 11.

Following the arrival of the first Messerschmitt Bf 109Bs in Spain in summer 1937, Fw. Peter Boddem became the first notable exponent of this type. Claiming his first I-16 on 12 July, he gained his fifth victory on 13 August and his tenth on 9 September – seven I-16s, two I-15s and an SB-2. After his return to Germany he was killed in an accident in a Ju 52/3m on 20 March 1939. After gaining one victory on an He 51 early in 1937, Major Harro Harder also converted to Messerschmitts, gaining his 11th victory on 5 December to pass Boddem's total. He later served in World War II in III/JG 53, claiming six more victories before being killed during the Battle of Britain. His score remained the Legion's highest until August 1938 when Wolfgang Schellmann, commander of 1 Staffel, J/88, claimed his 12th. In 1940 he would claim 10 more, becoming Kommodore of JG 27 in 1941. He collided with debris from an I-16 – his 25th victory – on the first day of the Russian invasion, and baled out. It was believed that he was subsequently shot by the NKVD.

Although not one of the leaders, Wilhelm Balthasar was notable for shooting down four SB-2 bombers in a single engagement on 7 February 1938 – a record at that time. With seven victories in Spain, he later emerged as one of the Luftwaffe's most important fighter pilots of 1940. There was never enough opposition for more than one high scorer to appear at a time in the Legion, but the greatest was yet to emerge. Already a highly trained officer and ex-instructor when he arrived in Spain in July 1938, Werner Mölders took over J/88's 3 Staffel as it converted from He 51s to the latest Bf 109Cs. During the next four months he built up a steady score until on 15 October, when he shot down two I-16s, he became the Legion Condor's top scorer with 14 victories. During 1940 he became a living legend to the German people, and Germany's greatest fighter pilot of the early years of the war.

On the Republican side, Major Andres Garcia Lacalle was considered to be the 'Ace of Aces' of the Republican Spaniards (although according to a Russian source, Leopoldo Morquillas Rubio, commander of the 2nd Chato Escuadrilla – I-15s – achieved 21 victories, later serving with the Soviet Air Force during World War II). An NCO pilot before the war, Lacalle rallied to the Republic and was involved in the earliest fighting flying a NiD 52 and other available aircraft. He was the first Spaniard to command a unit of Russian-built I-15s, and subsequently went to Russia to organize the training of new pilots. In many ways he was to the Republicans what Garcia-Morato was to the Nationalists. He was reputed to have gained at least 11 victories, some sources indicating that he claimed five of

Garcia-Morato – ace of the Civil War

Already a highly experienced pilot who had seen service against Arab guerrillas in Morocco, and served as a fighter instructor, Spain's Joaquin Garcia-Morato y Castano was on holiday in England when the civil war broke out. Hastening home to join the Nationalist cause, he gained his first victory in a Nieuport-Delage 52 on 12 August 1936 – one of three Vickers Vildebeeste over Antequera. He then flew one of the first Heinkel He 51s to be received from Germany, shooting down a Republican NiD 52 and a Potez 540 on 18 August and another NiD 52 on 2 September. He began flying an Italian Fiat CR 32, gaining his fifth victory in one of these on 11 September – another NiD 52. After a short period flying with the Italians, he was allowed to form his own Patrulla Azul (Blue Patrol) of three CR 32s, and from this grew the greater part of the Nationalist fighter force, as under his leadership it expanded first into an escuadrilla, and then a grupe, and finally an escuadra of two grupes. During the early Autumn of 1936 he added six more aircraft of French manufacture to his score, plus a British-built Hawker Fury; on 5 November his 12th victory (over a Potez 540) was followed by his first against a Russian aircraft – an I-15.

On 3 January 1937, with 15 victories already to his credit, he climbed high on a standing patrol in an effort to catch one of the fast, high-flying Tupolev SB-2 bombers, which outperformed the Cr 32 in terms of speed. Two appeared, and diving on these he shot both down. Further victories followed during the hard summer fighting of 1937, and on 1 August he claimed his 27th victory. Five more followed by mid-1938, but he now flew combat less frequently as he had been appointed Chief of Operations. Keen to fly on every opportunity he also undertook missions in many other types including He 112 and Bf 109B fighters, Ju 52/3m, He 111 and Do 17 bombers, and He 70 reconnaissance aircraft. During the second half of 1938 he flew with his old unit on numerous occasions, shooting down four more fighters by early October. On 24 December 1938 he enjoyed his best day when he claimed three Polikarpov R-5 attack bombers, and when his next victim – an I-15 – fell on 19 January 1939 his score had reached 40 – a total far higher than any other pilot was to achieve in Spain. Gained in 1012 hours of operational flying, this score included a dozen I-15s, five I-16s and nine R-5s. All but his first four victories were gained in the same aircraft – his faithful Cr 32, which carried the numbers 3-51 on the fuselage. On 3 April 1939, the war over, he took up 3-51 to undertake some low aerobatics for newsreel cameras, but the engine for once let him down, and he crashed to his death.

these in one day.

Most other early Republican aces were foreign volunteers. The only World War I fighter pilots to see combat in Spain were some Frenchmen serving in André Malraux's 'Esquadra Espana.' Abel Guides led the pilots in this unit and remained in Spain after its disbandment in November 1936, reputedly claiming six fighters and five bombers shot down. It was claimed that another French pilot, Darré, had been an ace in the earlier war, although his name does not appear on the official French list; he may have made five claims, not all of which were confirmed. In Spain however, he claimed three victories, including a two-seat reconnaissance aircraft in mid-August 1936. Most successful of the foreigners was Teniente Frank G Tinker, an American, who joined Lacalle's I-15 unit in January 1937, claiming his first CR 32 over Guadalajara on 14 March. After three victories (two CR 32s and an He 51) he was posted to a Russian-led I-16 unit, and with this gained five more victories during June and July, including three CR 32s and two of the new German Messerschmitt Bf 109Bs. Highly thought of by the Spaniards, he was in grave trouble for his adventures in Spain with the US State Department on his return home. He was not permitted to rejoin his previous flying service, the US Navy, and subsequently took his own life after publishing his autobiography, *Some Still Live*. Albert J 'Ajax' Baumler also joined the Lacalle unit, claiming two, one shared and a probable while flying I-15s, and subsequently claimed two and a probable in I-16s. He later went to China to join the American Volunteer Group (Flying Tigers), arriving after the United States had come into the war. Inducted into the USAAF, he flew in the 23rd Fighter Group, which the

AVG had become, and claimed five more victories, two of them at night. His score has been quoted as 13, but this includes two probables and one shared.

Other volunteers included Yugoslavian Bozko Petrovik with seven victories on I-15s in Lacalle's unit, including the first claim against a Bf 109 on 8 July 1937, and Czech Jan Ferak, who also claimed seven flying Dewoitine D.510s and I-16s. Petrovik was killed in action soon after his seventh victory, while Ferak went down at sea while aboard ship during World War II.

The Russians, better trained and organized than most of the volunteers, proved to be the most successful as a group. Operating under the *nom de guerre* 'Pablo Palencar,' Pavel Rychagov commanded the first I-15 escuadrilla to go into action in the Madrid area in November 1936. He is credited with shooting down four He 51s during that month, although he was shot down himself and baled out safely. He is reported to have gained 15 victories by the time he returned to Russia. Rapidly promoted to senior rank, he was shot during one of Stalin's purges before the outbreak of World War II.

Son of a fomer Polish nobleman, Boris Turshanski flew I-16s late in 1936, but was wounded in combat following his sixth victory, and lost an eye. He was, like Rychagov, rapidly promoted to Brigade Commander after his return to Russia, and was the first Soviet airman to be made a Hero of the Soviet Union for action in Spain. However, he too was shot in 1938. Known in Spain as 'Carlos Castejon,' Anatoli Serov was considered the most successful of the Russian pilots here, with a reputed 16 victories. In the summer of 1937 he formed a small nightfighter detachment of I-15s and during the early

Above left: A successful American in Spain was Albert J 'Ajax' Baumler who gained four and one shared plus two more probables. He is seen here in China with the USAAF in 1942 when he gained five more victories.
Above: A trio of Republican fighter pilots flanked by their mechanics and with a Polikarpov I-15 'Chato' in the background. Left to right: Harold 'Whitey' Dahl, 'Chang' Selles and Frank G Tinker. Tinker was the most successful of the American volunteers in Spain with eight victories. Although it was reported that Selles was shot as a spy for Japan, he survived the war and still lives in Spain.

hours of 26 July shot down a Junkers Ju 52/3m bomber – the first nocturnal victory of the war. After his return to Russia he was killed in a flying accident in May 1939. IT Yeremenko commanded an I-16 escuadrilla during 1937; he was reputed to have gained 14 victories.

One of the few successful Russian fighter pilots in Spain to see service during World War II was Vladimir Bobrov, who gained 13 victories during the Civil War. He was a unit commander in 1941 when Germany attacked Russia, and flew throughout the war as a fighter pilot. Much of his service was in Col Pokryshkin's 9th Guards Fighter Division, where he flew P-39 Airacobras. He was credited with 30 more victories during this conflict, three of them early in the Lvov operations of July 1944. Ivan Lakeiev commanded the 1ª Escuadrilla de Moscas (I-16s) early in 1937, and during his time in Spain was credited with 12 victories and shares in others. The year 1939 saw him gain one further victory while fighting the Japanese in Mongolia, but he then saw no further combat during World War II, as he had risen to command rank, later becoming a general.

Three pilots of the Republican forces who received their training after the outbreak of war are believed to have achieved scores of 10 or more during the conflict. Capitano Miguel Zambudio Martinez trained in Spain, first seeing action on the Northern Front in March 1937. During 1938 he commanded the 3rd I-15 Escuadrilla, and later that year became commander of Grupo 26. He survived the war, later settling in France. Captain Jose Bravo Fernandez trained in Russia during 1936/7, joining an I-15 unit at Belchite on his return to Spain. He then joined the 1st I-16 Escuadrilla at Belchite, becoming a flight leader. Subsequently he commanded the 3rd I-16 Escaudrilla, and in September 1938 became second in command of the grupo of which it formed part, operating throughout the rest of the Catalonian campaign. Escaping to Russia, he flew with the Red Air Force during World War II, but returned to Spain in 1948. Like Zambudio, Major Manuel Zarauza Claver trained at the start of the war, joining an I-15 Escuadrilla in the north in spring 1937, although trained to fly I-16s. He took command of the 4th Escuadrilla, flying the I-16s fighters at the end of the year, and subsequently commanded Grupo 21 on the Teruel front, becoming a Major in December 1938. This diminutive pilot escaped to Russia at the end of the war, but died there in an aerial accident.

ACES OF THE SPANISH CIVIL WAR

Spanish Nationalist Air Force

Comondante Joaquin Garcia-Morato y Castano	40	Patrulla Azul, 2-G-3, 3-G-3 KIFA
Comondante Julio Salvador Diaz Benzumea	25	Patrulla Azul, 2-G-3
Capitano Manuel Vazquez Sagaztizobal	21⅓	2-G-3 KIA
Capitano Aristides Garcia Lopez	17	2-G-3, 8-E-3
Comondante Angel Salas Larrazabal	16⅓	Patrulla Azul, 2-G-3 (+ 7 in WW II)
Capitano Miguel Guerrero Garcia	13	2-G-3
Capitano Miguel Garcia Pardo	12	2-G-3, 5-G-5 KIFA April 39
Teniente Joaquin Velasco Fernandez	11	3-G-3
Capitano Carlos Bayo Alexandri	11	2-G-3 (+ 2 in WW II)
Teniente Rodolphe de Hemricourt de Grunne	10	2-G-3 Belgian (+ 3 in WW II with RAF)

Right: Pavel Rychagov was reputedly one of the two most successful Russians in Spain with 15 victories. He was later shot in one of Stalin's purges.
Far right: Russian top scorer in Spain and the first pilot to claim a victory by night there was Anatoli Serov.

Legion Condor

Haupt Werner Mölders	14 (+ 101 in WW II)
Haupt Wolfgang Schellmann	12 (+ 14 in WW II)
Haupt Harro Harder	11 (+ al 6 in WW II)
Leut Peter Boddem	10
Ober Otto Bertam	9 (+ 13 in WW II)
Ober Wilhelm Ensslen	9 (+ ? in WW II)
Leut Herbert Ihlefeld	9 (+ 123 in WW II)
Ober Walter Oesau	9 (+ 115 in WW II)
Leut Reinhard Seiler	9 (+ 100 in WW II)

Russians

AK Serov	16
PK Rychagov	15
IT Yeremenko	14
VI Bobrov	13 (+ 30 in WW II)
IA Lakeiev	12 plus shares (+ 1 in Mongolia)
SP Denisov	12
VI Bobrov	12

Aviazione Legionaria

Maggiore Mario Bonzano	15 (+ al 2 in WW II)
Sergente Adriano Mantelli	15
Capitano Corrado Ricci	10–12 (+ 2 in WW II)
Maggiore Guido Nobili	10
Teniente Giuseppe Cenni	7 (+ 2 in WW II)
Maggiore Ernesto Botto	approx 6–7 and 15 shares (+ 1 al in WW II)
Colonello Riccardo Emo Seidl	6
Capitano Enrico Degl'Incerti	5 and 5 shares
Teniente Giuseppe Baylon	5 al
Capitano Aldo Remondino	5 al
Arrigo Tessari	5 al
Nicola Zotti	5 al

Spaniards and others reputed to be aces with the Republican Air Force

Leopoldo Morquilla Rubio	21 ?
Andres Garcia Lacalle	11 al
Abel Guides	11 (French)
Jose M Bravo Fernandez	10 al
Emilio Ramirez Bravo	10 al
Miguel Zambudio Martinez	10 al
Manuel Zarauza Claver	10 al
Frank G Tinker	8 (American)
Jan Ferak	7 (Czech)
Bozko Petrovik	7 (Yugoslav) KIA 1937
Felipe del Rio Crespo	7 KIA 1937

China

Following limited involvement on the Allied side during World War I, Japan became increasingly dominated by the military, becoming devoted to an expansionist policy in Eastern Asia. Hostilities with China broke out in February 1932, Japanese Navy aircraft supporting the action on the ground. The Chinese were virtually without an air force, but a single Boeing 218 demonstration biplane fighter was delivered to Shanghai, and was flown by the US test pilot, Robert Short, in defense of the city. This gallant crusader was shot down and killed on 22 February by three Nakajima A1N biplanes (license-built Gloster Gamecocks), one of his victors being NAP 3/C Toshio Kuroiwa. This was the first aerial victory credited to Japanese fighter aircraft.

Following five more years of inaction, the Sino-Japanese 'Incident' broke out in North China in July 1937, and soon spread to other areas of the country – an undeclared war that was to last for eight years. In mid-August 1937 the fighting reached Shanghai, and here the 14th of that month saw the first clashes with the new Chinese Nationalist Air Force. On this date, which later became Air Force Day for the Nationalists, Curtiss Hawk III biplane fighters intercepted unescorted Mitsubishi G3M bombers over Hangchow, claiming six shot down without loss.

Japanese Navy carrier fighters (Nakajima A3N biplanes) were thrown in, and there was some severe fighting, but it was clear that in equipment the Chinese had the edge. Consequently the carrier *Kaga* was rushed to Japan to bring across the 13th Fighter Kokutai (Ku), newly equipped with Mitsubishi A5M monoplanes, which were to prove far superior to anything the Chinese had – particularly in the hands of the very highly trained pilots of the IJNAF. One of the first claims made by these new arrivals was a Hawk on 7 September by one of *Kaga*'s resident fighter pilots, Watari Handa. Operating from land bases, the 13th Ku appeared over Nanking a few days later and took so great a toll of the Chinese defenders that by December they had all-but disappeared from the skies, the survivors being withdrawn into the hinterland. Despite this Japanese pre-eminence, the first ace of the campaign was Chinese, Captain Yuan Pao-Kang. Yuan flew Curtiss Hawk III biplanes, gaining his first victory over an A3N fighter on 16 August 1937. He had claimed two further victories by the end of August, and another two on 20 and 21 September, the latter pair over Nanking. Subsequently he claimed a seaplane over the Yangtze Kiang River, and another aircraft in the same area, one wing from this victim being completely sheared off. A year later, in December 1938, he gained one further victory when flying a Russian-built Polikarpov I-15 to raise his total to eight.

The first Japanese pilot to become an ace

achieved this distinction on 6 October 1937. Ensign Kiyoto Koga claimed three victories on this date to raise his score to seven, two of his earlier successes having been achieved over Nanking on 19 September. By 9 December his total had risen to 13 in six combats, and it was to be some weeks before his position at the top was to be challenged. He was killed in a flying accident on 15 September 1938. Among the 13th Ku's other aces was one who became a national hero – Flight Petty Officer Kanichi Kashimura. Kashimura joined the 13th Ku as a reinforcement in October 1937, gaining two victories during his first combat on 22 November. On 9 December he had just shot down one aircraft over Nanchung when he collided with another enemy machine, cutting off more than a

third of his A5M's port wing. Despite this damage, he managed to fly back to base; his return was photographed and brought him much publicity. Returning to Japan in March 1938 after eight victories, he later served with the 12th Ku, flying again in China in 1940. In December 1942 he was posted to the Solomons where he was reported missing on 6 March 1943 over the Russell Islands, having raised his score to 12, 10 in China and two more over the Pacific.

The arrival early in 1938 of substantial quantities of war material in China from the Soviet Union brought a resumption of Chinese resistance in the air. Not only were I-15s and I-16s supplied to the Nationalist Air Force, but volunteer units of Russian fighter pilots equipped with these aircraft also appeared to fight alongside them. At the same time the Japanese were reinforced by more A5Ms of the 12th Ku, and with long-range tanks added, these fighters were able to reach to the Nanchung area. The Chinese had withdrawn their air units here, and had again been taking a heavy toll of unescorted Japanese bombers until the escorts were able to thus extend their range. Heavy fighting followed, and on 25 February 1938 Momoto Matsumura and Sadaaki Akamatsu of the 13th Ku claimed four and three probables, and four respectively over Nanchung, while the 12th Ku's Tetsuzo Iwamoto become the first Japanese pilot to claim five in a day (three I-15s and two I-16s). Iwamoto was to claim four more Polikarpov fighters in a single combat over Hangkow on 29 April, and when he returned to Japan in September he was the top-scorer of the fighting in China, with 14 victories in 82 sorties. He was later to emerge as one of Japan's two top fighter aces of World War II.

One of the victors of Japan's first aerial victory in 1932, Warrant Officer Toshio Kuroiwa (as he was by 1938), saw much service in China with the 12th Ku, claiming 13 victories in three months during 1938. Watari Handa, who has already been mentioned for his victory over a Hawk on 7 September 1937, claimed three more victories in one day on 20 September. He left the carrier *Kaga* during 1938, returning to China to serve with the land-based 15th Ku. With this unit he added six more victories to the seven gained during his first 'tour,' so that by November his score stood at 13.

Following the appearance of Capt Yuan as the first Chinese ace, Lt Chen Chie-Wei became the second, credited with five victories in two combats on 17 and 19 October 1937. China's greatest ace was also operational at this time, but his rate of scoring was more modest. Col Liu Che-Sheng served in the 4th Fighter Group of the Nationalist Air Force, taking part in the combats on the first day of the air war – 14 August 1937 – when he shot down one Japanese bomber and shared another with two other pilots. He did not again claim until February

Top: The first Japanese ace was Ensign Kiyoto Koga who claimed 13 victories over China before his death in a flying accident in 1938. Above: The first ever Japanese fighter victory was gained by this trio of Navy pilots over Shanghai on 22 February 1932. NAP 3/C Toshio Kuroiwa (center) was later to become a leading ace. He is flanked by Lt Ikuta (left) and NA 1/C Takeo. Right: Pilots of the 12th Kokutai, IJNAF, in China 1938. In the center of the front row with the moustache is Wt Off Toshio Kuroiwa (13⅔). Middle row, far left: is one of Kuroiwa's wingmen, top scorer in China NAP Tetsuzo Iwamoto (14).

Japan's Greatest – Tetsuzo Iwamoto

Japanese Navy pilot Tetsuzo Iwamoto flew in China in 1938 with the 12 Kokutai, seeing considerable combat flying the Mitsubishi A5M fighter. On 25 February 1938 he became the first Japanese pilot to claim five in a day (three I-15s and two I-16s) and was to claim four more Polikarpov fighters in a single combat over Hangchow on 29 April. When he returned to Japan in September he was top-scorer with 14 victories in 82 sorties. He later served aboard the aircraft carrier *Zuikaku* from 1941 until late 1942. He claimed four victories against the RAF during the raid on Trincomalee, Ceylon, on 9 April 1942, and two during the Coral Sea battle on 8 May. In November 1943 he was posted to Rabaul in the Solomons with the 204th Ku, and here he claimed 15 and five probables in his first month; this total included two P-38s, two P-39s and three SB2C Helldivers on 20 November, and two F4U Corsairs and four bombers on 10 December. Late in February 1944, having added 25 more victories to his total, he was evacuated to Truk, to fly with the 253rd Ku. Here on 6 March he claimed five B-24 Liberators, which he destroyed by dropping a phosphorus bomb on their formation. After one further victory he returned to Japan, where he was commissioned. October 1944 saw him in the Philippines with the 252nd Ku, but he gained no victories here. During 1945 he flew on home defense with the 203rd Ku, claiming a further 23 victories in the period February-April 1945. Again this period saw many multiple claims, including four Corsairs and three other fighters over the Kanto area on 16 February, three Hellcats and three Corsairs off Okinawa over the sinking battleship *Yamato* on 6 April, four Hellcats on 15 April, and finally three more Corsairs off Okinawa late in April. This total of 94 claims included many probables, and his total of confirmed claims is believed to be about 80.

Above: Col Liu Che-Sheng, believed to be China's top-scoring ace.
Below: Liu Che-Sheng in his Polikarpov I-16.

1938, by which time his unit had exchanged its Hawk III biplanes for I-16 monoplanes. With the Russian fighter he claimed an A5M and a share in a second over Hankow on 18 February, sharing another fighter on the last day of May. He next saw action during the renewed fighting in 1940, claiming a bomber over Chunking on 10 June and added two individual and one shared victory on the 12th. Another double claim on 16 July was followed by one and one shared in August, again all claimed over the Chungking area. His final victory was claimed over Lanchow on 23 May 1941, raising his total to nine individual and five shared victories (11$\frac{1}{3}$).

Among the Russians operating in China, two were particularly notable. Piotr K Kozachenko was made a Hero of the Soviet Union after claiming 11 Japanese aircraft shot down. He later commanded a fighter regiment during World War II and gained several more victories. He was killed just before the end of the war, over Berlin in April 1945. A former TskB and NII V-VS test pilot, Lt Col Stepan Suprun led two eskadrilli of I-16 fighters to China in 1938, seeing much fighting over the Buir-Nur Lake area. He returned to test-flying in 1939, but is

Imperial Japanese Naval Air Force

NAP Tetsuzo Iwamoto	14	12th Ku (+ approx 80 in WW II)
FWO Toshio Kuroiwa	13⅓	*Kaga* and 12th Ku
FWO Watari Handa	13	*Kaga* and 15th Ku
Ens Kiyoto Koga	13	13th Ku. Killed in flying accident, 1938
NAP Kuniyoshi Tanaka	12	13th Ku (+ 5 in WW II)
NAP Sadaaki Akamatsu	11	13th Ku (+ al 16 in WW II)
Lt Motonari Suho	11	12th and 14th Ku (+ 5 in WW II)
Ens Mamoto Matsumura	10	12th and 13th Ku (+ 3 in WW II)

Leading Aces of the Imperial Japanese Army Air Force

Capt Tateo Kato	9	(+ 9 in WW II)
Lt Kousuke Kawahara	8½	KIA
Lt Mitsugu Sawada	7	(+ 5 in WW II)
Lt Yonesuke Fukuyama	7	KIA

(*NB all members of the 2nd Hiko Datai*)

Pilots of the Nationalist Chinese Air Force known to be aces in the period 1937–41

Col Liu Che-Sheng	11⅓	4th Fighter Group
Maj Kao Yu-hain	8	4th Fighter Group
Capt Yuan Pao-Kang	8	
Lt Chen Chi-Wei	5	

Chinese pilots reputed to be aces between 1937–45

·(*no further details are available*)

Capt Li Kwei-tan	12
Capt Liu Tsui-Kan	11
Capt Lo Chu	11
Capt Chen Jui-tien	6
Lt Chow Ting-fong	6
Lt Col Huang Shing-Yui	6
Capt Kwang Hsin-Jui	6
Capt Liu Chung-Wu	6
Capt Chu Chin-hsun	5
Capt Hwang Pei-yang	5
Capt Lo I-ching	5
Capt Mao Yin-chu	5

Above: Test pilot Stepan Suprun led a fighter unit in China, claiming about eight victories.

believed to have seen action against the Japanese again later in that year over Mongolia. In 1940 he was made a Hero of the Soviet Union for his test-flying activities, but at this time his total claims against the Japanese are believed to have reached eight. On the outbreak of war with Germany, he joined a volunteer regiment, the 401st IAP, flying MiG 3 fighters. He was killed in action shortly afterward, on 4 July 1941, while defending an airfield in the Tolochinsk region. He became the first pilot of the war to receive a second award of the HSU, which was made posthumously on 22 July. His final score was reputed to be of the order of 12 to 15.

Most air fighting over China up to 1941 was the province of the Japanese Naval Air Force, but the Army Air Force did see some limited combat over North China. Of the three fighter units involved, only the 2nd Hiko Datai saw any sustained action. This unit claimed 86 victories between October 1937 and May 1938. Equipped initially with Kawasaki Ki 10 biplanes, it received some of the first Nakajima Ki 27 monoplanes before the end of this period. The unit produced five aces, the leading one being the commander of the 1st Chutai, Capt Tateo Kato. A pilot since 1929, Kato gained nine victories over China in three combats, all during the first four months of 1938. The first two combats, were flown in Ki 10s and during the second combat he claimed four I-15s. However, his final successes -- three I-15s on 10 April -- were gained with the new Ki 27. He subsequently commanded the 64th Sentai at the outbreak of the Pacific War in December 1941, flying the new Nakajima Ki 43 Hayabusa ('Oscar') fighters. Operating over Malaya, the Dutch East Indies and Burma, he added nine further victories — mainly against the RAF – to raise his total to 18. On 22 May 1942 he and two companions gave chase to a single Bristol Blenheim bomber as it fled across the Bay of Bengal after attacking Akyab Island. His two wingmen were forced to withdraw, and Kato was finally hit after a 20-minute chase, crashing into the sea in flames; the bomber escaped unscathed. Kato was promoted posthumously to the rank of Major General.

One of his pilots in the I/2nd Hiko Datai was

Lt Kousake Kawahara, who shot down a Vought Corsair biplane on 25 October 1937 and shared a second for his first victories. On 20 January 1938 he claimed three I-15s in one dogfight, adding another on 8 March and then a further three on 25 March. During this fight, which occurred over Shanghai, he was himself shot down and killed.

During September 1940 the 12th Kokutai returned to China, taking with it the first of the famous Mitsubishi A6M-1 Zero fighters to see action. With the range necessary to reach the areas where the remaining Chinese fighters were then based, this single unit virtually wiped out the opposing fighter force in a matter of weeks. On 13 September, in their first combat, the Zero pilots claimed all of the 27 I-15s and I-16s which were engaged five being claimed by FWO Koshiro Yamashita. Several more successful combats followed, including one on 14 March 1941 when 24 more victories were claimed, five and one probable by Ens Masayuki Nakase alone. When the unit withdrew from China with all other IJNAF units in September 1941, the Zeros had been credited with 99 victories and four probables in one year. (Nakase got at least three more victories in China; he was killed over the East Indies on 9 February 1942 with his score at 18.)

Mongolia

While fighting in China continued, Japanese ambitions in their puppet state of Manchuria toward areas of the border with Russian Mongolia, led to an armed clash during the summer of 1938, and then to a major undeclared war in May 1939, which continued until mid-September of that year. Because of the tense political situation and the outbreak of war in Western Europe during this period, until recent years little was known about this conflict by the Western nations. Known as the Nomonhan or Khalkin Gol Incident, the fighting was of greater intensity than in Spain, and saw the use of forces, both land and air, of a size not seen since World War I. On the ground the Japanese Army suffered two severe defeats at the hands of the Russian forces commanded by Georgi Zhukov, later to be the most successful Soviet general of World War II. In the air however, although outnumbered, the well-trained and efficient Imperial Japanese Army Air Force achieved considerable ascendency at first. The maneuverable Nakajima Ki 27 monoplane fighters proved more than a match for most Russian types, and very considerable claims were made. Conditions were near-ideal for air fighting – units were close to the front, and the open steppe offered no obstructions to force-landings, or to the swift construction of airstrips close to the fighting; pilots could fly several sorties a day without long approach flights. In these circumstances over 50 Japanese Army pilots became aces, the 1st, 11th and 24th

Sentais seeing most of the action. Indeed, 30 of these aces came from the 11th Sentai alone. However Russian forces were built up fast, and newer types such as the latest Polikarpov I-153 fighters were introduced as the fighting progressed. There was little chance of resting the Japanese pilots and gradually, overwhelmed by numbers and fatigue from constant action, they fell. Fourteen of the aces were killed during the later stages of the fighting, and several others were wounded, or died in accidents. Many saw further service in World War II, but only one of the four top scorers was among them.

The highest scorer was to prove the most successful Army fighter pilot of all conflicts. Wt Off Hiromichi Shinohara flew with the 11th Sentai, claiming four victories during his first combats on 27 May 1939. Next day he claimed six more, including five I-15s in one sortie. His next fight on 27 June set a world record at the time; defending his own base at Tamsay against reconnaissances and dawn attacks, he claimed 11 I-15s and I-16s, all before watchers on the ground. More multiple victories followed – six on 6 July, eight on 10 July – and by 27 August his score stood at 54 or 55. On that day he was seen to shoot down three more, but was then shot down in flames himself, and was killed.

There were several rescues of shot-down pilots made by both sides on the flat and open steppe, undoubtedly the most dramatic involving Shinohara. On 25 July, after four vic-

Above left: Wt Off Hiromichi Shinohara, top scorer of the Japanese Army Air Force during the Nomonhan fighting of 1939 (58 victories).
Above: Capt Kenji Shimada (foreground).
Right: Sgt Mitsuyoshi Tarui, most successful pilot of the 1st Sentai in Mongolia with 28 victories. He later gained at least ten more in the Pacific war.
Above right: The Russian top scorer at Nomonhan was probably Grigori Kravchenko (right foreground). Next to him is Ivan Lakeiev, credited with 12 and 20 shared in Spain and one further victory over Mongolia. On the far left is Lt Gen Yakov Smushkevich, one of the senior Russian commanders in Spain, (where he was known as General 'Douglas') who claimed four victories there. They are seen at the May Day Parade in Red Square, Moscow, in 1940. One month later Smushkevich and Lakeiev were shot on Stalin's orders as 'traitors, spies and Nazi agents'.

flying accident on 7 October 1939, immediately after the end of the Incident.

Undoubtedly one of the most bizarre events of the Nomonhan fighting occurred on 7 August when M Sgt Daisuke Kanbara of the 11th Sentai landed alongside a Russian fighter which he had shot down and which had force-landed. Leaping from his cockpit, he attacked the vanquished pilot with his Samurai sword (which many Japanese pilots carried with them in their cockpits) and killed him. Kanbara ended the conflict with nine confirmed and three probable victories.

Few Russian pilots had the chance to build up big scores in Mongolia in the circumstances of the fighting there. However, the most successful appears to have been Grigori P Kravchenko. Like Stepan Suprun, Kravchenko was a test-pilot before going to China as a volunteer, where he claimed at least three victories, although he was once shot down by four Japanese fighters, taking to his parachute. He then led an I-16 unit in Mongolia, becoming a Hero of the Soviet Union and reportedly being credited with some 15 victories. He later served as a Lieutenant general, but was killed in action on 22 February 1943.

Probably the most famous Russian pilot to fight at Nomonhan was Maj Arsenii Vorozheikin, who served as a political commissar as well as a pilot in an I-16 eskadrill during this campaign, claiming six victories against the Japanese. In 1940 he flew against Finland, and in 1941 was still flying I-16s with the 728th IAP (Fighter Regiment) of the 256th IAD (Air Division), his unit retaining these obsolescent fighters until 1943, when it was at last re-equipped with Yak 7Bs. During World War II Vorozheikin was credited with 46 more victories, most gained during the latter part of the war. He was twice made a Hero of the Soviet Union, once in February 1944 and one in August of that year, his total score of 52 making him the Soviet Union's fifth equal leading ace.

tories, he was hit and obliged to force-land. Another ace, Yutaka Aoyagi (10 victories) landed alongside, but his aircraft was hit by fire from a Russian tank, and he was wounded. A third ace, Koichi Iwase (10 victories) then also landed and took off with both his fellow pilots crammed into the little aircraft with him.

The second most successful pilot of the 11th Sentai was Capt Kenji Shimada, commander of the 1st Chutai. He claimed 27 victories between 27 May and 21 August, including five in a day on three occasions. He was killed in action on 15 September, the last day of the Incident. Master Sergeant Mitsuyoshi Tarui was top-scorer of the 1st Sentai, claiming two victories during his first combat on 26 June; his score reached 28 by the end of the fighting. He was killed in 1944, having added at least 10 more victories. Wt Off Tomio Hanada was the 11th Sentai's No 3 ace with 25 victories, his first two claims being made on 28 May. On 4 July he landed near his Chutai leader, Capt T Fujita, who had baled out, and flew him back to base. He claimed five victories in a day on 25 July, but was killed in a

ACES OF THE IMPERIAL JAPANESE ARMY AIR FORCE IN THE NOMONHAN INCIDENT

Wt Off Hiromichi Shinohara	58	11th Sentai	KIA
M Sgt Mitsuyoshi Tarui	28	1st Sentai	(+ al 10 in WW II)
Capt Kenji Shimada	27	11th Sentai	KIA
M Sgt Tomio Hanada	25	11th Sentai	KIFA, 1939
M Sgt Shogo Saito	25	24th Sentai	(+ al 1 in WW II)
M Sgt Shoji Kato	23	11th Sentai	KIFA, 1941
Wt Off Saburo Togo	22	11th Sentai	
Sgt Zenzaburo Ohtsaka	22	11th Sentai	
Wt Off Hitoshi Asano	22	1st Sentai	(possibly additional score in WW II)
M Sgt Isamu Hosono	21	1st Sentai	(+ 6 in WW II)
M Sgt Chiyoji Saito	21	24th Sentai	(+ al 7 in WWII)
Sgt Goro Furugori	20	11th Sentai	(+ 5–10 in WW II)
Lt Jozo Iwahashi	20	11th Sentai	(+ al 2 in WW II)
M Sgt Bunji Yoshiyama	20	11th Sentai	KIA

Finland

Late in November 1939, some three months after the outbreak of war in Western Europe, and following the conclusion of its successful venture against the Japanese in the East, the Soviet Union launched an invasion against its small Baltic neighbor, Finland. This followed a sustained political campaign designed to obtain territory and bases from the Finns for the defense of the Baltic port of Leningrad. Expecting little resistance, the Russians did not commit their best forces – land or air – to the venture. However the Finns possessed units in both media which, though small, were highly efficient and extremely determined. Aided by the onset of a particularly severe winter, the Finns were able to bring the lumbering Goliath to a halt for some time, and to inflict staggering casualties. The Soviets were obliged greatly to strengthen their forces, and to throw in much more modern equipment before they were finally able to force Finland into an Armistice which ceded the land required by the Russians early in March 1940.

The Finnish Air Force possessed two fighter squadrons at the outbreak of war, only one of which, LeLv 24, had modern equipment – Fokker D.XXI monoplanes. Help from several Western countries – initially France and the United Kingdom, and subsequently Italy and the United States – brought more fighters later in the campaign, allowing the second unit to be re-equipped from its old Bristol Bulldog biplanes. During the three months of combat 10 Finns became aces, and many other pilots who later built up big scores when Finland became involved in the main conflict achieved their initial victories. First and leading ace of this conflict was Lt Jorma Sarvanto who gained his first victories on 23 December 1939 when he shot down two SB-2 bombers. His most notable combat occurred on 6 January 1940 when he intercepted a formation of seven unarmored Ilyushin DB-3 bombers and attacked repeatedly, shooting down no less than six! The seventh fell to another pilot who appeared on the scene. Sarvanto continued to meet bombers frequently, engaging in six more successful combats before the end of February. During February he brought down an SB-2 and three more DB-3s, and shared in the destruction of one more of each. He was to gain four more victories during the conflict of 1941–44.

Other pilots who became aces during this war include Viktor Pyötsiä, who claimed seven and two shared, Pentti Tilli with five and one shared, and Tatu Huhanantti who claimed five and three shared. All three were pilots of LeLv 24, flying D.XXIs. Tilli was shot down and killed on 20 January 1940, while Huhanantti rammed a Russian fighter on 28 February, then crashed

to his death. Pyötsiä later added 10 and four shared to his score, flying Brewsters and Messerschmitts.

One of the older, experienced N.C.O. pilots of the Finnish Air Force (aged nearly 32 at the outbreak of this war), Flt Sgt Ylikersantti Oiva Tuominen was serving with LeLv 26, the second fighter squadron, but was attached to LeLv 24 to fly D.XXIs, as was Risto Olli Puhakka. Tuominen shared in the destruction of an SB-2 on Christmas Day, and shot down one single-handed on 19 January 1940, while Puhakka claimed four bombers during the latter month.

Returning to his own unit when it was re-equipped with Gloster Gladiators, Tuominen claimed two I-16s on 2 February, and on 13 February shot down three SB-2s and a Polikarpov R-5, and shared a fourth SB-2. His seven individual and two shared victories make him the second-highest scoring ace of the war. Puhakka rejoined LeLv 26 a little later than Tuominen, flying one of the first Fiat G-50s which were arriving to replace the biplane Gladiators. In one of the Italian fighters he claimed two victories, the last a DB-3 on 11 March 1940 – one of the last victories of the conflict. Before the next round of fighting in 1941, the unit was to be fully re-equipped with G-50s, these two pilots becoming the highest scorers on this type.

FINNISH ACES IN THE WINTER WAR

Luuttnantti Jorma K Sarvanto	12	LeLv 24	(+ 4 in WW II)
Ylikersantti Oiva E Tuominen	8	LeLv 26	(+ 36 in WW II)
Lentomestari Viktor Pyötsiä	7½	LeLv 24	(+ 12 in WW II)
Luuttnantti Tatu M Huhanantti	6	LeLv 24	KIA
Luuttnantti Risto Olli P Puhakka	6	LeLv 26	(+ 36 in WW II)
Ylikersantti Kelpo JT Virta	6	LeLv 24	KIA, 1941
Luutnantti Per-Erik Sovelius	5¾	LeLv 24	(+ 7 in WW II)
Ylikersantti Pentti T Tilli	5	LeLv 24	KIA
Luutnantti Paavo D Berg	5	LeLv 26	(+ 3½ in WW II)
Luutnantti Urho A Nieminen	5	LeLv 26	(+ 6 in WW II)

3. WORLD WAR 2 Carnage over the Globe

The outbreak of war in Europe in September 1939 was to bring forth nearly six years of aerial combat right across the globe, involving dozens of nations. It brought many developments, and there were to be significant differences between the tactics, conditions and results obtained in the various areas involved. Air fighting took place over the frozen wastes of North Russia and the Aleutian Islands, over the arid deserts of North Africa, the jungles of Burma, New Guinea and the Solomons; over the vast sea areas of the Pacific, the bitter gray waters of the North Atlantic, and the sunny, limited distances of the Mediterranean. The densely-populated temperate heartlands of both Western Europe and Japan were to be as much the scenes of desperate fighting as were the vastness of the Russian steppe, or the beleaguered islands of Malta or Guadalcanal. From dirt strip, concrete runway or heaving carrier deck, the fighter pilot operated — and from every region came the aces until their numbers ran into thousands as the aircraft of all combatant nations fell to earth in their tens of thousands. It was a global war to an extent never imagined during 1914–18.

Right: The first RAF ace of World War II was New Zealander Flg Off EJ 'Cobber' Kain of 73 Squadron, seen here with his Hurricane.
Far right: One of the Armée de l'Air top scorers of 1940 was Curtiss 75A pilot, Sous Lt Camille Plubeau (14 victories) of GC I/4.
Below: French top scorer of the 1940 period was Cdt Edmond Marin la Meslée of GC I/5.

Poland and the West, 1939–40

The campaign in Poland was short and bloody, but the Polish Air Force put up a much longer, harder and more effective struggle than is generally realized. Most fighting here for the Luftwaffe was in the hand of the big new twin-engined Messerschmitt Bf 110 Zertörer (destroyers), the Jagdgeschwadern (fighter units) being kept well to the rear to defend the home bases. Despite this, the one pilot who would emerge as outstandingly the most successful, was flying an early-model Messerschmitt Bf 109D — although with a Zerstörergruppe which had not yet received its Bf 110s — I/ZG 2. Hauptmann Hannes Gentzen claimed seven victories in two days; on 3 September he shot down a PZL Los medium bomber and two PZL P.XI fighters, while next day he claimed four PZL P.XXIII Karas attack-bombers. With the conclusion of fighting, he led his unit to the Western Front, where in November he brought down a French Curtiss Hawk, although the Gruppe suffered disproportionate casualties in return. At last the Bf 110s arrived, and in April 1940 another Hawk was added to his tally, but now his position of Luftwaffe No 1 was challenged by Werner Mölders who had 10 victories by the end of this month. During the Blitzkrieg of May 1940 Gentzen added nine further successes, but he was killed in a crash on the 26th of that month.

The only other notable fighter pilot in Poland was Lt Stanislaw Skalski who was credited with four and one shared victories in three days, flying the elderly PZL P.XIC fighters with the Polish 142 'Wild Duck' Squadron. He escaped to fly with the RAF in England in 1940.

Over the Western Front there was considerable desultory combat from September 1939 to April 1940, British and French fighter pilots frequently being involved in clashes. The first Allied ace to appear was a New Zealander with 73 Squadron of the RAF's Advanced Air Striking Force in France, Flg Off EJ 'Cobber' Kain shot down two reconnaissance Dornier Do 17s during November 1939, and claimed three Bf 109s during March 1940, receiving considerable publicity. When the German offensive began on 10 May 1940 he was much in action, and by 27 May had raised his total to 17. Ordered back to England for a rest, he took off to 'beat up' the airfield before leaving, but during a low roll the wingtip of his Hurricane caught the ground and he crashed to his death. His squadron mate, Flg Off N 'Fanny' Orton, was the only other RAF pilot to gain five victories before 10 May, and by the end of the Battle of France had raised his total to 15 and had been wounded. He was lost in action in September 1941 after gaining two more victories.

The fighting in France brought many RAF reinforcements over from England, and in the many desperate combats which followed many new aces appeared. Flt Sgt Geoffrey Allard of 85 Squadron claimed his first on 10 May, and within seven days had 10 victories. In the same unit Plt Off Albert Lewis, a South African, gained seven victories; five of these, all Bf 109Es, were claimed during two sorties on 19 May.

The most successful Luftwaffe fighter pilot of the Battle of France was Oblt Wilhelm Balthasar who claimed 23 aircraft shot down

and 13 destroyed on the ground, flying with III/JG 27. This score included three Gladiators and a Morane 406 on 11 May, three Hurricanes on 23 May, three LeO 451 bombers and two Moranes on 5 June, and another three LeOs and one Morane next day. Mölders too had done well, with 15 victories, becoming the first to reach 20; these two were the first fighter pilots to receive the coveted *Ritterkreuz* (Knights' Cross), Mölders on 29 May and Balthasar on 14 June. Other leading pilots were now appearing, who would add greatly to their scores during the summer months as the fighting moved over Britain – Helmuth Wick of JG 2 and Adolf Galland of JG 27 particularly. French pilots too had soon become notable – particularly those flying Curtiss H-75A Hawks and Dewoitine D.520s. French scores of course now included both shares and 'probables' in the totals, but the achievements of these pilots in adverse circumstances were none the less praiseworthy for this. Sous Lt Camille Plubeau, who flew the Curtiss with GC I/4 had gained two shared victorious during 1939. In the heavy fighting of May and June 1940 he was to add 12 more confirmed and three probable victories to his total.

Groupe de Chasse I/5 was the most successful French unit of the 1940 campaign, producing the Armée de l'Air's top ace of the period. Commandant Edmond Marin la Meslee was a regular airman with several years' service when war broke out. He already had one shared victory before May 1940, and on 12 May was credited with two Ju 87 'Stuka' divebombers and one shared. By the evening of 7 June he had added 12 more confirmed victories, 10 of which were shared, plus four probables to give him a total of 20; his shares included three halves, five thirds, a quarter, two sevenths and a ninth. Capitain Michel Dorance of this unit was credited with 14 confirmed and three probables during 1940, but was later killed, while Capt Jean Accart was credited with 12 and three probables, including seven victories in two days. Twice wounded, he was badly hurt on 1 June, but managed to escape to England at the end of that month. Another of GC I/5's successful pilots was Lt Frantisek Perina, an escapee from Czechoslovakia who was credited with 11 confirmed and two probables with the unit. Escaping again, this time to England, he served with the Czech 312 Squadron, but was killed.

Most successful of the D.520 pilots was Capt

Michel Madon of GC I/3; he was credited with seven confirmed victories (three shared) and three probables during the summer of 1940. He later flew against the British in Algeria on 8 November 1942, claiming a Sea Hurricane shot down and sharing in the destruction of three US C-47 transports. Lt Georges Blanck of the same unit claimed three, three shared confirmed and one shared probable in 1940; on 8 November 1942 he shot down two Royal Navy Albacore biplane torpedo-bombers and also shared in the victory over the three C-47s to raise his score to 12.

Lt Georges Valentin gained one and three shared confirmed and one shared probable during 1940 with GC II/7. In 1943 his unit flew with the Anglo-American forces and, now equipped with Spitfires, he gained seven more victories, three of them over Corsica in September of that year. He was killed in action on 8 September 1944.

One of France's leading pilots, Lt Pierre Le Gloan, was flying Morane 406s with GC III/6 in 1939, gaining one shared victory in November of that year, and another on 2 March 1940 – both Do 17s. In May he shared two He 111s, one of them a probable, but the unit then withdrew to the South to convert to D.520s. When Italy entered the war in June he was involved in intercepting Italian air raids, shooting down two Fiat BR 20 bombers on 13 June, and another of these plus four Fiat CR 42 biplane fighters on

the 15th (several of these were shared victories). In June 1941 his unit moved from North Africa to Syria where he fought against the RAF, claiming four Hurricanes and a Gladiator shot down and two more Hurricanes as probables, to raise his score to 18–15 and three probables. In 1943 his unit was flying with the Allies again, now equipped with Bell P-39 Airacobras, but on 11 September 1943 he crashed while return-

Left: Pierre Le Gloan in his GC III/6 Dewoitine D 520 which he flew over Syria in summer, 1941.
Below left: Several of the RAF's new aces cheer King George VI at Hornchurch in June 1940 after being decorated for their parts in the Dunkirk operation. Left to right: Plt Off JL Allan (8⅓ victories) 54 Squadron; Flt Lt RRS Tuck (29) 92 Squadron; Flg Off AC Deere (21½) 54 Squadron; Flt Lt AG Malan (32) 74 Squadron; Sqn Ldr JA Leathart (8) 54 Squadron. Scores given are for the whole war.
Right: Le Gloan was an ace against both the Italians in summer 1940 and the RAF over Syria a year later. He also shot down some German aircraft becoming one of the French top scorers of the war with 18 confirmed and two probable victories.

ing from a shipping patrol with an overheating engine, and was killed.

Another Czech who flew with the Armée de l'Air and enjoyed a most varied career was Sgt Josef Stehlik. Flying Morane 406s and D.520s with GC III/3, he was credited with five victories during 1940; he then served with the RAF in 312 Free Czech Squadron, gaining two more shared victories and a probable during 1941. In 1944 he served with 1 Czech Fighter Regiment with the Russian forces, flying Lavochkin La 5s, claiming a Ju 88 shot down on 19 September and sharing a Ju 87 on 7 October of that year.

The evacuation of the British Expeditionary Force from France at Dunkirk in late May and early June 1940 brought many home-based fighter squadrons of RAF Fighter Command into action, including the first Spitfire units to join the fray. Over Dunkirk the British pilots

gained local air superiority over the Luftwaffe, and many future notable pilots like Malan, Tuck, Bader and others 'cut their teeth' in combat here. The man who was initially pre-eminent was Michael Crossley (the 'Red Knight' to his squadron mates). A flight commander in 32 Squadron flying Hurricanes in May 1940, the 6 feet 3 inches tall Crossley had operated twice over the Channel before getting his first victory over a Bf 109E on 19 May. Claiming steadily, his score stood at eight by mid-June when the evacuation was all over, this experience standing him in good stead for the fighting which followed over England. Flying Spitfires with 54 Squadron, New Zealander Plt Off Al Deere claimed two Bf 109Es and a probable during his first combat on 23 May, and by the end of the month had added another four and one shared. Flt Lt Bob Stanford Tuck was a flight commander with 92 Squadron, flying Spitfires also. On his first sortie over Dunkirk on 23 May he shot down a Bf 109, claiming a Bf 110 later the same day. Three victories on 2 June brought his score to six and one shared. Sgt JH 'Ginger' Lacey was a member of the RAF Volunteer Reserve before the war, having been taught to fly in his spare time. Called up into 501 Squadron in 1939, he went to France with the unit in May 1940, claiming five victories in two days.

From July onward the defense of the United Kingdom got underway, firstly with a series of costly fighter battles over off-shore shipping convoys in the English Channel. This was followed in August by the main Luftwaffe bomber assault against the RAF's airfields and radar sites in southeast England, and then in September

'Sailor' Malan

South African Adolph Gysbert Malan served as a Merchant Navy officer for several years before joining the RAF in 1935 at the age of 25. He was already a most efficient flight commander with 74 Squadron at Hornchurch at the outbreak of war, flying Spitfires; indeed his flight had won the Sir Phillip Sassoon Trophy in the previous year. He first saw action during the Dunkirk evacuation late in May 1940, and here in a period of little more than a week he was to claim five German aircraft shot down (two of them shared) and two probables, for which he received the DFC. On the night of 19 June a heavy raid was launched on southern England in moonlight conditions, and Malan was one of those airborne, intercepting and shooting down two He 111 bombers within 20 minutes. For this virtuoso performance he was awarded a Bar to his DFC.

In July the Battle of Britain began, and from the start Malan – now commanding the squadron – was much involved. He had claimed five more destroyed by mid-August, when the unit left Hornchurch for a rest. Now he produced his '10 Rules of Air Fighting' based on his experience; this was printed and widely circulated by Fighter Command,

virtually becoming the RAF fighter pilot's Ten Commandments for the rest of the war. Returning south to Biggin Hill in September, the squadron was much in action throughout the autumn, combating high-flying Messerschmitt Bf 109E fighters. By the end of the year Malan's score had reached 18, of which four had been shared. He then became one of the first wing leaders, heading the Biggin Hill Wing. Early offensive operations brought two further victories, but it was in June and July 1941 that the level of activity once more rose to a peak. In a period of slightly over one month he was to claim 14 Bf 109Es shot down (two of them shared), plus one more probable and seven damaged. With a total of 34 destroyed or shared destroyed, seven probables and 14 damaged he had become Fighter Command's top scorer and he was then sent on a liaison mission to the USA. On return he served as a gunnery instructor, and then became an airfield commander with the rank of group captain. In 1944 he took command of the Advanced Gunnery School at Catfoss. He left the RAF in 1946 to return to South Africa, where he had a distinguished business and political career, fighting apartheid until his death from Parkinson's Disease in September 1963.

'Vati' Mölders – first to 100 Victories

Already a highly trained officer and ex-instructor when he arrived in Spain in 1938 to fly with the Legion Condor, Werner Mölders took over J.88's 3 Staffel as it converted to the latest Bf 109C fighters from the old He 51 biplanes. During the next four months he built up a steady score. By 15 October, when he shot down his last two I-16s, he had become the Legion's top scorer with 14 victories. A year later he was serving as a Staffelkapitän with I/JG 53, the most active Luftwaffe fighter unit on the Western Front at the start of the war, and by the end of 1939 he had claimed four victories in the new conflict, despite the paucity of action. Promoted to command the new III/JG 53, he gained his fifth victory of World War II on 2 March 1940, and when the Blitzkrieg at last began on 10 May, he had already amassed a total of 10 – the highest of this period. When France fell late in June his score had risen by 15, although on the 5th of that month he had been shot down by a French Dewoitine 520, and had spent the final two weeks of the campaign as a prisoner. By now he had already become the first fighter pilot to receive the Ritterkreuz and, even ignoring his Spanish victories, was the Luftwaffe's top scorer.

Mölders was considered the 'Father' of German fighter tactics during World War II – indeed his nickname was 'Vati' (Daddy). He was now given command of Jagdgeschwader 51, and during the Battle of Britain vied with Adolf Galland, and later the mercurial Helmut Wick, to retain his lead. His score (excluding Spain) reached 40 on 20 September 1940, and next day he was

awarded the Oak Leaves to his Knights' Cross. On 22 October he became the first to reach 50, but within the next few weeks Wick pulled ahead of him before being killed in combat with Spitfires during November. With the Battle of Britain over, victories became less frequent during the winter, although he was one of the first to fly the new Bf 109F version of the classic Messerschmitt fighter. His 60th victory of the war was credited on 26 February 1941, and by early May he had added nine more. The unit was withdrawn to the East, ready for the Russian invasion; on the first day, 22 June, he was to shoot down four Soviet aircraft. During the month his World War II score passed 80 – the first to overtake Richthofen's score of World War I, and on 30 June he gained five further victories to reach 96. His final two confirmed victories came on 15 July, raising his score to 101 in the war (115 overall); much was made

of his 100th victory of the war, but the point at which his joint score passed this mark was overlooked; he was the first to reach the century!

Forbidden to fly further operations, the award of the Diamonds was added to the Swords to the Knights' Cross which he had received the previous month; pilots who flew with him indicate that even now he continued to fly unofficially, adding further victories which were never submitted as official claims. He was then promoted Oberst and appointed to the new post of Inspector of fighters. On 22 November 1941, flying back from a visit to the Eastern Front as a passenger in an He 111 for Ernst Udet's funeral, he was killed when the aircraft crashed on take off near Breslau. JG 51 was given the name 'Mölders' in honor of his memory.

---

with an attack on London. The later months of the year saw a series of fighter battles as the Luftwaffe, its bombers forced from the daylight skies over England by the losses inflicted by Fighter Command, sent over fighter sweeps and nuisance-type fighter-bomber raids in an effort to draw up the defenders and wear them down in an air superiority battle. Many of the pilots who had flown in France and over Dunkirk and the Channel, were much involved in this fighting. For 32 Squadron's Mike Crossley, July brought one and one shared victories, but between 12 and 25 August he was to claim 12 and one shared; this total included two Ju 88s, a Do 17 and another shared on 15 August, a Bf 109, a Bf 110 and a Ju 88 on 16 August and a Bf 109, Ju 88 and a Bf 110 probable on the 18th. He had been shot down and baled out after his second fight on this last date, and when the squadron withdrew to rest, his score of 21 and two shared plus two probables made him Fighter Command's top-scorer at this time.

Now commissioned, Geoffrey 'Sammy' Allard of 85 Squadron had claimed 13 and two shared plus two probables by 1 September, to overtake Crossley, raising his score to 23 and two shared. After two further victories with 85 Squadron in

August, Albert Lewis had been posted to the new 249 Squadron, and by 27 September his score stood at 11, but on that day he flew four times, claiming four Bf 109Es, two Bf 110s and a probable, and a Ju 88 to raise his total to 18. Next day his Hurricane was shot down and he was badly burned, though he managed to bale out and survived.

No. 54 Squadron was much involved in the early fighting of the Battle of Britain, and by the end of August its pilots were exhausted. Al Deere's score now stood at 16 and two shared, plus several probables, but he had come down himself seven times – on 9 July after colliding with a Bf 109 which also crashed. On 31 August his section was taking off from Hornchurch when bombing of the airfield began; all three Spitfires were totally destroyed, but the pilots all survived virtually unscathed! After that they were rested!

Early in the battle, Bob Tuck of 92 Squadron shared Ju 88 bombers shot down on three occasions, and by 25 August, when he brought down a Do 17, his score stood at 14 – 10 and four shared. Posted to command 257 Squadron on Hurricanes, he added seven more (one claimed in a Spitfire on 12 October while visiting

Right: Resplendent in his dark blue Royal Australian Air Force uniform, Flt Lt Pat Hughes (second from right) is seen at 234 Squadron dispersal during the Battle of Britain. Before being killed in a collision with a Dornier Do 17 on 5 September 1940 he had claimed 13 and three shared.

his old unit). With 501 Squadron 'Ginger' Lacey had gained one further victory in July after the return to England, and then five and three probables in August, nine (including three in one day on the 15th and the He 111 reputed to have bombed Buckingham Palace on the 13th) in September, plus three and one probable in October.

Many new aces appeared during this period, like Australian Flt Lt PC Hughes. Pat Hughes had gained two shared victories in July, but between 14 August and 6 September this 234 Squadron pilot added 13 and one shared, claiming three Bf 110s on 4 September, and getting two a day on five other occasions. Next day his Spitfire was seen to fly into the wreckage of a Do 17 he had just exploded and he crashed to his death. Others who did well during the battle included Desmond McMullen, who claimed 12 and three shared plus eight probables, flying Spitfires with 54 and 222 Squadrons (final score 17 and four shared); Robert Doe with 14 and two shared with 234 (Spitfires) and 238 (Hurricane) Squadrons; New Zealander BJG Carbury with 15 and one shared, including five Bf 109Es in a day on 31 August, all gained flying Spitfires with 603 Squadron.

Flt Lt AA McKellar, a Scot who flew Hurricanes with 605 Squadron, had been involved in shooting down the first He 111 to fall on British soil earlier in the war. On 15 August and 9 September he was reported to have shot down three He 111s on each occasion. However records seem to indicate that he was involved in the destruction of one only in each case. He certainly gained three victories and a probable on 15 September, while on 7 October he was credited with five Bf 109s shot down, four of them in 10 minutes. By the end of October his score stood at 14 and three shared at least, and possibly 19 and two shared. On 1 November he was engaged in a dogfight and was seen to spin down and crash; an unclaimed Bf 109 was found nearby and was credited to him.

Possibly the most successful RAF fighter pilot of the Battle period was Flt Lt Eric Lock. Flying Spitfires with 41 Squadron, he claimed his first two victories on 15 August, followed by four more on 5 September. By 20 October his score stood at 19 and one shared, and on 17 November he added two more Bf 109s, but was hit and wounded. He crash-landed but it was two hours before help came. Several months in hospital followed before he was able to return to action in June 1941 with 611 Squadron. Four

further victories followed during July, but on 3 August he failed to return from a sweep across the Channel.

One of the unusual features of the May–August 1940 period was the RAF's employment of the ill-fated two-seater Defiant turret fighter. While the two squadrons equipped with these aircraft suffered savage losses, they did enjoy their occasional successes, and outstandingly the most successful Defiant 'team' were Flt Sgts ER Thorn (pilot) and FJ Barker (gunner), of 264 Squadron. Over the Channel on 28 May this pair claimed three Bf 109s shot down, adding two Ju 87s and a Bf 110 next day, plus an He 111 and a second shared on the 31st. During August they claimed four more victories, including two Do 17s and a Bf 109 on the 26th to raise their score to 11 and one shared. They gained one further victory at night on 9 April 1941.

Numerous foreign nationals escaped from occupied Europe to fly with the RAF, many of these seeing service during the Battle – most notably the Poles of 302 and 303 Squadrons. Two achieved particularly noteworthy results, both serving with the 303 Squadron. Sqn Ldr Witold Urbanowicz had already gained at least one victory over the Polish border area before the outbreak of the war. Attached to the RAF, he first flew Hurricanes with 145 Squadron, claiming two victories during August 1940. Moving to the new 303 Squadron next month, he added at least 13 more by 30 September, including four

Top: German propaganda photo showing a captured RAF Spitfire I being pursued by a Messerschmitt Bf 109E.
Left: Messerschmitt Bf 109Es, the aircraft with which the German fighter pilots fought the Battles of France and Britain in 1940.
Right: Map showing the bases and areas of operation of the opposing airforces – RAF and Luftwaffe – during the Battle of Britain.

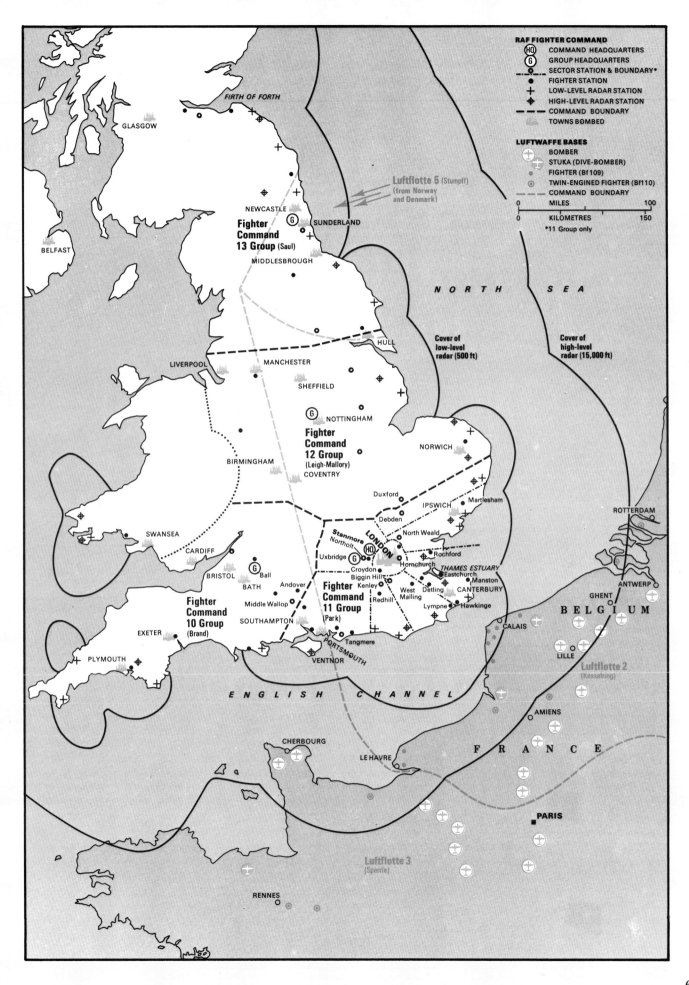

RAF FIGHTER COMMAND

- HQ COMMAND HEADQUARTERS
- G GROUP HEADQUARTERS
- G SECTOR STATION & BOUNDARY*
- FIGHTER STATION
- LOW-LEVEL RADAR STATION
- HIGH-LEVEL RADAR STATION
- COMMAND BOUNDARY
- TOWNS BOMBED

LUFTWAFFE BASES

- BOMBER
- STUKA (DIVE-BOMBER)
- FIGHTER (Bf 109)
- TWIN-ENGINED FIGHTER (Bf110)
- COMMAND BOUNDARY

MILES 0 ———— 100
KILOMETRES 0 ———— 150

*11 Group only

GLASGOW

FIRTH OF FORTH

BELFAST

NEWCASTLE
SUNDERLAND

Fighter Command 13 Group (Saul)

MIDDLESBROUGH

Luftflotte 5 (Stumpff)
(from Norway and Denmark)

N O R T H   S E A

HULL

Cover of low-level radar (500 ft)

Cover of high-level radar (15,000 ft)

LIVERPOOL   MANCHESTER

SHEFFIELD

NOTTINGHAM

Fighter Command 12 Group (Leigh-Mallory)

BIRMINGHAM

COVENTRY

NORWICH

Duxford
IPSWICH   Martlesham

Debden

North Weald

ROTTERDAM

SWANSEA

CARDIFF

BRISTOL   Ball

BATH   Andover

Middle Wallop

SOUTHAMPTON

Fighter Command 10 Group (Brand)

EXETER

PLYMOUTH

Stanmore
Northolt
Uxbridge   LONDON
HQ
Croydon   Rochford
Biggin Hill   Hornchurch
Kenley   THAMES ESTUARY
Eastchurch
West   Detling   Manston
Malling   CANTERBURY
Redhill   Lympne   Hawkinge

Fighter Command 11 Group (Park)

Tangmere
PORTSMOUTH
VENTNOR

ANTWERP
GHENT

B E L G I U M

CALAIS

LILLE

Luftflotte 2 (Kesselring)

E N G L I S H   C H A N N E L

AMIENS

CHERBOURG

LE HAVRE

F R A N C E

PARIS

Luftflotte 3 (Sperrle)

RENNES

67

in a day on the 27th and 30th. Indeed some sources quote his score as having reached 17 by this date, although records do not seem to confirm this. He subsequently led the Polish fighter wing as a Wing Commander and then went to the US as Assistant Air Attache. He then volunteered to fly with the US 14th Air Force in China, joining the 23rd Fighter Group late in 1943. Here, flying P-40 Warhawks, he claimed three further victories, at least two of which were confirmed.

Sgt Joseph Frantisek escaped to Poland from his native Czechoslovakia in March 1939, and then in September to France, and subsequently England. It was reported that he gained 11 victories with the Armée de l'Air in May/June 1940, but French records do not confirm this. It is believed that the 11 victories of Frantisek Perina were mistakenly credited to him, due to confusion arising from the common name. In England Frantisek joined 303 Squadron, flying with the Poles rather than with his fellow Czechs in 310 Squadron. Here his achievements were little short of phenomenal, and he was the most successful single pilot during September 1940. Between 2 and 30 September he claimed 17 victories, including three in a day on the 11th. On 8 October he crashed while landing at Northolt and was killed.

figure – and receive Knights' Crosses – as the year wore on. Several of these will be dealt with later, but the following list indicates the point at which each reached a total for the war of 20 or just over:

20 August	Horst Tietzen	II/JG 51 (also seven in Spain)
22 August	Walter Oesau	III/JG 51 (also eight in Spain)
27 August	Helmuth Wick	I/JG 2
3 September	Hans-Karl Mayer	I/JG 53
5 September	Werner Machold	I/JG 2
11 September	Gerhard Schöpfel	III/JG 26
13 September	Herbert Ihlefeld	I(J)/LG 2 (also seven in Spain)
14 September	Joachim Müncheberg	II/JG 26
16 September	Hermann-Friedrich Joppien	I/JG 51
24 September	Hans Hahn	II/JG 51
1 October	Gustav Sprick	III/JG 26
19 October	Josef Priller	II/JG 51
22 October	Hans Philipp	II/JG 54
22 October	Heinz Bretnütz	II/JG 53
9 November	Siegfried Schnell	II/JG 2

Meanwhile however Mölders had reached 40 victories by 21 September, followed by Galland on 25 September, and by Helmuth Wick on 6 October, and by this time all three had been promoted to command full Geschwadern – JG 51, JG 26 and JG 2 respectively. Wick's rate of claiming had been particularly high during the

Thus by the end of 1940 Fighter Command's victory list was as follows:

Flt Lt G Allard	23 and two shared	85 Squadron
Plt Off JH Lacey	23	501 Squadron
Sqn Ldr MN Crossley	21 and two shared	32 Squadron
Plt Off ES Lock(WIA)	20 and one shared	41 Squadron
Flt Lt AA McKellar (Scot) (KIA)	20 and one shared	605 Squadron
Flt Lt WD David	19 and two shared	87 and 213 Squadrons
Flg Off AG Lewis (South African) (WIA)	18	85 and 249 Squadrons
Sqn Ldr AG Malan (South African)	17 and five shared	74 Squadron
Sqn Ldr RRS Tuck	17 and four shared	92 and 257 Squadrons
Sqn Ldr RG Dutton	17 and two shared	145 Squadron
Plt Off HJL Hallowes	17 and two shared	43 Squadron
Sgt J Frantisek (Czech) (KIFA)	17	303 Squadron
Sqn Ldr W Urbanowicz (Polish)	17 (?)	145 and 303 Squadrons
Flg Off EJ Kain (New Zealander) (KIFA)	17	73 Squadron
Plt Off AC Deere (New Zealander)	16 and two shared	54 Squadron
Plt Off CF Gray (New Zealander)	16 and one shared	54 Squadron
Flg Off WL McKnight (Canadian) (KIA)	16 and one shared	242 Squadron

Among the German pilots operating over Southern England, three were particularly outstanding. The fighting over France and the Channel had provided most Luftwaffe fighter units with good experience, and most pilots who had gained victories here were to continue to expand their scores throughout the summer. As has been seen, Mölders and Balthasar had already taken their scores over 20 when France fell, but on 4 September Balthasar, now Kommandeur of III/JG 3, was seriously wounded, this removing him from the field. On 15 August 1940 a third pilot, Adolf Galland of JG 26 who had claimed 13 victories over France, raised his total to over 20, and a steady stream of other pilots were to reach this

later, mainly fighter-versus-fighter period of the battle. He claimed five Spitfires and Hurricanes on 5 October, and again on 6 November. On 28 November he shot down a Spitfire for his 55th victory, having passed both Mölders and Galland to become top-scorer. Two hours later, on another sortie, he attacked more Spitfires near the Is of Wight and shot one down, but was himself at once shot down by Flt Lt JC Dundas (13½ victories) of 609 Squadron, and baled out. Dundas was in turn shot down by Wick's wingman, Oblt Rudi Pflanz (52 victories). Neither Wick nor John Dundas were ever found. Wick's total of 56 included 14 claimed over France During May and June.

Top right: Luftwaffe fighter leaders with their commanding general at the end of 1940. Left to right: Adolf Galland (104 victories), Kommodore JG 26; Gunther Lützow (108) Kommodore JG 3; General Theo Osterkamp, Jagdführer Kanal, ace of two world wars with 32 victories in the first and six in the second; Werner Mölders (115) Kommodore JG 51; Günther von Maltzahn (68) Kommodore JG 53.

Top far right: 303 Squadron's top scorer of the Battle of Britain – and indeed one of the most successful of all pilots during the Battle – was Czech Sgt Joseph Frantisek (17 victories) seen here with his Hurricane shortly before his death in a crash.

Center right: Maj Helmuth Wick (56 victories) was the Luftwaffe top scorer during the Battle of Britain until his death at the hands of RAF ace John Dundas of 609 Squadron.

Below right: 74 Squadron was one of the most experienced Spitfire units at the start of 1941. Flg Off HM Stephen, who at this time had claimed some 18 individual victories and 9 shared, talks to one of the flight commanders, Flt Lt JC Mungo-Park, who was to be killed in action in June 1941 after 12 and four shared victories. The photograph was taken on 30 November 1940 just after the pair had shared in the shooting down of a Bf 109E for Biggin Hill's 600th confirmed victory.

When the battle drew to a close at the end of November, Mölders and Galland were firmly in the lead, followed by Oesau, whose score was close to 40, and by Joppien and Ihlefeld who had both reached 25. Losses among these leaders had generally been light, and apart from Wick, only Tietzen (killed 18 August) and Hans-Karl Mayer (killed 17 October with his score at 38) had been lost among the leaders. Other successful pilots had included Hans-Joachim Jabs, the top-scoring Zerstörer pilot of 1940, with 19 victories with II/ZG 76, Arnold Lignitz of III/JG 51 and Hans-Ekkehard Bob of III/JG 54 also with 19, Heinz Ebeling of III/JG 26 and Erich Schmidt of III/JG 53 with 18 each, and Dietrich Hrabak of II/JG 54 with 16.

Western Europe 1941–43

Early in 1941 Fighter Command began offensive operations over France and Belgium, although Luftwaffe fighter sweeps still came in over southern England. Both sides introduced new models of their standard fighters – Bf 109Fs, Spitfire Vs and Hurricane IICs, the two latter types introducing cannon armament on a wide scale to RAF units. Although many units on both sides had been withdrawn to rest, activity remained high. Wings of RAF fighters, Spitfires predominating, flew sweeps over the occupied coastal belt of Western Europe, or escorted small formations of light bombers to bomb targets here – mainly in an effort to tempt the German fighters up to give battle.

During the early summer many Luftwaffe units were withdrawn to the East for the attack on Russia, others moving to the Mediterranean and Balkans, but the cross-Channel 'leaning into Europe' was to be the RAF's main daylight activity during much of the next three years. While initially many ex-Battle of Britain pilots added to their scores here on both sides, and new aces appeared, these operations were to prove costly to the RAF. Claims were undoubtedly well above actual results, with combats taking place at high altitude, over enemy territory and far from home. The Germans who remained in Western Europe were to have opportunities for

Left: Plt Off AG Lewis (18 victories) climbs from the cockpit of an 85 Squadron Hurricane during the Battle of Britain.
Above: Spitfire I of 72 Squadron over the Channel.

building up big scores against the steadily-increasing numbers of the RAF, which was to introduce many units of foreign nationals to the fight, notably Poles, Czechs, French, Belgians, Norwegians and Americans. Despite the introduction of the first bombers of the US 8th Air Force to the scene late in 1942, following the American entry into the war, these tactics were not to differ greatly until the end of 1943.

During 1941 the Luftwaffe veterans of 1940 remained at the top of the high scorers on the Channel Front, Mölders until JG 51 moved East in June, but particularly Adolf Galland. When the bulk of the Luftwaffe moved East, just two Jagdgeschwadern were left in the West — JG 2 and 26 — together with the nucleus of JG 1, at that time at about one Gruppe strength. This unit was to defend North Germany and Holland, while the two main units faced the RAF fighters along the French and Belgian coastlines. When Mölders and his JG 51 departed for the East, his score stood at 68, but on the day the offensive against Russia began, Galland became top-scorer in the West with his 69th victory. Within days Josef 'Pips' Priller of JG 26, Balthasar — now back as Kommodore of JG 2 — and Siegfried Schnell of JG 2 all gained their 40th victories, while Hans 'Assi' Hahn of the latter unit also reached this score during August.

While the Germans were undoubtedly getting the best of this fighting, it was by no means without cost. Lt Robert Menge, who had claimed four victories in Spain, had been clear top-

scorer of the campaign in Norway and Denmark the previous spring, where he had been credited with shooting down 12 bombers, flying with II/JG 77. Now with JG 26 as wingman to Galland, he had claimed two Spitfires, but on 14 June was shot down and killed by 92 Squadron's commander, Jamie Rankin. Just two weeks later Lt Gustav 'Micky' Sprick of III/JG 26 (31 victories) was also killed by Spitfires, while on 3 July JG 2's commander, Hpt Wilhelm Balthasar, went down to a similar fate after 47 victories. Walter Oesau was brought back from Russia later in the month to take over JG 2, having added 44 Soviet aircraft to his score in less than a month. On 26 October he would achieve his 100th victory — the third pilot to do so.

With the RAF, several of the most successful unit commanders of 1940 were promoted to the new post of Wing Leader, among them being AG 'Sailor' Malan, Bob Tuck and the famous and indomitable legless ace, Douglas Bader. By early July, Malan had become Fighter Command's top-scorer with a stated total of 32, while Tuck's score had reached 29 (in both cases these totals included a number of shared victories counted as wholes). Both were stood down to go on a mission to the USA. Bader, at the head of the Tangmere Wing, had added eight and one shared Bf 109s and three probables during June and July, to his 1940 score of 12 and one shared. On 9 August he shot down two more Messerschmitts, but then collided with a JG 26 machine and was obliged to bale out. He was entertained by

Left: In July 1941 Walter Oesau returned to the West from Russia with his score around 90 to take command of JG 2. He is seen (right) here in 1940 by the tail of his Bf 109E when serving with III/JG 51. At least 39 victory bars are painted on the aircraft, but at least 12 of these appear to be for aircraft destroyed on the ground (the down-pointing arrowheads).
Below left: The indomitable legless fighter ace Douglas Bader is seen (center) when commanding 242 Squadron late in 1940. On his right is Canadian ace Flg Off Willie McKnight (16 and 1 shared) while on his left is one of his flight commanders, George Ball (6). Only Bader survived the war.
Above: Joachim Müncheerg was one of the most successful Luftwaffe pilots against the Western Allies. He took over II/JG26 in August 1941 after a detachment to the Mediterranean. His score of 135 included 102 British and American aircraft; 58 in the West and 44 over the Mediterranean area. He was killed in action in Tunisia in March 1943.

Galland and the Germans agreed to a spare set of artificial legs being dropped by parachute for him during a raid, his own having been damaged in the fall.

It was not only the high-scorers of 1940 who were now doing well. Sqn Ldr JE Rankin, an ex-instructor, had taken command of 92 Squadron – one of Fighter Command's top-scoring units – at the start of the year, after only one shared victory with 64 Squadron. On 11 April 1941 he shot down an He 59 floatplane, and then added 12 and one shared Bf 109s by the end of August. Promoted to lead the Biggin Hill Wing after 'Sailor' Malan, he had added four more by mid-December to raise his total to 18 when he was rested.

Irishman BE 'Paddy' Finucane had claimed five and one shared with 65 Squadron during 1940 and early 1941, but then became a flight commander in 452 Squadron, the first fighter unit of the Royal Australian Air Force to operate with the RAF. Between 11 July and 13 October 1941 he was to claim 19 and two shared Bf 109s shot down, but then broke his ankle and was off operations for a time. Don Kingaby of 92 Squadron had claimed nine and one shared during 1940, including four Bf 109s on 15 November, adding eight more by early October 1941.

By mid-1941 a large proportion of British effort was being diverted to the Middle East, both squadrons and many pilots being posted to North Africa or to Malta at this time. Increasingly their place in England was taken by the foreign units, which preferred to fight in the West. As a result, while new British and Commonwealth aces did appear during 1941 and 1942, many pilots were posted away after a few victories. In

JG 2 and 26, most of the Germans stayed, and their victories continued to grow. From 16 June to 8 November 1941 JG 26's 'Pips' Priller had his most fruitful days, claiming 37 Spitfires and Hurricanes, and a single Blenheim, to raise his total to 67. In August Joachim Müncheberg returned from a high-scoring detachment to the Mediterranean, taking over II/JG 26 where he would add 34 more Spitfires and a Hurricane to his score before being posted to Russia in June 1942. Galland meanwhile sustained his position as top-scorer in the West, gaining his 94th victory on 5 December. He was then taken off operations to take over the position of Inspector of Fighters left vacant since Mölders' death the previous month. Here he was to become the youngest general in the German forces. However JG 26 suffered a severe loss at this time when Hpt Johann Schmid, who had claimed

Above: Brendan 'Paddy' Finucane, the greatest Irish-born fighter pilot of World War II, with his Spitfire when a flight commander in 452 Squadron, RAAF, in 1941.

41 victories, 15 of them during August 1941 alone, was shot down by Spitfires and killed on 6 November.

New names were now appearing, particularly in JG 2. Egon Mayer, who had been a slow starter, brought his total since spring 1940 to 20 on 1 August 1941, but would add another 30 during the next 12 months. Kurt Bühligen claimed his 21st victory during September, and Josef 'Sepp' Wurmheller his 24th, while Erich Rudorffer also had well over 20 by this time. Late in 1941 the first of the new radial engined Focke-Wulf Fw 190s were introduced to the Western Jagdgeschwadern, establishing a marked ascendency over the RAF's Spitfire Vs. For the next year, until quantities of the improved Spitfire IX became available, RAF claims fell and losses rose.

The Japanese attack in the Far East in December 1941 brought the USA into the war, but led to a further drain of RAF fighter units and pilots to this new war zone. Not until mid-1942 did the first units of the USAAF begin to reach England, some of their fighter pilots – flying Spitfires provided by the RAF – taking part in the biggest operation in the West since 1940 – the landings made at Dieppe on 19 August 1942 by Anglo-Canadian forces (Operation 'Jubilee'). Fighter Command provided a massive air umbrella – and suffered its greatest losses in a day, over 100 fighters. JG 2 provided much of the opposition, Siegfried Schnell claiming five

Stanislaw Skalski – Poland's Greatest

Stanislaw F Skalski was a 23-year-old regular officer of the Polish Air Force in September 1939, flying PZL P.XIe fighters with the 142 (Wild Duck) Squadron. During the brief fighting over his country he became top scorer, shooting down two Dornier Do 17s on the 2nd and claiming two more individual and a shared victory over the next two days. Escaping from the invading Germans via the Mediterranean, he reached London where he enlisted in the RAF in January 1940. After training, he was posted to 501 Squadron to fly Hurricanes, claiming four further victories during the Battle of Britain, and being shot down once himself. After brief service with several other RAF squadrons, he joined the Polish 306 Squadron as a flight commander on Spitfires in June 1941. During the next three months he added a further five victories to his total, receiving a DFC to add to his Polish Silver Cross and Cross of Valor. After a period as an instructor, he took command of 317 Squadron in April 1942, claiming a single Fw 190 shot down during that month and received a Bar to his DFC. Early in 1943 he headed a unit of experienced Polish pilots, the 'Fighting Team,' which was sent to Tunisia to fly Spitfire IXs with Lance Wade's 145 Squadron. Here during the closing weeks of the campaign, he claimed three further victories, and at the start of May took command of 601 Squadron in the same Desert Air Force Wing – the first Pole to lead a British squadron. Returning to England late in the year, he received a second Bar to his DFC and the Polish Gold Cross. He was promoted to wing commander in April 1944 and took over 133 (Polish No 2) Fighter Wing, now flying Mustang IIIs. With this unit he gained his last victories – two Fw 190s which he caused to collide and crash on 24 June 1944 – to raise his official score to $18^{11}/_{12}$, although $19^{1}/_{4}$ victories have been found for him. He ended the war as an instructor at the Advanced Gunnery School at Catfoss under 'Sailor' Malan, and added a DSO to his long list of decorations. Returning to Poland after the war, he was imprisoned for a time by the Russians. He was subsequently released and worked in Warsaw as a taxi driver.

Main picture: Messerschmitt
Bf 109Es of I/JG 27 flying
over the Libyan Desert,
1941.
Inset left: Messerschmitt
Bf 110C 'zerstörer' in Libya;
this is an aircraft of III/ZG 26
Inset right: Wreckage of
RAF Blenheim bombers in
Greece, 1941, after the
German occupation.

victories to reach a score of 70, and 'Sepp' Wurmheller, with a leg in plaster and concussion from a crash-landing, claiming seven, while Egon Mayer gained his 50th on this date.

Early in November a substantial element of Fighter Command and the new US Eighth Air Force left England to support the Anglo-American landings in French Northwest Africa (Operation Torch). II/JG 2 was also sent to Tunisia as part of the force opposing this venture, taking with it Bühligen and Rudorffer, whose scores had now reached 30 and 48 respectively. During the same month 'Assi' Hahn departed for the East after 68 victories, but JG 2 still retained many successful Experten in the West – notably Wurmheller, whose score now stood at 60, Oesau and Mayer. The Geschwader's main loss of the year had been Rudi Pflanz, shot down by Spitfires on 31 July after 52 victories.

Many promising RAF aces and future aces went with the force to North Africa, but 1942 was to see Jamie Rankin back in action as Wing Leader, Biggin Hill, again, adding three more victories to his score to reach 21. Don Kingaby also returned as a flight commander in 64 Squadron, claiming his 19th over Dieppe. In early 1943 he would lead 122 Squadron, adding three more fighters to his growing score. Another returning to action was 'Paddy' Finucane, who appeared at the head of 602 Squadron in January 1942. He claimed five and two shared Fw 190s by the end of May, and in June was promoted Wing Leader, Hornchurch, his score standing at 29 and six shared – at least equal to 'Sailor' Malan's total. On 15 July 1942, at the head of his wing as it left the French coast after a sweep, his Spitfire was hit by a machine gun on the beach. He ditched in the sea; the aircraft sank at once, and he was not able to get out.

Initial US heavy-bomber raids began against targets in France during August 1942, opposition coming from JG 2 and 26. Egon Mayer, particularly, was responsible for developing tactics for use against the formidable, heavily armed B-17 Flying Fortresses and B-24 Liberators. The withdrawal of many units to North Africa slowed down the development of these raids, but during 1943 they grew steadily in strength and frequency. Those directed into North Germany were met by elements of JG 1, now at full Geschwader strength, and soon battles with the big bombers became a major element for the Luftwaffe. Initially the most successful opponents of the bombers were to be the pilots of this unit – Günther Specht, Gerhard Sommer and Heinz Knoke, who soon had scores in double figures against the big aircraft.

The threat was obvious, and the force deployed for Home Defence began to grow. JG 1 was split to form the cadre of a new JG 11, while III/JG 54 and I/JG 3 returned from Russia, I/JG 27 arriving from the Mediterranean. Further north, elements of JG 5 now defended Norway against attacks by aircraft from RAF's Coastal and

Left: New Zealander JAA
Gibson gained 13½ victories
by 1942 when he was a
flight commander in 457
Squadron RAAF. He later
flew Kittyhawks with the
RNZAF in the South Pacific,
returning to the RAF late in
1944 and ending the war
with a score of 14½.
Center left: A typical Wing
Leader's Spitfire IX in 1943.
This one was the personal
mount of Canadian Wg Cdr
EJ 'Jack' Charles (15½
victories) when leading the
Middle Wallop Wing.
Below left: JR 'Johnny'
Baldwin became the
highest scoring Typhoon
pilot of the war. He is seen
here in the cockpit of his 609
Squadron Typhoon IA (an
early model with the older
style cockpit canopy) after
his initial victories.

Bomber Commands. As the year wore on, more US fighter units moved to England to replace those which had gone to Africa, and soon P-38 Lightning and P-47 Thunderbolt pilots were gaining experience, flying sweeps with the RAF. Later in the year they began making limited escort sorties toward Germany, and soon these new opponents were locked in mortal combat with the Luftwaffe fighters. At first they suffered some severe losses to the experienced pilots of JG 2 and 26, but by winter their successes were beginning to mount, and their first aces had appeared.

For the RAF, 1943 was to see a steady improvement of the situation over the Channel Front, as more Spitfire IXs, and new types such as the Typhoon became available in numbers. Also, experienced and successful pilots returned from the Mediterranean to begin second tours as flight commanders or squadron leaders in Fighter Command. Late in the year the new 2nd Tactical Air Force was formed, ready for the planned 1944 invasion, although for the time being operations continued as before. Again, the foreign squadrons saw much of the action, together with the growing fighter contingent of the Royal Canadian Air Force, but several RAF pilots continued to do well. Wg Cdr Ray Harries brought his score to 19 and two shared, flying the powerful new low-altitude Griffon-engined Spitfire XIIs with the Westhampnett Wing, while Sqn Ldr JR Baldwin was well on his way to becoming the top-scoring Typhoon pilot of the war with 14½ victories, twice getting three in a day. In 1944 Harries would add one further victory, and Baldwin three. One of those returned from the Mediterranean was New Zealand Malta ace, Ray Hesselyn, who claimed eight and one shared during 1943, including three in a day, to add to his 12 earlier victories. Another New Zealander, Al Deere, also returned as Biggin Hill Wing Leader to add four Fw 190s to his 1940/41 total of 17 and two shared. Most notable however was the Kenley Wing Leader, Wg Cdr JE 'Johnny' Johnson, whose total had reached 25 by the end of the year.

Among those various foreign nationals, a number of leading pilots had emerged, as follows:

Poles

Plt Off Michal Maciejowski	12 and one shared	249, 316, 317 and 601 Squadrons
Sqn Ldr Jan Zumbach	12 and one shared	303 Squadron
Flg Off Anthoni Glowacki	11 and one shared	501, 303 Squadrons
Wg Cdr Marian Pisarek	10 (+ 2 and 1 shared in Poland)	303, 308 Squadrons, No 1 Polish Fighter Wing
Flt Lt Jan Falkowski	9	315, 308 and 303 Squadrons
Flt Sgt Aleksander Chudek	9	315 and 303 Squadrons
Sqn Ldr Stanislaw Skalski	9 (+ 4 and 1 shared in Poland)	501, 306 and 315 Squadrons

Among these pilots, who had gained their totals between 1940 and 1943, Glowacki had claimed five in one day, Maciejowski had been shot down and made a prisoner on 8 August 1943, and Pisarek had been killed in action on 29 April 1942. Six more Poles had by this time gained eight victories while flying from England.

French

Sqn Ldr Jean Demozay	21	1, 242 and 91 Squadrons
Capt Michael Boudier	10 (+ 3 in France with GC II/5)	340, 341 Squadrons

Demozay's score included 14 with 91 'Jim Crow' Squadron on lone shipping reconnaissance sorties between July 1941 and October 1942, three of them Fw 190s all claimed on 31 October.

Belgians

Flg Off Count Yvan DuMonceau de Bergandael	8	609, 350 Squadrons
Flt Lt Jean Offenberg	6 (+ 1 in Belgium, 1940)	145 and 609 Squadrons

Offenberg had been killed in a mid-air collision on 22 January 1942.

Norwegians

Flt Lt Svein Heglund	11 and one shared	331 Squadron
Wg Cdr Kaj Birksted	8 and one shared	331 Squadron and Norwegian Fighter Wing

Although flying with the Norwegians, Birksted was in fact a Dane.

Americans

Sqn Ldr Carroll W McColpin	8	71 and 133 'Eagle' Squadrons
Sqn Ldr G Augustus Daymond	7	71 'Eagle' Squadron
Sqn Ldr Chesley G Peterson	6	71 'Eagle' Squadron

Far right: Two American aces of the original 'Eagle' squadron, both of whom became commanding officers of this unit. Chesley Peterson (right) was succeeded by 'Gus' Daymond.

Far right inset: Capt Gerald W Johnson (17 victories) became the first ace of the Eighth Air Force's top-scoring 56th Fighter Group on 19 August 1943.

Center right: Flt Lt Svein Heglund, Norwegian top scorer, after a fierce combat in which his Spitfire IX suffered damage to the propeller boss. Heglund was credited with 11½ victories by day, later adding three as a night fighter with 85 Squadron, flying Mosquitos.

Near right: The most successful Frenchman to fly with the RAF was Jean Demozay, known by the

'nom de Guerre' of Moses Morlaix (21 victories). Above: The first USAAF Eighth Air Force ace was Capt Charles 'Joppo' London of the 78th Fighter Group. He was also the first pilot to gain five victories flying the P-47 Thunderbolt.

American volunteers served with the RAF from 1940 onward, and three special 'Eagle' squadrons were to be formed, which would eventually be transferred to the USAAF in September 1942 to become the 4th Fighter Group. Peterson commanded the group, adding a seventh victory to his score with it in April 1943. First 'Eagle' Squadron ace of the war was William R Dunn, who claimed two Bf 109Es on 27 August 1941 to reach five victories, but was then wounded. Daymond and McColpin were both reputed to have been credited with nine victories, but records do not substantiate this; McColpin and Dunn both claimed further victories with the USAAF in 1944.

Once the USAAF fighters got into their stride, the first aces were to come from the 78th Fighter Group. Capt Charles P 'Joppo' London claimed his first victory on 22 June 1943, then twice claimed two in a day to become an ace on 30 July. On this latter date the unit's Lt Col Eugene P Roberts claimed his first three, becoming an ace on 24 August when he raised his total to six; he had nine by 20 October. The 78th

did not retain its lead for long, another P-47 group – the original one, the 56th – soon overtook it. On 19 August Capt Gerald W Johnson became the unit's first ace, followed on 2 October by the group commander, Col Hubert Zemke. Before October was out five more of the unit's pilots were to have become aces together with one each from the 4th and 353rd Fighter Groups. By the end of the year one more from the 353rd and another five from the 56th had joined these ranks. Of the Eighth Air Force's 17 aces of 1943, no less than nine were to become high-scorers, none of them getting less than 18 victories. Indeed by the end of 1943 Walker Mahurin of the 56th already had 13½, followed by Robert S Johnson from the same group and the 353rd's Walter 'Turk' Beckham with 10 each.

The year 1943 brought a substantial increase in losses to the Luftwaffe – many of them in combat with the new American opponents. As with the RAF, many leading Experten of the fighting in both the Mediterranean and in Russia were posted home to lead units, but numbers of these were killed. With JG 2 Egon Mayer was at

Above: A number of leading pilots of the Norwegian Fighter Wing after a medal presentation ceremony. Left to right: Wg Cdr Kaj Birksted, the Danish-born Wing Leader (8 and 1

shared); **Maj Arne Austeen (5 and 1 shared) 331 Squadron; Maj Werner Christie (9 and 2 shared) 332 Squadron; Capt Nils Jörstad (7 and 1 shared) 331 Squadron.**

this time the most successful pilot in the Luftwaffe against the US heavy bombers. Oesau gave up command of the Geschwader in June 1943 for a command job, but not for long. On 8 October Oberstlt Hans Philipp, Kommodore of JG 1 (206 victories) was killed in action soon after joining the unit on return from Russia, and Oesau was sent to take over. Kurt Bühligen, back from Tunisia, was still a stalwart, as was Wurmheller. Kurt Goltzsch, who had claimed 14 in Tunisia, had brought his score to 43 by November 1943, but was then badly wounded in combat with Spitfires and died some months later. JG 2 lost two other long-serving high-scorers during the year. In January Erich Leie, Kommandeur of I Gruppe, was posted to I/JG 51 in the East after 43 victories, while Siegfried Schnell was posted to command III/JG 54 in May. At the end of the year he moved to the East after 87 victories, but was killed there on 25 February 1944 with his total at 93.

Priller was now Kommodore of JG 26 and a number of his pilots continued to do well. Adolf Galland's brother, Wilhelm-Ferdinand ('Wutz')

reached 40 by May, but on 17 August, his score at 55, was killed in combat with P-47s. He was the second of the Gallands to be killed with JG 26; Paul had died on the ground in a bombing raid some months earlier after 17 victories. At the turn of the year Fritz Geisshardt had joined the unit as Kommandeur III Gruppe after gaining 100 victories, the 18 most recent in the Mediterranean area. After two more early in 1943, he was shot down and badly wounded on 5 April, dying next day. Johannes Seifert, Kommandeur of II Gruppe, had gone with the unit to Russia on detachment from February to May 1943, claiming 11 victories to add to the 40-odd he had claimed prior to this. After his return he raised his total to 57, but on 25 November he collided with the last of these, a P-38, and crashed to his death. However, Klaus Mietusch reached his 50th victory by 30 November, and Adolph Glunz, a steady scorer, had claimed his 40th during the late summer. Toward the end of 1943 more reinforcements for the Home Defense arrived in Germany – notably the rest of JG 3 (II, III and IV Gruppen).

The Mediterranean Area

Mussolini's declaration of war on France and the United Kingdom on 10 June 1940 brought the whole area of the Mediterranean Sea and most of the countries bordering it into the fighting zone. Initially Italy attacked Southern France, Malta and French North Africa, while small British forces in Egypt made some limited strikes against the Italian army in Libya. There was also an immediate outbreak of hostilities in East Africa, between Italian forces in Ethiopia and Eritrea and British forces in Sudan, Aden and Kenya – soon joined in the latter colony by a substantial South African contingent. With the French surrender late in June, the Italians were able to turn all their attention to the British, who were in a desperately weak situation at this time. However they made few serious offensive moves, their own forces being ill-prepared, and in October they further diluted their efforts by invading Northwest Greece from Albania.

Unable to consider action in Western Europe, and with the immediate threat of invasion abated, the British sought to expand much of their initial military effort in the Middle East, which was seen as a critically important sector. Consequently a fighter defense was established – with great difficulty – on Malta, where an aerial siege which was to last for over two years was underway. Reinforcements were also rushed to Egypt and to the Sudan, both from Britain and from many of the Commonwealth nations, and it was to be here that aircraft purchased from the USA – and later provided under Lend Lease – were first to be put fully to use by the RAF.

In December 1940 a major offensive was launched from Egypt which rolled the Italians back through Libya almost all the way to Tripoli, while at the same time offensives from Kenya and the Sudan rolled up the numerically larger Italian colonial defenders, bringing the main fighting there to an end by April 1941, and allowing the dispatch of a large part of the Commonwealth forces to Egypt – and to Greece, where a growing proportion of British military support was directed early in 1941. In the early fighting in the Western Desert of Libya, the Gladiators and Hurricanes of the RAF gained a marked ascendency over the Regia Aeronautica, the outstanding pilot of the First Libyan Campaign being Flg Off EM 'Imshi' Mason of 274 Squadron, who claimed over 15 Italian aircraft shot down at this time. In March 1941 he led a detachment over to aid in the defense of Malta, but here he would be shot down and wounded after one further victory. Several other pilots also did well, but those of 33, 80 and 112 Squadrons were all posted to Greece between October 1940 February 1941. In East Africa pilots of the SAAF bore the brunt of the aerial fighting and several became aces here, notably Maj KW Driver with

Above: Bearded during service at forward desert landing grounds during the First Libyan Campaign is the RAF's top-scoring Hurricane pilot of that period, Flg Off EM 'Imshi' Mason of 274 Squadron.

Top right: This group of 80 Squadron pilots in Greece in 1941 includes most of the RAF's top scorers in this campaign. Left to right: Sgt EWF Hewett (15); Flg Off W Vale (20+); Flg Off PT 'Keg' Dowding; Plt Off Trevor-Roper; Flt Lt MT StJ Pattle (40+); Flg Off HDW 'Twinstead' Flower and Plt Off JJ Lancaster.
Right: RAF top scorer on Malta during the first 18 months of defense was Sgt FN Robertson of 261 Squadron, who claimed ten victories there from his final total of 12.
Right center: Oblt Erbo Graf von Kageneck was the most successful pilot of III/JG 27 in 1941. After service over France and Britain he flew briefly over Malta in spring 1941, gaining four victories there. He was killed late in 1941 in Libya having meanwhile flown in Russia and raised his total to 67.
Far right: SAAF top scorer of the war, Maj JE 'Jack' Frost, who gained 15 and two shared over East Africa and the Western Desert before being killed in summer 1942.

Gloster Gladiator I
L8011 of 80 Squadron,
carrying the code letters
YK-D. Seen over the
Egyptian desert in 1940,
this aircraft is flown by Flt Lt
MT StJ Pattle, soon to
become probably the RAF's
top-scoring ace of the war.

desert during August 1940, adding 10 more in Greece before the end of the year, and then by early March 1941 raising his total by a further 10 and one shared, nine after converting from Gladiators to Hurricanes. At this point he was posted to command 33 Squadron, and thereafter lost records fail to indicate his further score in detail. Various sources indicate that this could have been as high as 27 and two shared, plus five on the ground, during the final month before he was shot down and killed over Athens. This estimate is almost certainly too high, but it seems highly likely that his score may well have reached or even exceeded 40.

With Pattle in 33 Squadron had been several more outstanding pilots, the most successful of whom was Canadian Vernon Woodward. After five and a shared victories in the early weeks of the war in the desert, Woodward flew Hurricanes during the First Libyan Campaign, adding five more. In Greece he added a further nine and one shared, including three Cant Z.1007 bombers on 6 April 1941, to raise his total to 19 and two shared. He later gained two more after returning to North Africa.

The failures of Italy's forces led Mussolini to seek aid from Germany, although Adolf Hitler considered the Mediterranean an unimportant area, in which he was loath to become involved. However when the Greek Campaign also turned against the Italians early in 1941, the threat to the Balkans and to his planned invasion of Russia, brought the dispatch of German units to stabilize the position. From January onward units arrived in Sicily to neutralize Malta, and bolster the Italian army in Libya, while on 6 April 1941 a major offensive was launched against Yugoslavia and Greece.

A single Staffel of Bf 109Es operated over Malta from mid-February to early June, but had quite disproportionate success, gaining some 42 victories here. Some 19 of these were credited to the unit commander, Oblt Joachim Müncheberg, including one over Yugoslavia during a brief detachment to Eastern Italy in April. Throughout 1940–41 fighting over Malta ebbed and flowed, Müncheberg being the only really outstanding high scorer of this period over the island. During the 18 months of fighting no Italian pilots achieved five victories here, while about a dozen or so RAF pilots achieved this score at least. The most successful were Sgt FN Robertson (10) Wg Cdr AC Rabagliati and Flt Lt JAF MacLachlan (8 each). Over the seas around the island Royal Navy pilots also achieved some success – particularly those of 806 Squadron flying Fairey Fulmar fighters from HMS *Illustrious*. Perhaps eight became aces, and three had scores over eight (Lt Cdr CLG Evans, Lt (A) WL LeC Barnes and Sub Lt (A) SG Orr).

The Luftwaffe swept all before them in the Balkans, elements of three Jagdgeschwadern wiping out the Yugoslav, Greek and RAF forces facing them in the air and on the ground. Their

10 and Capt JE Frost with 8½ plus 21 and three shared on the ground. Ken Driver of 1 SAAF Squadron became a POW in Libya with his score at 11, while 'Jack' Frost of 3 SAAF Squadron later became SAAF top-scorer after adding 7⅓ more in Libya before his death in action.

However the East African Campaign was to see probably the most effective Regia Aeronautica involvement of any, and it was an Italian pilot who was the outstanding ace of the fighting here. Capt Mario Visentini was believed to have gained some 20 victories (four of them shared) before his death in a flying accident on 13 February 1941, including three Gladiators in one fight on 6 November 1940. He also took part in three very successful strafing attacks during which 32 British aircraft were claimed destroyed on the ground. He was awarded the Medaglia d'Oro.

It was in Greece that the RAF achieved much glory, 80 Squadron particularly claiming many successes first with Gladiators and then with Hurricanes over the Tepelene Front. Notable among an outstanding unit were Australian Plt Off RN 'Ape' Cullen, who claimed 16½ victories between 30 December 1940 and 4 March 1941 when he was shot down and killed; Plt Off W Vale, whose score exceeded 20; Sgt EWF Hewett, who claimed 15, and above all, Flt Lt MTSt J 'Pat' Pattle. Pattle, widely believed among historians to have been the top-scoring RAF pilot of the war, had claimed four victories in the

Malta Ace

George Frederick Beurling was not accepted into the national Royal Canadian Air Force owing to lack of educational qualifications, although he was already a qualified civil pilot. After two attempts, he joined the RAF in England and, after training, was posted to 403 Squadron, RCAF. However he was transferred to 41 Squadron as he was not a member of the RCAF. A loner and a dedicated fighter pilot, who gave much thought to the theory and practice of deflection shooting and lived only to shoot down enemy aircraft, he broke away from formation on several occasions. Although this brought him victories over two Fw 190s during May 1942, it gained the wrath of his superiors, who did not object when he applied for posting to the 'fighter pilot's paradise' – Malta.

On the besieged island he flew with 249 Squadron – the RAF's top-scoring unit of the war. He was quickly in his element, shooting down three fighters on 6 July and three more on the 11th to raise his total to 11 and receive a DFM. Six more fighters were claimed by the end of the month, four of them on the 27th, and he gained one more and a shared Ju 88 during the quieter month of August. A Bar to his DFM followed and he was persuaded with some difficulty to accept a commission. Two further victories in September brought his total to 20⅓. During the final October Blitz on the island he claimed eight more victories in three days of actual combat, but on the last day – the 14th – he was shot down and wounded in the leg. With 26⅓ hits over the island he had achieved more than twice the score of any other Allied pilot during the Gibraltar siege. Surviving an air crash at Gibraltar during which many other passengers aboard

the Liberator taking them back to England were drowned, he joined 'Johnny' Johnson's Canadian Wing at Kenley in the late Summer of 1943 as a flight commander in 412 Squadron. He added three more Fw 190s by the end of the year to bring his total to 31⅓, but then became a gunnery instructor at Catfoss. He was killed in 1948 when an aircraft he was ferrying out to the new state of Israel, crashed on takeoff in Italy – it was believed as a result of sabotage.

Italian Number One

Adriano Visconti flew in the Libyan Desert in 1940 as a reconnaissance pilot, claiming one Gladiator fighter shot down while in this role. He subsequently became a fighter pilot, flying with the 7° and 16° Gruppo of the 54° Stormo CT. Operating over Malta during 1941 to 1942, he claimed two Hurricanes and two Blenheims shot down, later adding 14 more victories over Tunisia and Sicily between late 1942 and August 1943. When the Armistice of 8 September 1943 was announced, he flew from Sardinia to Guidonia with three groundcrew crammed into the fuselage of his MC 205 fighter, and joined the air force of the new Fascist Republica Sociale Italiana, commanding the 1° Gruppo CT 'Asso di Bastoni.' With this unit he claimed seven more victories – three P-47s, a P-38 and three bombers – to raise his score to 26. However, on 29 April 1945 he was shot in the back and killed in Milan by anti-Fascist partisans. With 26 victories he was the top-scoring Italian pilot of World War II.

Commonwealth Top Scorer?

Marmaduke Thomas St John Pattle, born in South Africa of English parents, joined the RAF in 1936, and served with 80 Squadron in Egypt from 1938. During early battles with the Italians over the desert, he claimed four victories and a probable, although he was shot down himself on 4 August 1940. The squadron then moved to Greece where by the end of the year he had claimed 10 more victories and shared in two others. During February 1941 the unit received some Hurricanes to replace its aging Gladiator biplanes and, flying one of these, Pattle claimed two Fiat BR 20 bombers and two CR 42 fighters, plus a probable, on 28 February, plus three Fiat G 50 fighters on 4 March to bring his score to 24⅔. Posted to command 33 Squadron, also Hurricane-equipped, he also received a Bar to the DFC he had been awarded late in 1940. At the head of 33 Squadron he led an attack on an Italian airfield in Albania on 23 March, claiming a G 50 and one probable in the air, and three on the ground.

On 6 April 1941 Germany entered the Balkan war, and on the first day he shot down two Bf 109Es of III/JG 27 over the Rupel Pass. Thereafter details vary as to his score as all records were destroyed. According to a diary kept by one of his groundcrew, he claimed eight more victories by 12 April. He destroyed two Bf 109s on the ground, thereafter claiming five in a day on the 14th and six on the 19th. However, this is believed to be a considerable overestimate, and may have indicated the claims of the squadron as a whole. On 20 April he led the surviving RAF fighters up over Athens to intercept a heavy raid, reportedly flying with a fever and a high temperature. He was seen to shoot down two Bf 110s and possibly a Bf 109, but was himself shot down by other Bf 110s as he went to the aid of another Hurricane. He crashed to his death in Eleusis Bay. If all claims made for him were in fact correct, his total would be in excess of 51. However, it can be stated with a degree of confidence that his final score was at least 40.

Regia Aeronautica Ace

France Lucchini first saw action in Spain in 1938 with the 23° Gruppe CT, claiming five victories here over Russian-built aircraft. He was twice shot down, on the second occasion falling to escorting I-16s after shooting down an SB-2 bomber on 22 July, and baling out to become a prisoner; he managed to escape in February 1939. In 1940 he was posted to Libya with the 10° Gruppo of the 4° Stormo CT, flying Fiat Cr 42 biplanes. Here he shared in the shooting down of two Gladiators, a Blenheim and a Sunderland flying-boat before the unit was withdrawn to Italy. In mid-1941, now flying Macchi C.200 monoplanes, he operated over Malta from Sicily, claiming a Hurricane on 27 June, and sharing in many more victories. However on 27 September he was wounded, and was out of action until spring 1942. By now his unit had received MC 202s, and again over Malta, he added two more victories to his total before the unit moved back to Libya. Here he saw much action throughout the second half of 1942. He claimed at least 14 victories during this period, plus shares in others. He was shot down on 16 July, and again on 24 October after claiming a P-40 and a Boston. This time he was wounded again, and was evacuated home with his score at 25. He rejoined the Gruppo once more in June 1943, by which time it was fighting in defense of Sicily. On 5 July he was seen to shoot down a Spitfire while intercepting an escorted formation of B-17s, but was then shot down and killed. He received a posthumous award of the Medaglia d'Oro.

The RAF's Deadliest Foe

No German pilot was to take a heavier toll of the aircraft of the Western Allies than Hauptmann Hans-Joachim Marseille. Something of a maverick, with a tendency to wear his hair long and a fondness for jazz music, Marseille was marked out as troublesome from the start, and was moved from unit to unit during 1940. In this period he claimed seven Spitfires shot down over the English Channel, but was shot down himself four times. Finally early in 1941 he was posted to I/JG 27 which was about to leave for Africa – still at the time an Oberfähnrich (officer cadet), not yet considered suitable for his commission.

In Africa he gradually began to improve his flying and shooting, and although shot down once more, only just escaping with his life, he had added 11 more British aircraft to his score by mid-September 1941. On 24 September came his best day yet, when he claimed four Hurricanes, but it was in December that things began to speed up. Now the unit received Bf 109Fs to replace the earlier E version, and with this superior aircraft with its engine-mounted cannon, Marseille really found his form; the month bringing 11 more successes to raise his total to 36 by the end of the year. By now he had developed a superb and virtually unrivalled skill at the difficult art of deflection shooting and, as well being a magnificent pilot, was able to wring the last vestiges of performance from his aircraft. In his next dozen engagements between February and May 1942 he never claimed less than two in a day,

twice more getting four. February brought the award of the Knights' Cross with his 50th success, but June saw him reach his peak. On 3 June over Bir Hakeim he shot down six Curtiss Tomahawks in a single combat (five actually went down and a sixth crash-landed on the way back to base due to damage – all aircraft of 5 SAAF Squadron). This raised his total to 75 and brought an immediate award of the Oak Leaves. The rest of June brought 26 more victories, including four in a day on four occasions and six on 17th, raising his score to 101, which occasioned the award of the Swords to the Knights' Cross.

A period of leave before the Alamein battles brought a lull in his scoring until the Battle of Alam el Halfa at the end of August. On 1 September, in three sorties, he claimed an incredible 17 victories – 16 of them claimed as Curtiss fighters and one a Spitfire (research shows that he actually got at least 12, with others damaged). Next day saw the award of the Diamonds – and five more victories. This was followed by another six on the 3rd, and then 26 more during the rest of September, including seven on the 15th and 26th, the latter day bringing his total to 151 of them over the desert. On 30 September he piloted a new Bf 109G for the first time. No enemy aircraft were seen, but on return over the lines a fractured connecting rod started an engine fire. Blinded by smoke and fumes, he baled out with the aircraft inverted, but struck the tailplane and fell unconscious to his death with his parachute unopened.

83

top scorer was Oblt Gustav Rödel of II/JG 27, who claimed six victories in two days during April to raise his personal score to 20. The main zone in which the Luftwaffe was to operate however, was the Libyan-Egyptian Desert. Following the arrival of some Bf 110s early in 1941, I/JG 27 reached Libya and began operations during April. The Gruppe had a number of pilots already well-experienced over France and Britain who were to do well, but it was several of the younger pilots who were to shine particularly. Young and individualistic, but brilliantly gifted as a fighter pilot was Lt Hans-Joachim Marseille, whose score soon began to mount. By September 1942, when he died in an accidental crash, he was to claim 151 of his total of 158 victories – the greatest score of any German pilot against the Western Allies. In the same unit were Werner Schroer with 61 in the Desert by October 1942, Hans-Arnold Stahl-schmidt with 59, all in Africa, Gerhard Homuth with 46 here, and Gunther Steinhausen with 40. Stahlschmidt and Steinhausen were both killed in September 1942, a few days before Marseille. Late in 1941 the rest of JG 27 arrived to join I Gruppe, and these Gruppen too had their Mediterranean high scorers. Rödel of II Gruppe, who had done well in Greece added 50 between

October 1941 and November 1942, Otto Schulz of this unit running his score from nine to 51 by his death in action on 17 June 1942; Karl-Heinz Bendert of this unit claimed 36.

Against the 'crack' Gruppen of JG 27, the Italians and the various other units operating in Africa with the Axis forces, the RAF fought a long, hard and costly battle. At first Hurricanes provided the mainstay of the fighter force, but from mid-1941 American-built Curtiss Tomahawks and then Kittyhawks, gained air superiority. Sqn Ldr CR 'Killer' Caldwell, an Australian, was one of the early Tomahawk pilots with 250 Squadron, claimed 18 victories in this type between June and December 1941. Later heading 112 Squadron on Kittyhawks, he raised his total to 20½. He would subsequently lead the special No 1 Spitfire Wing in the defense of Darwin, Northern Australia, against the Japanese in 1943, adding eight victories here to become Australia's top-scorer, and also one of the Commonwealth top-scorers in the Far East. Sqn Ldr Billy Drake took over 112 Squadron from Caldwell. He already had five or six victories to his credit elsewhere; by the end of the year he had claimed 14 and two more shared. Other successful Tomahawk and Kittyhawk pilots in the Libyan Desert included:

Above: Sqn Ldr Billy Drake (22½ victories) commanding officer of 112 'Shark' Squadron in North Africa in 1942.

Flt Lt JL Waddy (Australian)	12½ (plus 3 on Spitfires)	250, 260, 4 SAAF, 92 Sqns
Sqn Ldr AW Barr (Australian)	12½	3 RAAF Sqn
Maj AC Bosman (South African)	10½	4 SAAF, 2 SAAF Sqn
Sqn Ldr RHM Gibbes (Australian)	10¼	3 RAAF Sqn
Flt Lt JF Edwards (Canadian)	12½ (of which 4 over Tunisia in 1943)	94, 260 Sqn

Main picture: 94 Squadron Kittyhawk flown by James F 'Stocky' Edwards when a Flt Sgt. This Canadian pilot was to achieve a final score of 15½ in the Mediterranean war.

Above left: Leading pilots of I/JG 27 at Appollonia, Libya in 1942. Left to right: Lt Karl Kugelbauer (4 victories); Oblt Hans-Joachim Marseille (158 – Luftwaffe top-scorer in Africa and most successful pilot of the war against the RAF); Lt Werner Schroer (114, 61 in Africa); Oblt Hans-Arnold Stahlschmidt (59 – third highest scorer in the Desert after Marseille and Schroer). Only Schroer survived the war.

Above: Clive 'Killer' Caldwell, Australia's top scorer of the war (28½ victories) gained the highest score in the Western Desert Campaigns (20½) flying Tomahawks and Kitty-hawks. We later became one of the Commonwealth's most successful pilots against the Japanese, leading the No 1 Wing Spitfires in the defense of Darwin.

Far left: Luftwaffe top scorer over Malta was Hpt Gerhard Michalski of II/JG 53 (26 out of a total of 73). Near left: Top scorer of JG 53 in the Mediterranean area

Most successful with the Hurricane were American Flt Lt LC Wade, who claimed 15 victories with 33 Squadron, F/Sgt J Dodds who claimed 14 with 274 Squadron, Flt Lt AE Marshall who claimed 14 with 73 Squadron, adding three more on Kittyhawks with 250 Squadron, and Sqn Ldr PG Wykeham-Barnes, who claimed 13 with 80, 274 and 73 Squadrons.

Over Malta meanwhile, the arrival of Spitfires early in 1942 following a renewed Luftwaffe 'blitz' on the island, led to eight months' intensive fighting which saw the appearance of many new Commonwealth aces. Three of the first were New Zealander Ray Hesselyn (12), Australian Paul Brennan (10) and Rhodesian Johnny Plagis (11), all of whom served with 249 Squadron. They were followed by Canadian George 'Screwball' Beurling, who became the island's greatest ace and his country's top-scoring pilot, claiming $26\frac{1}{3}$ here before being shot down and wounded in October. Fellow Canadian HW 'Wally' McLeod claimed 13 with 603 and 1435 Squadrons and was the island's second-highest scorer. Many other pilots scored well on the island, including Sqn Ldr MM Stephens who added six and two shared to 14 earlier victories over France, England and Africa, to reach a total of 22. The Luftwaffe found Malta one of the hardest locations for aerial combat, and during 1942 its experienced pilots did no better than the RAF here, in direct contrast with other fronts. Top scorer was Hpt Gerhard Michalski of II/JG 53 with 26 victories, followed by Oblt Siegfried Freytag of I/JG 77 with about 25 and Lt Herbert Rollwage of II/JG 53 with 20.

By late 1942 the RAF's Desert Air Force, reinforced during the summer by Spitfires, had gained superiority in the air in Africa – mainly by virtue of superior numbers. In November came the Anglo-American landings in French North-west Africa, and at once units of the Luftwaffe were rushed to Tunisia from Sicily, France and the Eastern Front. With substantial USAAF elements involved for the first time, the next six months saw an extremely severe period of fighting in the air and on the ground, with the first serious fighting between German fighters and escorted formations of US four-engined bombers. German pilots from all fronts did well here, although by April 1943 their position had become untenable, threatened on the ground and totally overwhelmed numerically in the air. I/JG 77 had flown over Malta since June 1942, then in Libya since October, being joined by the rest of the Geschwader from Russia late in 1942. Major Joachim Müncheberg was now Kommodore of this unit, adding 19 final victories over Africa before his death in collision with a US Spitfire – his 135th victim – on 23 March 1943. One of the greatest pilots of the war, his total included 102 against the Western Allies, 44 of them in the Mediterranean area.

In I Gruppe, Heinz Bär was to prove one of the most successful Germans in the area, claim-ing four over Malta, 22 over Libya by the end of 1942, and then 39 more during early 1943 over Tripoli and Tunisia. II Gruppe's Ernst-Wilhelm Reinert was credited with 51 in Tunisia between January and April 1943, later adding 12 more over Italy by the end of the year. He had previously claimed 103 in Russia, and would end the war with his score at 174. Heinz-Edgar Berres of I Gruppe claimed 47 of his 53 in the Mediterranean area, 11 over Malta, 26 over Africa, and the balance over Italy before being shot down and killed in August 1943. JG 53, which saw much action throughout the campaigns here, had Oblt Franz Schiess as Mediterranean top scorer – he had 52 successes here between December 1941 and September 1943, when he was shot down and killed. II/JG 2, sent from France, had with it Oblt Kurt Bühligen, who claimed 40 over Tunisia and Lt Erich Rudorffer, who claimed 27, together with several other successful pilots. II/JG 51 from Russia produced as its top scorer in the area firstly Fw Anton Hafner, who gained 20 swift victories, but was then shot down and wounded on 2 January 1943, and then Obfw Otto Schultz (not to be confused with Otto Schulz of II/JG 27) who claimed 18 and 8 unconfirmed over Tunisia, then 8 more over Italy and a further six against the USAAF over Rumania in summer 1944.

Several Desert Air Force pilots continued to do well for the Allies. Flt Lt Neville Duke who had eight earlier victories, six of them on Tomahawks and Kittyhawks with 112 Squadron, was most successful in Tunisia, gaining 14 flying Spitfires with 92 Squadron. He later added six more over Italy to become Desert Air Force top scorer of the war. (He subsequently became a famous test-pilot, gaining the World Air Speed Record in a Hawker Hunter on 7 September 1953.) The American Lance Wade, now flying Spitfires at the head of 145 Squadron, gained eight over Tunisia, adding two more over Italy in October 1943 to head DAF with 25 until overtaken by Duke; he was killed in a flying accident on 12 January 1944. From Malta another American with 249 Squadron, Sqn Ldr JJ Lynch, claimed nine and three shared, adding one more in July 1943 – mainly against transport aircraft flying between Sicily and North Africa. Also preying on this traffic was an ex-bomber pilot, Wg Cdr JK Buchanan of 272 Squadron; with 10 confirmed, four shared shot down and one destroyed on the water, he was the most successful of all the Beaufighter intruder pilots by day.

Many experienced pilots arrived in Algeria and Tunisia from England and continued to do well, among them Wg Cdr Colin Gray. He claimed five and one shared over Tunisia, then five over Sicily and Italy to become New Zealand's top scorer with 26 and four shared. South African Wg Cdr Petrus 'Dutch' Hugo claimed eight and one shared over Tunisia, and then three over Italy to raise his score to 20 and four shared, while several Poles also did well – sent to Tunisia

Main picture: New Zealand top scorer, Wg Cdr Colin Gray, leading 322 Wing in Sicily in 1943 with his personal Spitfire. Gray flew in England, Tunisia and Sicily, claiming 27 victories. Inset top: Most successful American pilot serving with the RAF was Lance Wade. He claimed 25 victories over North Africa and Italy. He is seen here as commanding officer of 145 Squadron in 1943.

Inset bottom: Top-scoring pilot of the Desert Air Force during the whole of the Mediterranean was Neville Duke (25 out of 27 and 2 shared). He is in the cockpit of his 92 Squadron Spitfire during the Tunisian Campaign.

as a special experienced Polish Fighting Team to fly Spitfire IXs with 145 Squadron. Sqn Ldr Stanislaw Skalski added three victories to his growing score. Flt Lt Eugeniusz Horbaczewski claimed three more in Italy at the head of 43 Squadron, but died in combat over Normandy on 18 August 1944, having added five and one shared flying Mustangs to raise his total to 16½.

The Americans were now also producing aces in their own units. The P-40-equipped 57th Fighter Group was the first unit to enter action in Egypt in 1942, Capt Lyman D Middleditch claiming three Bf 109s on 27 October to become the unit's first ace; he subsequently claimed one more. Over Tunisia some 28 US pilots claimed five or more victories flying P-38s, P-40s and Spitfires. Capt Levi Chase of the 33rd Fighter Group was top scorer with 10, gained flying P-40s. Lt Sylvan Feld of the 52nd Fighter Group got seven, to which he added two more in June to become the USAAF's top-scoring Spitfire pilot of the war. Among those flying P-38s, Lt William J Sloan was at the front with the 82nd Fighter Group, claiming five over Tunisia and then seven more over Sardinia, Sicily and Italy by late July –

he was the US Twelfth Air Force's top scorer of the war.

Following the end of the fighting in North Africa in May 1943, the Germans and Italians put up a stiff resistance to attacks on Sicily until the landings there on 10 July. Having already suffered severe losses, they were virtually wiped out on the island within the first two or three days, the survivors withdrawing to Italy. Several of Italy's top aces were killed at this time, including Capt Franco Lucchini and Sottoten Leonardo Ferrulli, both lost over Sicily on 5 July 1943. Lucchini had five in Spain and 21 in World War II, the latter all gained with 10° Gruppo of 4° Stormo CT, flying CR 42s, and later Macchi MC 202s. Twenty of his victories were claimed over Malta and North Africa by 24 October 1942, when he was shot down and wounded; he also shared in at least 13 other victories. Ferrulli also had 21 in World War II with the same unit and over the same areas, plus one earlier in Spain. Another pilot of this Stormo who did well was Serg Teresio Martinoli, who claimed four over Malta in 1941, and four in 1942, plus about 10 in North Africa from a total of 22 and 14 shared.

Above: The RAF's highest-scoring Beaufighter pilot was Wg Cdr JK Buchanan, an ex-bomber pilot who claimed ten and two shared while flying day intruder operations from Malta.
Above right: Top scorer of the USAAF during the Tunisian Campaign was Maj Levi Chase, a P-40 Warhawk pilot in the 33rd Fighter Group. He claimed nine German and one Italian aircraft shot down between November 1942 and May 1943, later adding two Japanese aircraft.
Far right top: Sottotenente Leonardo Ferrulli of the 10° Gruppo, 4° Stormo CT gained 22 victories (1 in Spain) before being killed by Spitfires over Sicily on 5 July 1943.
Far right center: Serg Magg Teresio Martinoli who claimed 21 and 14 shared while with the Regia Aeronautica, added 1

German aircraft while flying with the Allies.
Far right below: Highest-scoring Italian ace to survive the war was Capt Franco Bordoni-Bisleri (19 victories).

He later flew with the Allies in the Co-Belligerent Air Force, claiming a German Ju 52 shot down while flying a P-39 Airacobra in November 1943; he was killed in a flying accident in August 1944.

Flying on the mainland in defense of Rome in the summer of 1943 was Capt Franco Bordoni Bisleri of the 18° Gruppo, 3° Stormo CT. He had claimed 12 in Africa in CR 42s and MC 202s before being wounded in November 1942; he later added seven US bombers to his score over Italy. Ten Col Furio Lauri of the 53° Stormo CT flew Fiat G-50bis fighters in North Africa, claiming 11 by late 1941. He then flew over Tunisia and in defense of Italy, raising his score to about 18.

On 8 September 1943 the Italians accepted an armistice as the Allies invaded Italy, but a long, hard campaign against the Germans followed. Luftwaffe fighters remained active with varying degrees of success until June 1944, being withdrawn to Germany at the time of the Normandy invasion. Most fighting on both sides involved pilots who had already flown over Tunisia and Sicily, and few names appeared, although many aces added to their scores. After

June 1944 there was very little aerial fighting, the whole defense of Northern Italy resting in the hands of two Gruppi of the new Italian Fascist air force of the Republica Sociale Italiana. While like Duke and Wade added to their scores, so did others – Wg Cdr Tony Lovell, who had claimed 10 and two shared over England and five and two shared over Malta, added a further three in Italy in 1944 to bring his total to 18 and four shared; Sqn Ldr SW Daniel had claimed seven over Tunisia with 72 Squadron, and added a further seven and one shared by late 1943. With 92 Squadron, New Zealander Sqn Ldr Evan Mackie claimed three in 1944 to add to 12 and one shared over Tunisia and Sicily, raising his personal total to 16, while Flt Lt James Edwards added two more in the same unit to reach 15½.

In November 1943 the strategic bombers and their escorts of the US 9th and 12th Air Forces joined to form the new strategic Fifteenth Air Force, which was soon joining the English-based Eighth Air Force in its attacks on Europe. Throughout the spring and summer of 1944, the units of this air force, including three P-38 groups and three, later four, P-51 groups (one of which first flew P-47s for some time), attacked targets in northern Italy, Greece, Bulgaria, Yugoslavia, Hungary, Austria, Rumania and south Germany. They were met by fighters of the Luftwaffe, RSI, Bulgarian, Hungarian, Rumanian, Slovak and Croat air forces, and were to achieve many successes. The most successful units were the 31st Fighter Group, formerly Spitfire-equipped, the 325th, formerly P-40 and P-47-equipped, and the P-38-equipped 82nd. All were originally part of the Twelfth Air Force, and all gained in excess of 500 victories. Top scorer was Capt John J Voll of the 31st who claimed 21 victories between June and November 1944, including five and two probables during his last combat on 16 November. Maj Hershel H Green of the 325th claimed 18 (three of them while flying P-40s and 10 on P-47s, including six in a day on 30 January 1944 – four Ju 52s, a Do 217 and a Bf 109). Capt James S Varnell of the 52nd claimed 17.

During late 1943 British landings in the Aegean brought some fairly heavy air fighting here, III and IV/JG 27 being heavily involved on the Luftwaffe side. Flying against RAF Beau-fighters and Baltimores, and US bombers raiding Greece, several pilots from these units did well. US fighter involvement was brief but spectacular, P-38s of the 14th Fighter Group slaughtering a formation of Ju 87 dive-bombers on 9 October; Maj William L Leverette claimed seven of these shot down and Lt Harry T Hanna five.

Among the Italians with the RSI, facing both the RAF and US Twelfth Tactical Air Force units over central Italy, and the Fifteenth Air Force heavy bombers and their escorts over the north, several aces continued to score and others appeared, although losses were high. Magg

Adriano Visconti, who had claimed four over Malta in 1941 and 14 over Tunisia and Sicily in 1943, to add to one earlier victory, claimed seven more with 1° Gruppo CT of the RSI, becoming Italian top scorer of World War II. He was killed by partisans on 29 April 1945. Serg Luigi Gorrini had claimed four in the desert and 11 in defense of Italy during Summer 1943, adding a further four with the RSI before being wounded in action in Spring 1944. Top scorers of the RSI were Capitani Ugo Drago and Mario Bellagambi of the 2° Gruppo CT, who each claimed 11 victories with this unit. Drago had previously claimed five over Sicily flying Bf 109Gs with the 150° Gruppo in 1943, while Bella-gambi had claimed one in Greece in February 1941, where he was wounded, and had then claimed the last Regia Aeronautica victory of the war on 8 September 1943, also with 150° Gruppo.

Top left: One of the lesser-known high scorers of the RAF was New Zealander Evan Mackie who had raised his score to 16 by early 1944. He later flew in Western Europe, raising his score to 21½.
Center left: The only USAAF pilot to achieve a score in excess of 20 while flying in the Mediterranean war zone was the Fifteenth Air Force's Capt John J Voll, a P-51 Mustang pilot who claimed 21 victories with the 31st Fighter Group.
Bottom left: Serg Magg Luigi Gorrini was the second top Italian ace to survive the war. He achieved 15 victories with the Regia Aeronautica and 4 more with the 1° Gruppo CT of the Republica Sociale Italiana.
Above: Maj Herschel H Green was top scorer of the US 325th Fighter Group and for some time was No 1 of the Fifteenth Air Force until overtaken by Voll. He gained victories flying P-40s, P-47s and P-51s, including six in one day on 30 January 1944, for a total of 18.

TOP-SCORING GERMAN FIGHTER PILOTS IN THE MEDITERRANEAN AREA 1940–45

	Mediterranean Score	Units	All Fronts Total
Hpt Han-Joachim Marseille*	151	I/JG 27	158
Hpt Werner Schroer	86	I, II/JG 27	102
Hpt Heinz Bär	65	I/JG 77	220
Oblt Ernst-Wilhelm Reinert	62–3	II/JG 77	174
Oblt Hans-Arnold Stahlschmidt*	59	I/JG 27	59
Hpt Gustav Rödel	57	II, Stab /JG 27	98
Oblt Franz Schiess*	52	Stab, III/JG 53	52
Hpt Gerhard Homuth*	46	I/JG 27	63
Hpt Heinz-Edgar Berres*	45	I/JG 77	52
Maj Joachim Müncheberg*	44	7/JG 26, Stab/JG 77	135
Oblt Siegfried Freytag	50	I/JG 77	102
Oblt Otto Schulz*	42	II/JG 27	51
Lt Willi Kientsch*	41	II/JG 27	52
Oblt Kurt Bühligen	40	II/JG 2	112
Maj Jürgen Harder*	40 al	III/JG 53	64
Lt Günther Steinhausen*	40	I/JG 27	40
Hpt Gerhard Michalski	37	II/JG 53	73
Lt Karl-Heinz Bendert	36	II/JG 27	54
Oblt Friedrich Körner	36	I/JG 27	36
Ofw Herbert Rollwage	36	II/JG 53	102
Oblt Rudolf Sinner	32	I, II/JG 27	39

TOP-SCORING ITALIAN FIGHTER PILOTS IN THE MEDITERRANEAN AREA AND EAST AFRICA, 1940–45

Magg Adriano Visconti*	26 (7 RSI)	Desert/Tunisia/Italy	4° Stormo/1°	Gr RSI
Serg Teresio Martinoli*	23 (1 Co-Bell)	Malta/Desert/Italy	4° Stormo	
Capt Franco Lucchini*	21 (+ 5 Spain)	Malta/Desert/Sicily	4° Stormo	
Sottoten Leonardo Ferrulli*	21 (+ 1 Spain)	Malta/Desert/Sicily	4° Stormo	
Capt Mario Visentini*	20	East Africa	412ª Squad	
Capt Franco Bordoni Bisleri	19	Desert/Italy	3° Stormo	
Serg Luigi Gorrini	19 (4 RSI)	Desert/Italy	3° Stormo/1°	Gr RSI
Ten Col Furio Lauri	18 approx	Desert/Tunisia/Italy	53° Stormo	
Capt Ugo Drago	16 (11 RSI)	Sicily/Italy	150° Gruppo/2°	Gr RSI

TOP-SCORING BRITISH COMMONWEALTH FIGHTER PILOTS IN THE MEDITERRANEAN AREA, 1940–45

	Nationality	Med. Scor	Areas Scored	Units	Total
Sqn Ldr MTStJ Pattle	South African	40+	Desert/Greece	80, 33 Sqn	40+
Flt Lt GF Beurling	Canadian	26⅓	Malta	249 Sqn	31⅓
Sqn Ldr NF Duke	English	25⅚	Desert/Tunisia/Italy	112, 92, 145 Sqn	27⅚
Wg Cdr LC Wade	American	25	Desert/Tunisia/Italy	33, 145 Sqn	25
Flg Off W Vale	English	22 approx	Greece	80 Sqn	22 app
Sqn Ldr VC Woodward	Canadian	21⅚	Desert/Greece	80, 274, 213 Sqn	21⅚
Sqn Ldr CR Caldwell	Australian	20½	Desert	250, 112 Sqn	28½
Sqn Ldr EM Mason*	English	17⅖	Desert/Malta/Iran	80, 274, 261, 94 Sqn	17⅖
Wg Cdr B Drake	English	17	West Africa/Desert/Sicily	112, 128 Sqn	22½
Flt Lt AE Marshall*	English	17	Desert	73, 250 Sqn	19½
Flg Off RN Cullen*	Australian	16½	Desert/Greece	80 Sqn	16½
Maj JE Frost*	South African	15⅚	East Africa/Desert	3 SAAF, 5 SAAF Sqn	15⅚
Flt Lt JF Edwards	Canadian	15½	Desert/Tunisia/Italy	94, 260, 417, 92 Sqn	15½

Sqn Ldr ED Mackie	New Zealander	15½	Tunisia/Sicily/ Italy	243, 92 Sqn	21½
Flt Lt JL Waddy	Australian	15½	Desert	250, 260, 4 SAAF, 92 Sqn	15½
F/Sgt EWF Hewett	English	15	Greece	80 Sqn	18
Wg Cdr PG Wykeham-Barnes	English	15	Desert/Sicily	80, 274, 73, 23 Sqn	15

TOP-SCORING BULGARIAN FIGHTER PILOTS, 1943–44

Lt Stoyan Stoyanov	14	6th Orliak
Lt Marinopolsky	8 app.	
Maj Toplodolski	8	

TOP-SCORING USAAF FIGHTER PILOTS IN THE MEDITERRANEAN AREA, 1942–45

		Unit	Air Force
Capt John J Voll	21	31st FG	Fifteenth
Maj Herschel H Green	18	325th FG	Fifteenth
Capt James S Varnell	17	52nd FG	Fifteenth
Maj Samuel J Brown	15.5	31st FG	Fifteenth
Capt James L Brooks	13	31st FG	Fifteenth
Maj Robert C Curtiss	13	52nd FG	Fifteenth
Capt Harry A Parker*	13	325th FG	Fifteenth
Maj Michael Brezas	12	14th FG	Fifteenth
Capt Norman C Skogstad	12	31st FG	Fifteenth
Lt William J Sloan	12	82nd FG	Twelfth
Capt Robert J Goebel	11	31st FG	Fifteenth
Lt John B Lawler	11	52nd FG	Fifteenth
Maj William L Leverette	11	14th FG	Twelfth and Fifteenth
Lt Wayne L Lowry	11	325th FG	Fifteenth
Col Charles M McCorkle	11	31st FG	Twelfth and Fifteenth
Maj Norman McDonald	11	52nd and 325th FG	Twelfth and Fifteenth
Maj Leland P Molland	11	31st FG	Twelfth and Fifteenth
Capt Robert E Riddle	11	31st FG	Fifteenth
Maj Levi R Chase	10 (+ 2 in Burma)	33rd FG	Twelfth
Capt Walter J Goehausen Jr.	10	31st FG	Fifteenth
Flt Off Frank D Hurlbut	10	82nd FG	12th

*indicates killed in action or flying accident during World War II.

The Eastern Front

The massive invasion of the Soviet Union launched by the Germans in the early hours of 22 June 1941 brought a whole new dimension to the war. At dawn almost the full strength of the Luftwaffe, rested and strengthened since its campaigns of the previous year, swept over the Russian Western borders in a series of devastating attacks on the forward airfields of the Red Air Force. During that single day 322 Russian aircraft were claimed shot down and 1489 destroyed on the ground, all for the loss of 35. Four of the victories were credited to Mölders, Kommodore of JG 51, taking his score from 68 to 72, passing Galland's total of 69.

The Russian reaction was to throw in every aircraft available to try and slow the rot, as their

One of the early Luftwaffe success stories of the campaign in Russia in 1941 was Herbert Ihlefeld, seen here (center, with Knights' Cross at his throat) as a Hauptmann with I(J)/LG 2 in mid-1941. On his left is Oblt Wolf-Dietrich Huy (40 victories) during an inspection by Gen Förster (right); with his back to the camera is the Kommodore of JG 77, of which I(J)/LG 2 formed a part at this time, Maj Gotthardt Handrick (10 in Spain, 10 in World War II).

The World's Greatest Ace

The 20-year-old Erich 'Bubi' Hartmann was by no means one of the 'old guard' of the Luftwaffe. Not until October 1942 did he complete his training and join his first unit – 9 Staffel of III Gruppe, Jagdgeschwader 52 in South Russia. His first victory was claimed on 5 November of that year, but success was slow to come; after 100 sorties he had claimed only seven victories. Gradually the skills came as he flew every day in his Messerschmitt Bf 109G over the front. By July 1943 his 200th sortie was reached with his score at 34, but in two months his third 100 flights brought him 61 more successes, although after his 90th victory during August, he came down in Soviet territory and was taken prisoner for a few hours. Now well into the ways of air fighting, his score rose fast. His 100th victory fell on 20 September; by the end of this period, the Oak Leaves followed on 2 March 1944, by which time his score stood at 200. By now the German retreat had taken III/JG 52 into Rumania, and here for the first time Hartmann met US aircraft –

elements of the Fifteenth Air force. In two combats he was able to claim five P-51s shot down. Still the Russians remained his main opponents, and on 18 July 1944 he became the fourth to reach 250, having received the Swords to his Knights' Cross earlier in the month. The end of August brought the much-coveted Diamonds, for his total had reached the new record of 301. Promoted to command 4 Staffel in II/JG 52 in October, February 1945 saw a further promotion to lead I/JG 52. On 8 May 1945, out spotting for advancing Russian troops, he saw a fighter aerobatting over Brunn and shot it down for his 352nd and last victory – and possibly the last Luftwaffe claim of the war.

A great dogfighter, master of the hit-and-run tactic, his total included 260 fighters – seven of them P-51s, for he had met the Americans again in April 1945. On his best day he claimed 11 victories, four of them in one sortie, but he had crash-landed 12 times and once baled out in the course of over 800 operational sorites – although only twice

were these the result of enemy action. A prisoner of the Russians after the war, he was sentenced to 25 years hard labor for, 'sabotaging the Soviet war effort.' He was however released 10 years later after Conrad Adenauer's visit to Russian and returned to marry his sweetheart, who had waited for him. He subsequently served with the new West German Luftwaffe, commanding the Sabre unit, JG 71 'Richthofen.'

---

surprised and ill-prepared armies fell back before the blows of the Blitzkrieg. Many of the latest aircraft had been destroyed on landing grounds near the frontier on the first day, and much of what now appeared was obsolescent, the pilots were inexperienced and poorly prepared to face the cream of the Luftwaffe. Massive air battles were fought daily, and by the end of the first week it was estimated that 4990 Soviet machines had been destroyed for a loss of 179 German aircraft. While the majority were caught on the ground, victory tallies in the air rose swiftly against such opposition, and in just five days Herbert Ihlefeld of I(J)/LG 2 had claimed 15 to raise his total to 40. On 30 June massive formations of unescorted Russian bombers attempted to halt the German advance at Minsk, but fell foul of Luftflotte 2's fighters, which claimed 110 shot down! On the same day around Lvov, Luftflotte 4 claimed 41 in the air and 55 on the ground – such was the pace and scale of the new war front. By 15 July came the electrifying news that Mölders, who had already passed von Richtofen's World War I total of 80, had gained his 33rd victory in Russia to become the first to top 100 in this war. Indeed when added to his Spanish score, his total now stood at 115, and he was at once ordered to cease operations. JG 3's Walter Oesau was scoring at an even faster rate, gaining his 80th on the same day, but he was then withdrawn to take command of JG 2 in the West (despite this move he would still become the third pilot to reach 100 victories).

The Germans were not alone in their Russian adventure, either on the ground or in the air. From the start Rumania joined in the attack, being followed by Hungary and Finland – the latter only to retake the territory lost in March

1940. Subsequently an Italian legion would arrive – uninvited – together with contingents from Franco's Spain, from the puppet republic of Slovakia and from the Croatian areas of Yugoslavia. All these nations provided fighter units for the front, and all would produce fighter aces of note with the exception of the Italians. Aid for Russia was slower arriving; in an effort to show early solidarity the British launched a carrier aircraft attack on the northern ports of Kirkenes and Petsamo on the Norwegian/Finnish border area, but this was met by Luftwaffe interception and suffered severe losses. Later in the year a wing of RAF Hurricanes arrived in the far North of Russia, seeing some brief action before transferring their aircraft to the Red Naval Air Fleet with appropriate training – the main purpose of their arrival. Fighting in the north was on a more limited scale, but here a Bf 110 Zerstörer pilot, Hpt G Schascke of ZG 76, became the first big scorer, being credited with 20 victories before becoming a POW in early August.

On 30 August 1941 Jagdgeschwader 3 celebrated its 1000th victory over Russia, but already JG 51's score was higher, this unit claiming 77 bombers in two days while covering bridging operations over the River Dniepr at Rostov at the turn of the month, and by 10 September had claimed 1357 in Russia to raise its score for the war so far to 2000! The totals of many of the veteran Experten of 1940 were now rocketting up. On 24 October Günther Lützow, Kommodore of JG 3, became the second to reach 100, while on 18 October the Geschwader's Gordon Gollob, a former Zerstörer pilot, created a new German record, claiming nine in a single day; by the 26th his score stood at 85.

The onset of autumn and winter weather brought a reduction in action as the German armies stalled in the mud before Moscow, and a number of units were withdrawn – some to Germany, but most to the increasingly active Mediterranean Front. The great successes of the summer had not been gained without loss, and a number of the Experten had lost their lives, including Herman-Friedrich Joppien of JG 51, who crashed during a dogfight with his score at 70. The tremendous scores obtained in Russia had led to an upgrading of the requirements for the award of decorations on this front. The coveted Knights' Cross was awarded for 40, rather than 20 victories; later the requirement crept steadily upward, until eventually 100 victories became virtually the norm for this decoration in the East.

Although the Russian losses had been frightful, they had not been without their own successes. Capt Afanasi Karmanov of the 4th IAP (Fighter Regiment) had gained five victories during the first two days of the war, flying one of the scarce modern MiG 3 fighters, before he was shot down and killed. Lt Piotr Brinko, who had served earlier in Finland, fought over Leningrad until his death in action on 14 September, by which time he had been credited with 15 German and Finnish aircraft brought down in his Polikarpov I-16 – one of them by ramming. Indeed ram attacks were to be something of a feature of the desperate Russian defense during this period. The first deliberate ramming action occurred over Moscow in August, when 2/Lt Victor Talalikhin brought down a bomber at night by this method; he survived to amass a personal victory total of 27. Boris Korzan was to be the leading exponent of these 'Taran' attacks, bringing down four German aircraft by this method. Other pilots soon emerged as leading aces – included Aleksei Ryazanov of the 14th IAP who gained the first of 32 individual and 16 shared victories at this time, and a flight commander in the MiG 3-equipped 55th IAP, Alexander Pokryshkin, soon to be seen as the Red Air Force's greatest fighter tactician and leader.

The return of good weather in spring 1942 brought a resumption of activity in the air, initially in the Leningrad area, where during March Hpt Hans Philipp of III/JG 54 became the fourth to reach 100. On the Central Front in this one month Lt Hans Strelow of II/JG 51 claimed 26 victories; he was lost when he force-landed in Russian-held territory on 22 May with his score at 66. It was however in South Russia, in the Caucasus, that the most hectic fighting of the year was to be seen. The Germans launched their Operation 'Blau' offensive which initially achieved great success, sweeping through the great wheatlands and oil-producing areas of the South, and reaching the Crimea. It was here that JG 52, previously a relatively undistinguished unit, came to the fore. JG 77 also saw a lot of action in

this area before withdrawing to the Mediterranean later in the year. Between 19 and 22 April Hpt Herbert Ihlefeld, Kommandeur of I Gruppe, gained 17 victories to reach a total of 101, while his wingman, Lt Fritz Geisshardt, was credited with 26 between 1 March and 25 April. On 12 May Oblt Max-Helmuth Ostermann of III/JG 54 claimed his 100th victory, while two days later JG 52's first great 'star,' Lt Hermann Graf of III Gruppe, gained seven to raise his total to 104 – 47 of them in the past 17 days! In the same Gruppe, Oblt Adolf Dickfield equalled Gollob's record, claiming nine on 14 May, and then claiming 11 more on the 18th to pass the century also. Next day Hpt Heinz Bär of I/JG 51 (1940s top-scoring NCO pilot) gained his 100th, while on 20 May Hpt Gollob of II/JG 3 also reached this total.

During the short, fine summer nights, efforts were made to supply the besieged garrison of Leningrad by air. Several day fighters of JG 54 saw considerable success in this area; the notable example was Lt Erwin Leykauf, who claimed no less than six Polikarpov R-5 biplanes in one night. Scores continued to rise, and a new landmark appeared on 29 August when Gordon Gollob became the first to reach 150 victories. JG 52's Graf was close behind, equalling this score on 4 September. During this period he ran his total from 127 to 202 in just four weeks, being the first to 200 on 26 September; like Mölders before him, he was then rested, being withdrawn to Germany.

Many new pilots reached 100 during the year, but the onset of winter brought the disaster of Stalingrad, where General von Paulus's Sixth Army was wiped out in the greatest setback suffered by the Germans to date. This defeat occurred in November 1942, immediately after the almost equally damaging setback at El Alamein in the North African desert, and coinciding with the Anglo-American invasion of French Northwest Africa. While Stalingrad held, a single Staffel of JG 3 operated for some weeks from within the perimeter, claiming some 130 victories, 33 of them credited to Fw Kurt Ebener. The Stalingrad defeat led to the withdrawal of the Italians however, their Macchi fighters having been credited with 88 victories in 18 months, for the loss in combat of 19.

Action reduced as autumn turned to winter, but still the German roll of honor grew. On 17 December 1942 Maj Wolf-Dietrich Wilcke of JG 3 was fourth to claim 150 victories, while on 30 December Ofw Max Stotz of II/JG 54 claimed 10 in a day, reaching his 150 on 26 January 1943. On 2 February Hpt Johannes Steinhoff of II/JG 52 – a pilot who had been in action since 1939 – also reached this total with six in a day, while on 6 March Oblt Hans Beisswenger of II/JG 54 was shot down and killed immediately after shooting down his 152nd victory.

By now Russian aces of some standing were appearing – most of these early high scorers

Juutilainen – Finland's Number One

When Russia attacked Finland in late 1939, Eino Ilmari Juutilainen ('Illu' to his friends) was an experienced NCO pilot, approaching his 25th birthday. Flying Fokker D.XXI monoplanes with the country's leading fighter squadron, LeLv 24, he was credited with two individual and one shared victories during December, but had no further chance to add to his score before the fighting ceased in March 1940. The resumption of hostilities in June 1941 found his unit re-equipped with the Brewster 239s – an aircraft with which the 'crack' pilots of LeLv 24 were to achieve wonders. In the next six months he was to claim 13 victories over Soviet aircraft, twice getting three in a day. The year 1942 saw the I-153s and I-16s giving way to more modern types such as the MiG 3, Pe 2 and Lend-Lease Hurricanes, Tomahawks, and so on. Some 20 further victories were credited to

him during the year, and he received the first award of the Mannerheim Cross – Finland's highest decoration. In March 1943 he joined the new LeLv 34, formed to fly the first Messerschmitt Bf 109Gs received, and with this improved equipment he had claimed a further 18 victories by the end of 1943 to raise his total to 52 in the present war. Five successes in the early months of 1944 were followed by 21 more in June as the country fought for its very existence as the Russians launched their summer offensive; this total included four on the 10th, five on the 20th and six on the 30th. This best day yielding two Yak 9s, two Airacobras, an La 5 and an Il 2 to make him top scorer. He added a further 11 victories in the first six days of July before fighting tailed off as the Russians withdrew units to the Central Front. With a second Mannerheim Cross received at the end of June, he claimed one more Yak 9 on 15 July, and then an Li 2 transport aircraft on 3 September 1944 – the last Finnish victory against the Russians – to bring his total score in two wars to 941/6.

'Hasse' Wind – Brewster Exponent

Hans Hendrik Wind joined the Finnish Air Force in 1940 as he turned 20. Commissioned, he was posted to LeLv 24 as the Continuation War with Russia broke out in the summer of 1941, to fly the Brewster 239 fighter. With this splendid unit he achieved his first shared victory over an I-15bis biplane on 27 September. His early promise was maintained, victories coming steadily during the next year. By the end of 1942 he had been involved in shooting down 16 aircraft – three of them shared – for a score of 14½. He took command of his flight during October. The year 1943 was to bring much success; he added a further 23½ to his score by 28 September and was awarded the Mannerheim Cross. On 21 March 1944 he shot down an La 5 – no mean achievement in the old Brewster – to raise his total to 39 (36 individual and six shared) plus three observation balloons. This was the highest score gained by any pilot on this type of aircraft.

Promoted Kapteeni (Capt) in late 1943, he continued to command the 3rd Flight as the unit converted to Bf 109Gs in early 1944 and gained his first two victories with the new aircraft on 27 May. The heavy fighting of June saw his score rise rapidly, and the 34 victories he was to claim during the month included four Pe 2 bombers on the 13th, one more plus four fighters on the 20th, four fighters on the 28th. On 23rd, five on the 26th and five on the 28th. On this last date he and one other pilot engaged 27 Airacobras and Yak 9s but, despite his success, he was seriously wounded in the hand and was hospitalized. At the time he was the highest scoring pilot, and received a second Mannerheim Cross, his total amounting to 72 and three balloons.

Russia's Number One

Ivan Nikitich Kojedub was one of the new generation of young pilots who first saw service after the initial desperate struggles of 1941 to 1942 were past. He came to the front in July 1943 in time for the great Kursk battle. He was with one of the first units equipped with the new Lavochkin La 5 fighters, and although shot down during an early sortie, was able to claim his first victory over a Ju 87 on 6 July. At the end of the battle he had so distinguished himself that he was made an eskadrilli commander, and awarded the Order of the Red Banner. Over Kiev that autumn he was to claim 11 in 10 days but on 12 October, after shooting down a Ju 87, he was hit by return fire and had the wing of his aircraft set on fire. He managed to extinguish the fire by diving steeply.

During 1944 he served with the crack 176th Guards IAP, moving from front to front in a 'fire-brigade' role, and by 1945 was vice commander of this unit. After 45 victories with the La 5 he had converted to the newer La 7 fighter. He added 17 more victories during the late months of the war, to raise his score to 62, passing Pokryshkin's previous record of 59. His score included an Me 262 jet – the first seen over the Eastern Front – in February 1945, together with 22 Fw 190s, 19 Bf 109s, 18 Ju 87s and two He 111s, all claimed during 520 sorties in two years. His last two victories – Fw 190D 'long noses' – were claimed over Berlin when he and his wingman 'bounced' about 40 aircraft. He received three Hero of Soviet Union awards and the Order of Leni

Hungary's Best

2nd Lts Dezsö Szentgyörgyi (right) and György Debrödy (below) saw service in Russia late in 1942, flying Reggianne Re 2000 fighters with 5/1 Squadron. In early 1943 these aircraft were replaced by Bf 109Fs and both pilots gained their first victories during the summer of that year, Szentgyörgyi on 26 June and Debrödy on 5 July. In September Debrödy was shot down, crash-landing behind Russian lines. He managed to get back on foot, but in doing so had to swim the River Dniepr. Returning to Hungary late in the year, both had claimed six victories by mid-August, but Debrödy then added 12 more during late 1943/early 1944 with the 102 Independant Fighter Squadron. Throughout the summer of 1944 both flew in defense of their country against the US Fifteenth Air Force, serving with the 101 'Puma' Regiment. Here Debrödy claimed six US aircraft shot down – three fighters and three bombers – while Szentgyörgyi claimed at least five, including four B-24s. By late 1944 the Russians were appearing again, this time over Hungarian soil, and on 16 November Debrödy shot down two Yak 9s to raise his total to 26. However, he was then hit in the stomach and badly wounded, only an emergency operation after landing saved his life. Although he returned to the unit as a captain in 1945 to command the 101/IV Group, he saw no further action. Szentgyörgyi meanwhile was constantly in action against the Russians until the end of the war, claiming over 20 victories against them to raise his total to 34 and become Hungarian top scorer. Rehabilitated after years in prison, he became an airline pilot, but was killed in a crash in 1971.

Soviet Fighter Leader

Alexandr Ivanovich Pokryshkin joined the Red Air Force in 1933, and by 1941 was commanding a flight of the latest MiG 3 fighters in the 55th. IAP (Fighter Air Regiment). He claimed his first victory over a Bf 109E of JG 77 on 23 June 1941 while escorting SB-2 bombers, but on 20 July was shot down by flak over German-held territory while on a reconnaissance; he managed to make his way back to Russian lines on foot. He volunteered to undertake a lone reconnaissance on 20 November 1941, and discovered von Kleist's Panzers approaching Rostov in a snowstorm. An experienced pilot of outstanding ability, his score steadily began to climb during 1942, and by early 1943 had risen to nearly 20 in 350 sorties. He was now a captain and commander of an eskadrilli of P-39 Airacobras in the 16th Guards IAP, and was becoming a great teacher and a developer of fighter tactics – a role in which he would become to the Luftwaffe and Force what Mölders was to the Red Air Malan to the RAF. On one occasion he led his unit to attack 16 Ju 87s in two formations, and personally shot down four of them. Operating in the Caucasus, he became well-known to the Germans, who would radio 'Achtung! Der Ass Pokryshkin in der Luft' when they knew he was airborne.

Awarded the Hero of the Soviet Union title on three occasions, he rose to command the 16th Guards IAP. In the summer of 1944 as a colonel he commanded the 9th Guards Fighter Division. His units converted from P-39s to the Lavochkin La 7, but 48 of his 59 victories were achieved while flying American aircraft. He was shot down four times during the war, baling out on three occasions and crash-landing on the fourth. Considered the 'Father' of Russian fighter aviation during the war, 30 of the pilots who served under his command became Heroes of the Soviet Union, and between them claimed some 500 victories.

gained much of their success in the British and American Lend-Lease aircraft which were now available in quantity. The first really notable ace was Lt Col Boris Safonov of the Naval Air Force in the north. After early service with I-16s in the 72nd IAP, his first victory over an He 111 being recorded on 24 June 1941, he converted his unit to the first RAF Hurricanes in September, and then to Curtiss P-40s in March 1942. By May of that year his score had reached 22 and he became the first fighter pilot of the war to receive a second Hero of the Soviet Union (HSU) award. On 30 May he led three P-40s to cover British convoy PQ.16, and attacked 40 escorted bombers, four of which were shot down – two by Safonov to raise his score to 25 individual and 14 shared victories. However his engine was hit as he attacked a third and he came down in the icy sea, the first leading Soviet ace to die. In his unit, which had been redesignated 2nd Guards IAP, was Zakhor Sarokin, who returned to fly after losing both his legs in a crash; he achieved a total of 18 victories. Also under Safonov's command was Senior Lt Piotr Sgibnev, who gained 19 victories flying Hurricanes with the 78th IAP before his death in action on 3 May 1943.

Another unit on the Baltic Front, operating over Leningrad, was the 4th Guards IAP. With this regiment Senior Lt Mikhail Vasiliev gained 22

Above: Col Alexsandr Pokryshkin (centre in flying helmet) is congratulated by fellow pilots of his 16th Guards Fighter Regiment on one of the last of his 59 victories. Note the Bell P-39 Airacobra in the background with 54 victory stars on the nose.
Left: Lt Col Boris Safonov, the highly successful Soviet Naval ace is seen here (left) with two RAF pilots of 151 Wing in the Murmansk area in late 1941.

victories flying I-16s before being killed on 5 May 1942, while Senior Lt Gennadi Tsokolayev claimed 20. Capt Yevgenii Tsyganov later flew LaGG 3s with this unit, his score reaching 24 by early 1944.

Alexsandr Pokryshkin joined the 16th Guards IAP as a squadron commander during 1942, flying Bell P-39 Airacobras throughout the Caucasus fighting. By early 1943 his score had reached 20, and this total rose steadily, 48 of his 59 successes being achieved while flying Airacobras. A great leader, he inspired those who flew with him. Among pilots in his unit were Capt Grigorii Rechkalov, who claimed 56 and 5 shared, 44 of them with the Airacobra; and Capt Nikolai Gulayev, who had claimed four victories in earlier conflicts and was to add 53

more (including five in a day in March 1944) of which 36 involved the American-built fighter. Capt Alexsandr Khubov initially flew I-153 biplanes before joing the 16th and converting to P-39s; with the latter he added 31 of his final total of 50. On one occasion a comrade crashed and was killed because a spanner had been left loose in his aircraft. At a party to mourn the death, Khubov killed the mechanic responsible. He was stripped of his decorations for this, but later redeemed himself in combat. During the Jassy battle of early 1944 he was the most successful pilot, claiming nine in five days, and his decorations were later restored. He was killed in a crash in November 1944 when the unit converted to Lavochkin La 7 fighters.

Other successful 16th Guards IAP pilots in-

Below: Guards Major Vladimir Lavrinenkov (35 victories) of the 9th Guards IAP.
Bottom: Capt Grigorii Rechkalov, Russia's No 3 ace with 56 victories who flew Airacobras in the 16th Guards IAP under Pokryshkin's leadership.

cluded the Glinka brothers, Dmitri and Boris, who claimed 50 and 30 respectively, both having flown earlier with the P-40-equipped 45th IAP. By early 1943 they had 30 between them, but Dmitri then flew with Lt Ivan Babak as his wingman and between them, these two scored 16 over the Kuban. Later in the war the brothers shot down seven bombers between them in one day. Babak also became one of the unit's leading pilots with 35 victories after being shot down, becoming a prisoner and escaping again. Disgraced for having surrendered, his career seemed finished, but Pokryshkin overruled the NKVD repatriation officer and took him back into the unit. Another very successful Airacobra pilot was Senior Lt Alexei Smirnov who had 10 victories by March 1943, and ended the war with 27.

A very successful unit in the Stalingrad area was the 9th Guards IAP. This unit's leading pilots included Col Aleksei Alelyukhin, who claimed 10 over Rostov during early 1943, and then 15 in a two-month period. He ended the war with 40 and 17 shares. One of the regiment's first aces was Maj Vladimir Lavrinenkov, who had 26 by the start of May 1943, including 16 in one month over the Volga region. He too escaped after being shot down and captured. He ended the war as a fighter regiment commander with 35 and 11 shared. In all, the 9th produced 24 pilots who became Heroes of the Soviet Union, six of them receiving two awards. One of the latter was a member of the Soviet Union's Asiatic community, Maj Sultan Akhmet-Khan, who gained his 30th and last individual victory (he also shared in 19 more) over Berlin in 1945. He died in 1971 when testing a new delta-wing jet aircraft.

Defeated at Stalingrad and in Africa, the Germans launched a last desperate bid to win the war in the East on 5 July 1943 with a massive offensive to pinch off a vast salient in the Russian line at Kursk. Huge quantities of the latest tanks and aircraft were brought forward, but the opening of the attack was delayed, and Allied intelligence warned the Russians of an impending attack and they prepared defenses in extraordinary depth. As the Luftwaffe prepared to take off at dawn on 5 July, radar picked up an incoming Soviet pre-emptive strike, aimed at the German airfields. Intercepting Messerschmitts and Focke-Wulfs caught the Russians well short of their targets, and in the ensuing fighting claimed 120 shot down. With the offensive underway, aerial battles of unprecedented violence and scale took place throughout the day and by evening the toll had risen to 432. Some 77 of these, including 62 bombers, were credited to II/JG 3; Hpt Kurt Brändle, the Kommandeur, claiming five and Oblt Joachim Kirschner nine. In I/JG 52 Hpt Johannes Wiese claimed 12 and Oblt Walter Krupinski of III Gruppe claimed 11, but honors for the day went to Obfw Herbert Strassl of III/JG 51 who claimed 15 in four sorties

in an Fw 190. Next day 205 more victories were claimed, Strassl again claiming 10. Two days later, having claimed no less than 30 victories in four days, he was shot down and killed with his score at 67.

For the Russians too the Kursk battle produced many victories. On 6 July Lt Alexander Gorovetz reportedly shot down nine bombers from a formation of 20 before being shot down and killed by an escorting German fighter. The 10 victory ace's body was not found until 14 years later. Another pilot to do well at this time was Guards Maj Alexei Maras'yev. Maras'yev had crashed deep in German lines in April 1942 after shooting down two Ju 52 transports to bring his score to eight. With injured feet, he crawled through the snow for 19 days, living on berries, hedgehogs and insects, and on one occasion shooting a bear with his revolver. Finally picked up by partisans and air evacuated, he lost his lower legs due to gangrene, but rejoined his unit on recovery, just in time for the Kursk battle. On his first sortie on 6 July he shot down two of 20 Ju 87s, and next day claimed three Fw 190s, claiming a further three a week later. His final score was 19.

A new pilot at the front, flying one of the newly introduced Lavochkin La 5s, was a young Leutenant, Ivan Kojedub, who made his first claim on 6 July against a Ju 87 – the first of many, for he would eventually become Russia's top scorer. The fighting of Summer 1943 was to bring severe losses to the Red Air Force however, including their top woman ace of the war. Russia's women fighter pilots were unique. Short of trained pilots after the terrible losses of 1941, experienced female aircrew were allowed to fly operationally, and the all-woman 73rd IAP was formed. 2/Lt Lilya Litvak gained 13 victories, 12 in one year, but was killed over Orel on 1 August 1943 at the age of 21 after 66 aerial battles. She was survived by Lt Katya Budanova, who was credited with 11 victories, like her compatriot claiming most over Stalingrad.

By mid-September 1943 JG 51's score had risen to 7000, but other Geschwadern were catching up fast. During the month Walter Nowotny of JG 54, an Fw 190 pilot, and Erich

Hartmann of JG 52, each claimed 49 victories, Nowotny reaching a score of 200 on 4 September. On 12 September JG 52's Günther Rall also reached this total. Nowotny set new records on 14 October when he became the first to reach 250, Rall matching him on 28 November. Meanwhile Lt Emil 'Bully' Lang of JG 54 also set a new record which was never to be surpassed. Claiming 12 in a day on 21 October to raise his total to 73, he was to be credited with 72 victories in three weeks, including an incredible 18 in one day – surpassing even Marseille's record day in Africa. By the end of November another JG 52 pilot reached 200 – Hpt Gerhard Barkhorn – and even on the tough, frozen polar front in the far North, JG 5 had its first two 'century scorers' by the end of the summer, the Kommodore, Hpt Heinrich Ehrler, and Oblt Theodor Weissenberger of II Gruppe both passing the 100 during August.

After the great battles of summer 1943, the pattern of the air war in the East began to change inexorably. Even as the Kursk Offensive got

Top left: Ivan Kojedub, later to become Russian top-scorer of the war, with his Lavochkin fighter which carries the inscription 'From the Kolkhoze-worker Vassily Viktorovich Konev'. Top right: Although only claiming 8 victories (4 Russian and 4 US), Lt Col Aladar de Heppes led the successful Hungarian 'Puma' units throughout the war, although over 40 years of age. He is seen with his Bf 109G V-039 in 1943. Above: Gathered for an award ceremony are four of the Luftwaffe's greatest aces. On the right is Günther Rall of JG 52, whose score reached 250 in November 1943, while next to him is Walter Nowotny from JG 54, who had become the first to reach this total during the previous month. Hartmann Grasser,

Right: A trio of successful
Hungarian fighter pilots.
Top to bottom: 1/Lt Lajoz
Toth (24 victories); Capt
György Ujszaszy (5); Lt
Laszlo Molnar (25).

underway, news came of the Anglo-American
landings in Sicily, followed at the start of September by those in Italy. Now too the US daylight-bombing offensive on the Reich was really
getting into its stride, and soon bombers based
in Southern Italy would join in the attack,
raiding South Germany, Austria, Hungary,
Rumania and other targets in this area. Already
JG 53 and JG 77 had gone to the Mediterranean,
and now JG 3 and elements of JG 54 were withdrawn for Reich defense. JG 52 remained the only
full Geschwader in Russia, holding the line with
the remaining elements of JG 51 and 54, and with
part of JG 5 in the far north. As the attacks of the
US Fifteenth Air Force began to threaten their
homelands, Germany's allies withdrew their
air units for defense – during 1943 the Croat and
Slovakian contingents left, followed early in 1944
by the Hungarians and Rumanians. The changing
fortunes of war also saw the withdrawal of the
Spanish volunteers, who had flown successively
with JG 27 and then JG 51 since 1941. They
had gained 147 victories, in achieving which 15
pilots had become aces. The two most successful
were Capt Gonzalo Hevia with 12 and Cdt
Mariano Cuadra with 10. Probably the most
notable was the Civil War ace, Cdt Angel Salas,
who led the first contingent of volunteers,
gaining the first two victories on 4 October 1941,
and in two months adding seven air and two
ground victories to his 17 earlier successes. Two
of the new aces were killed in Spain, one in an
accident, while a notable 17-victory ace of the
Civil War, Capt Aristedes Garcia, was shot down
and killed by anti-aircraft fire soon after arrival
on the Eastern Front.

With JG 52 the Slovaks, flying first Avia
B.534 biplanes and then Bf 109Es, produced two
or three aces, most renowned of whom was
2/Lt Jan Reznak, credited with 32. The Croats
performed most creditably, at least 16 of their
pilots getting five or more, flying first Fiat G-50s
and then Bf 109Fs and Gs. Three of these pilots
had totals exceeding 20, the most successful
being Lt Cvitan Galic, Oblt Mato Dubovak and
Oblt Jan Gerthofer, who claimed 36, 34 and 33
respectively. Galic was later killed when his aircraft was shot up on the ground by US Mustangs
in Yugoslavia, and one other ace (Oblt Mato
Culinovic – 18 victories) was killed by ground
fire. The Croats' commander, Oberst Fanjo Dzal,
claimed 13, but after the war he was handed
over to Tito's government and hanged; his
brother Zivko, was also an ace with eight
victories.

The Hungarians – the only allies to continue
to fight alongside the Germans right to the end
in May 1945 – produced at least 20 aces, flying
both against the Russians and the Americans.

First Hungarian ace of the war was 2/Lt
Imre Pánézel who claimed five in 1942, three of
them in one sortie flying a Re2000. By the end
of 1943 their leading ace was Lt Miklos Kenyeres
with 19 victories against the Russians, closely

Kommandeur of II/JG 51
would end the war with 103,
while Heinrich Prinz zu
Sayn-Wittgenstein (far left)
was one of Germany's
top night fighters with 83
victories, 29 of them
claimed in Russia.

followed by Lt Laszlo Molnar and 2/Lt György Debrödy, who had 18 each. Kenyeres was shot down and became a prisoner in February 1944, just before the Hungarians withdrew their fighters to home defense.

Despite the withdrawal of so many fighter units, the loss was partially made good by the start of a re-equipment program to replace the aging Ju 87 dive-bombers with Fw 190 fighter-bombers, and the conversion of Stukageschwadern into Schlachtgeschwadern. Although the Schlachtflieger were not trained for air combat, a number of these pilots developed great skill in this secondary role as they were obliged to defend themselves and generally stand in for the greatly thinned Jagdflieger. SG 2 was to gain the most noteworthy success in this role, claiming 247 victories in the Crimea during the first half of 1944. One pilot alone accounted for more than a third of these; Oblt August Lambert had gained 20 victories when the battle reached its peak, and added 70 more in a period of just three weeks. He would later take his total to 116 before his death in action in 1945 — by far the most successful of the Schlachtflieger in aerial combat.

Because of the great reduction in opposition, the Russians — now increased in numbers, better equipped and with better tactics and training — were able to operate with much greater freedom and lower loss. When the German fighters did appear, however, they retained the upper hand right to the end. The numbers of pilots producing huge scores was greatly reduced, and the scores of Russia's aces rose faster against the lower caliber of Luftwaffe ground-attack and bomber personnel now reaching the front.

On 2 March 1944 Hpt Barkhorn of JG 52 became the third pilot to reach 250, and also during that month JG 54 recorded its 7000th victory of the war. In June however came the Allied invasion of Normandy, and the withdrawal of further units to face this new threat — though now mainly from Reich defense. Before the month was out a great Russian offensive began which was to drive the Germans from Soviet soil, and the beginning of the end was in sight. June also saw some desperate fighting over the Arctic coast as Russian Naval bombers attempted to destroy German supply convoys to this area. On 17 June Lt Walter Schuck of III/JG 5 claimed 12

Above left: Flt Mstr Urho 'Jätti' Lehtovaara flew in Finland's fighter squadron HLeLv 28, equipped with Morane 406 fighters like this one. He was top scorer on the Morane, with 15 of his 44½ victories claimed while flying this type (one of them in 1940). When this photograph was taken he had just shot down three I-16s on 9 September 1941 to raise his total in the Continuation War to 10.
Above: A group of successful Finnish fighter pilots serving with squadron HLeLv 24 in June 1943. Left to right: Sgt Jussi Huotari (17½ victories); Flt Mstr Ilmari Juutilainen (top scorer with 93); Sgt Emil Vesa (29½). Behind them is the tail of Juutilainen's Brewster 239, marked with his victories at that time.

Right: Finland's No 3 ace, Col Eino Luukkanen, commander of HLeLv 34 (56 victories) who claimed 36 of his successes while flying the Messerschmitt Bf 109G.

such bombers shot down during one attack, while 10 days later similar scores were recorded by Obfw Jacob Norz of II/JG 5 and Hpt Franz Dörr of III Gruppe. In three days fighting – 17, 27 and 28 June – 154 victories were claimed by these two Gruppen in this area!

During June, prior to the launching of their main offensive, the Russians had also launched a massive attack on the Leningrad/Karelian Isthmus Front, designed to take the Finns out of the war. The Finnish air force had fought magnificently since 1941, using a wide variety of diverse and generally obsolescent fighter types with great effect. Not until 1943 did the first few Bf 109Gs arrive. By early 1944 Capt Hans Wind had been credited with 36 individual and six shared victories, plus three observations balloons while flying the Brewster 239 (an early version of the Buffalo). Flight Master Eino Juutilainen had 34 victories on this type, others also having done well (Maj Jorma Karhunen $24\frac{1}{2}$, Lt Lauri Nissinen $22\frac{1}{2}$, and so on). With Curtiss H-75A Hawks, Lt Alto Tervo had 14 and four shared and Lt Kyösti Karhila 10 and seven shared. Flt Mstr Oiva Tuominen had 23 and Capt Risto O Puhakka 11 on Fiat G-50s, and Flt Mstr Urho Lehtovaara 14 on Morane 406s. Several of the leading pilots had begun flying Messerschmitts during 1943, but early in 1944 more of these became available, and were the main types used during the desperate fighting of June and July 1944. Scores rose at tremendous rates during these two months as the Finns fought to hold the Soviet steamroller, six pilots gaining 25 or more victories flying the Bf 109. Col Eino Luukkanen, who commanded the first Messerschmitt unit, claimed 39 with this fighter, but Hans Wind, who started to fly it only at the beginning of June, was one of the great stars. Claiming five in a day on three occasions in June, he had raised his score to 78 by 28 June, when he was wounded in action; at this time he was top scorer. Eino Juttilainen, who like Luukkanen had been on the Messerschmitts since the previous summer, claimed 21 in June, 11 in two days. He overtook Wind's score on 30 June, and by mid-July had reached a score of $93\frac{1}{6}$.

Unable to break the Finns before having to withdraw forces for the Central Front offensive, the Russians ceased the attack, and there was little aerial fighting after mid-July, but the Finns now sought an armistice. Bloody but unbowed, their resistance, and their unwillingness to advance beyond their 1939 boundaries, gained them the best terms of any of the Soviet Union's enemies. It was left to Juutilainen to claim the last victory against them on 3 September 1944 when he shot down an Li 2 transport; he was top scorer of any of Germany's European allies.

At the same time the Russian advance had flooded into Rumania and the Northern Balkans. The Rumanians signed an armistice in August 1944 and changed sides. Less is known of their aces than of any other nation involved in the war except the Bulgarians, but certainly they produced several during operations in Russia, and on home defense. The three most remarkable appear to be Capt Prince Constantine Cantacuzene (60), Capt Alexandre Serbanescu (50), who was killed in combat with US fighters on 18 August 1944, and Lt Florian Budu (40).

With only the Hungarians still supporting them, the Germans fought on. Even JG 52 on occasion found itself involved with US bomber formations over Rumania during the summer of 1944, but still the pilots of this unit continued to pile up the victories. On 18 July Oblt Erich 'Bubi' Hartmann had gained his 250th victory. Then, claiming 78 in four weeks, he became the first to reach 300 on 24 August, a day on which he claimed 11 victories for his best-ever performance. Hpt Wilhelm Batz of this unit claimed his 200th on 17 August, while on 2 September JG 52 recorded its 10,000th victory.

Still the fighting went on as the Germans were driven back into East Prussia, fighting now in defense of their homeland as well as of their forces on the ground. On 5 January 1945 Gerhard Barkhorn became the second — and last — to top

Left: A group of II/JG 52's top scorers in the Crimea in 1944. Left to right: Heinrich Sturm (157 victories); Gerhard Barkhorn (301); Wilhelm Batz (237); Otto Fönnekold (136). Sturm and Fönnekold were both to be killed later in the year.
Main picture: Ivan Kojedub's Lavochkin La 7 fighter at the end of the war, showing all his 62 victories and his major decorations painted on the fuselage.

300 victories. On 14 February Oblt Otto Kittel of I/JG 54 was shot down and killed in combat with an Il-2 Schturmovik; this 267-victory ace, fourth on the list of Luftwaffe top-scorers, was the highest-scoring pilot to be killed in action. On 8 April Hpt Helmut Lipfert, who had recently taken command of I/JG 53 after many months with III/JG 52, was the last to pass 200, while on 14 April Obfw Heinz Marquardt of IV/JG 51 was the last to reach 100. On 8 May, the last day of the war, Maj Hartmann claimed a Yak 11 over Brünn – his 352nd. Among those faithful allies, the Hungarians, Laszlo Molnar had become top scorer with 25 during the summer of 1944, but had been killed in combat with US aircraft. By the war's end two pilots had passed his score, Ens Deszö Szentgyörgyi with 34 and Capt Debrödy with 26.

The final 18 months of the war had seen many new Soviet aces appear. After his initiation at Kursk, Ivan Kojedub's score had mounted rapidly until in the last days of the conflict he passed Pokryshkin's previously unbeaten total of 59, to become Russia's leading ace with 62; he was by this time vice-commander of the 176th

Guards IAP. The air battles over Jassy during the summer of 1944 had been a particularly fruitful ground for the Russians; among those doing well were Col Kirill Yevstigneyev of the 13th Guards IAP, who had also been credited with 12 victories in nine air battles during October 1943. The score of this twice HSU stood at 52. Col Nicolai Skoromorokhov of the 31st IAP had gained 46 and eight shared flying Lavochkin fighters, while with the 5th Guards IAP Maj Vladimir Popkov, another Lavochkin pilot, had 41 in over 300 sorties. Among successful pilots of Yakovlev fighter types was Ivan Stepanenko (32). Sergei Luganskii, who flew I-16s in Finland, LaGG 3s, and then Yaks, claimed 37 and six shared. Shared victories by numbers of fighters were a feature of Soviet claims, and perhaps the outstanding example was Senior Lt Georgii Kostilev of the 3rd Guards IAP, who flew LaGG 3s and La 5s on the Leningrad Front, where he was credited with 11 individual and 32 shared victories. His La 5 was extraordinary in that, as well as having victory stars and his medals painted on as was normal, it also featured an enormous 'shark's mouth' on the nose. As with a number of Russians whose scores included many shares, Kostilev's score is sometimes quoted as though these were all individual victories – that is, 43.

On the Northern Front particularly, Curtiss P-40 fighters were widely used right up to the late months of the war. Among those who flew these aircraft with the 154th IAP on the Leningrad Front in 1942 were Maj Petr Pokryshev, credited with 22 and seven shared victories, and Capt N Zelenov, who claimed 24 and 10 shared before his death in action on 29 June 1944. Other P-40 pilots included Senior Lt Nikolai Kuznetsov, whose total is listed as 36, but may be an amalgam, as he is known at one stage to have had 15 and 12 shares, Maj Aleksei Khlobystov, who got three of his 30 victories by ramming (on the first occasion unintentionally!) and Petr Pilyutov (23). Both Khlobystov and Pilyutov got at least five victories on the early model Curtiss Tomahawk during 1942.

Like most nations deeply involved in the war, the Soviet Union produced a number of aces who were not true fighter pilots. Tactical-reconnaissance pilot Capt Vladimir Merkulov of the 15th Reconnaissance AP was credited with 29 victories in the Leningrad region; he flew a two-seater Yak 7 conversion. Ivan Mikhaili-chenko was one of the leading exponents of the Ilyushin Il 2 Shturmovik, flying 179 ground-attack sorties in these aircraft during which he was credited with ten aerial victories. His opposite number was one of the most famous, and undoubtedly the most highly-decorated, combat airmen in the world – the Luftwaffe's Oberst Hans-Ulrich Rüdel. Flying with Stuka-geschwader 2 'Immelmann', he undertook 2530 sorties – a world record – most of them with the Ju 87, but 430 with the Fw 190. Credited with nine aerial victories, he was also world top scorer against tanks – 519 destroyed – and also was credited with sinking the battleship *Marat*, a cruiser, a destroyer and 70 landing craft, and with the destruction of many other artillery and motor vehicle targets. Losing a leg in action, but still flying on recovery, he was the sole holder of the Golden Oak Leaves with Swords and Diamonds to the Knights' Cross.

During the later stages of the war units of foreign personnel were formed within the Red Air Force, Czech and Polish fighter regiments seeing action during the closing stages of the fighting. The most successful and famous however was the French Normandie unit. Formed late in 1942 as a Groupe of two escadrilles after France had rejoined the Allies, the unit first went into action in March 1943 equipped with Yak 1 fighters. Pilots joined the unit in considerable numbers, both from the Armée de l'Air in North Africa, and from Free French units with the RAF. One of the most outstanding to join initially was Capt Albert Littolff, who had been credited with six and a probable with GC III/7 in France in 1940, and then four more at least with 73

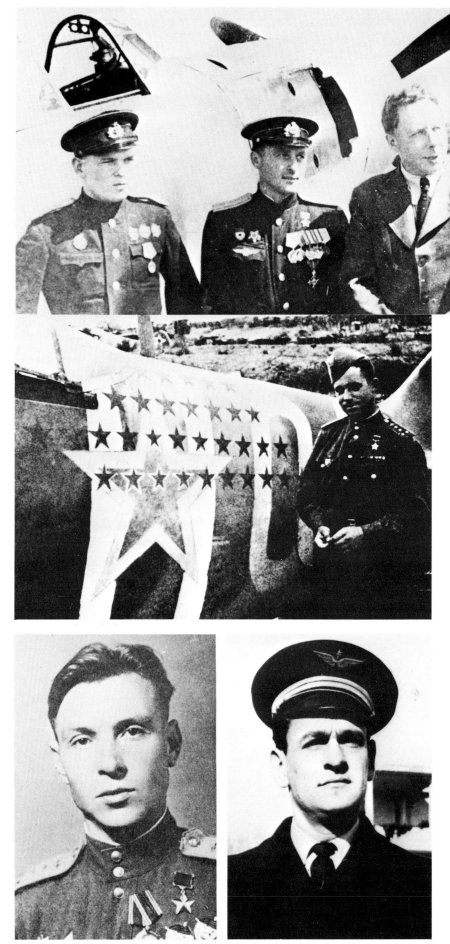

Squadron, RAF in the Libyan Desert. He was however killed in July 1943 with his score at 14. Another ex-RAF pilot, Sous Lt Albert Durand, became the initial top scorer during 1943 with 11 victories, but he too was killed during September of that year. With him from England came Capt Marcel Albert, later to command one of the unit's

escadrilles and to emerge as ultimate top scorer. Albert had claimed one shared confirmed and one probable flying Dewoitine 520s with GC I/3 in 1940; now he raised his score to 23 by 1945 — top-scoring Armée de l'Air pilot of the war.

So successful was the Normandie Groupe with the French that at the start of 1944 it was doubled in size to a full regiment of four escadrilles. It was to be credited with 273 confirmed and 37 probable victories, producing many aces, 14 of whom had 10 or more victories, while losses amounted to 52 pilots.

The Russian Front had certainly been the outstanding front numerically so far as the fighters were concerned, scores here outstripping all others. As has been seen here, circumstances and conditions favored the Luftwaffe as never before, and German pilots claimed some 45,000 Russian aircraft shot down. The figures look incredible, yet the Russians admit over 70,000 aircraft lost on operations during the war, and informed sources consider the total could have been as high as 90,000 — double the losses of the combined Anglo-American air forces in the West by night and day! The very intensity of action can be seen by the fact that the Russians, despite the appalling problems that they faced — the very problem of keeping pilots alive against the German Experten for long enough to gain their own expertise — nonetheless produced the overwhelming preponderance of high-scoring aces on the Allied side. Yet the Eastern Front saw hardly any of the important developments of aerial warfare; it remained a slogging match, a production slaughterhouse — in many ways a rerun of the Western Front of 1916–18, with more modern equipment.

TOP-SCORING FIGHTER PILOTS OF THE LUFTWAFFE ON THE EASTERN FRONT, 1941–45

Maj Erich Hartmann	352 (including 7 US)	JG 52
Maj Gerhard Barkhorn	301	JG 52, 6
Maj Günther Rall	271 (+ 4 West)	JG 52
Oblt Otto Kittel*	267	JG 54
Maj Walter Nowotny*	255 (+ 3 West)	JG 54
Maj Wilhelm Batz	237	JG 52
Oblt Walter Schuck	206	JG 5
Maj Heinrich Ehrler	204–220	JG 77, 5
Oberst Hermann Graf	202 (+ 10 West)	JG 51, 52
Hpt Helmut Lipfert	203 (including 3 US)	JG 52, 53
Hpt Joachim Brendel	189	JG 51
Oblt Anton Hafner*	184 (+ 20 West)	JG 51
Oblt Günther Josten	178	JG 51
Obstlt Hans Philipp*	177 (+ 29 West)	ZG 76, JG 54
Maj Walter Krupinski	177 (+ 20 West)	JG 52, 5
Maj Theodor Weissenberger	175 (+ 33 West)	JG 77, 5
Hpt Gunther Schack	174	JG 51, 3
Hpt Heinz Schmidt*	173	JG 52
Hpt Maximilian Stotz*	173 (+ 16 West)	JG 54
Hpt Joachim Kirschner*	167 (+ 21 West)	JG 3
Maj Horst Adameit*	165 (+ 1 West)	JG 54
Maj Werner-Kurt Brandle*	160 (+ 20 West)	JG 53, 3
Hpt Heinrich Sturm*	157	JG 52
Oblt Gerhard Thyben	152 (+ 5 West)	JG 3, 54
Oblt Hans Beisswenger*	151 (+ 1 Yugoslavian)	JG 54
Lt Peter Düttmann	150 (including 2 tanks)	JG 52

TOP-SCORING FINNISH FIGHTER PILOTS OF THE CONTINUATION WAR, 1941–44

(figures in brackets are scores in the Winter War of 1939/40)

			Scores on Type	Unit (HLeLv)
Flt Mstr Eino I Juutilainen	92	(+ $2\frac{1}{6}$)	BW 34; MT 57	24, 34
Capt Han H Wind	78		BW 42; MT 36	24
Col Eino A Luukkanen	$53\frac{1}{2}$	(+ $2\frac{1}{2}$)	BW $14\frac{1}{2}$; MT 39	24, 34
Flt Mstr Urho S Lehtovaara	$43\frac{1}{2}$	(+ 1)	MS 14; MT $29\frac{1}{2}$	28, 34
Flt Mstr Oiva EK Tuominen	36	(+ 8)	FA 23; MT 13	26, 34
Capt Risto O Puhakka	36	(+ 6)	FA 11; MT 25	26, 34
Lt Kauko O Puro	36		IT 2; BW $5\frac{1}{2}$; MT $28\frac{1}{2}$	24, 30
Sgt Maj Nils E Katajainen	$35\frac{1}{2}$		BW $17\frac{1}{2}$; MT 18	24
Lt Kyösti K Karhila	$32\frac{1}{4}$		CU $13\frac{1}{4}$; MT 19	32, 34
Lt Lauri V Nissinen*	$28\frac{1}{2}$	(+ $3\frac{5}{6}$)	BW $22\frac{1}{2}$; MT 6	24
Sgt Maj Emil O Vesa	$29\frac{1}{2}$		BW $9\frac{1}{2}$; MT 20	24
Maj Jorma Karhunen	$26\frac{1}{2}$	(+ $4\frac{7}{12}$)	BW $26\frac{1}{2}$	24
Sgt Maj Tapio T Järvi	$28\frac{1}{2}$		BW $9\frac{1}{2}$; MT 19	24
Sgt Klaus J Alakoski	26		FA 1; MT 25	26, 34
Lt Alto K Tervo*	$23\frac{1}{4}$		BW $\frac{1}{2}$; CU $15\frac{3}{4}$; MT 7	24, 32, 34
Lt Jorma K Saarinen*	23		BW 5; MT 18	24
Sgt Maj Antti J Tani	$21\frac{1}{2}$		MS 7; MT $14\frac{1}{2}$	28, 34
Lt Urho PJ Myllylä	21		MS $1\frac{1}{2}$; MT $19\frac{1}{2}$	28, 34
Flt Mstr Eero A Kinnunen*	18	(+ $3\frac{1}{2}$)	BW 18	24

(BW – Brewster 239; MS – Morane 406; FA – Fiat G-50;
IT – Polikarpov I-153; MT – Bf 109G)

TOP-SCORING HUNGARIAN FIGHTER PILOTS, 1941–45

Ens Dezsö Szentgyörgyi	34	(6 Russian 1943; 5 al US 1944; 12 al Russian 45)
Capt György Debródy	26	(18 Russian 1943/4; 6 US 1944; 2 Russian late 1944)
Lt Laszlo Molnar*	25	(18 Russian 1943/4; 7 US 1944)
1/Lt Lajoz Toth	24	(11 app. Russian 1943/4; 4 US 1944; 5 al Russian 45)
Lt Miklos Kenyeres	19	(19 Russian 1943/44)
Sgt Istvan Fabian	13	(Approx 10 Russian, 3 US)
Capt Laszlo Pottyondy	13	(all Russian)
Lt Ferenc Malnasy*	12	
Lt Jozsef Malik	11	al (6 Russian, 5 US)

TOP-SCORING RUSSIAN FIGHTER PILOTS, 1941–45

Maj Ivan N Kojedub	62	176th IAP
Col Aleksandr I Pokryshkin	59	55th IAP, 16th Gu IAP
Capt Grigorii A Rechkalov	56	16th Gu IAP
Capt Nikolai D Gulaev	53 (+ 4)	16th Gu IAP
Col Kirill A Yevstigneyev	52	13th Gu IAP
Maj Dmitrii B Glinka	50	45th IAP, 16th Gu IAP
Capt Aleksandr F Klubov	50	16th Gu IAP
Ivan M Pilipenko	48	
Maj Arsenii V Vorozheikin	46 (+ 6 in Mongolia)	728th IAP
Vasilii N Kubarev	46	
Col Nikolai M Skomorokhov	46	31st IAP
Sergei N Morgunov	42	
Maj Vitalii I Popkov	41	5th Gu IAP
Maj Viktor F Golubev	39	4th Gu IAP
Vasilii F Golubev	38	
Sergei D Luganskii	37	
Mikhail Y Pivovarov	37	
Grigorii K Gul'tyaev	36	
Anatolii G Dolgikh	36	
Snr Lt Nikolai F Kuznetsov	36	
Aleksandr I Koldunov	36	
1st Lt Ivan I Babak	35	16th Gu IAP
Capt Pavel M Kamozin	35	
Maj Vladimir D Lavrinenkov	35	9th Gu IAP
Nikolai S Pavlushkin	35	
Petr A Gnido	34	
Aleksandr V Kotchekov	34	
Sergei I Luk'yanov	34	
Ivan N Sytov	34	
Aleksandr M Chislov	34	
Lt Fedor M Chubukov	34	
Andreii Y Bcrovykh	32	
Viktor V Kirilyuk	32	
Mikhail S Komel'kov	32	
Nikolai F Krasnov	32	
Aleksei K Ryazanov	32	14th IAP
Maj Gen Ivan N Stepanenko	32	
Mikhail M Zelenkin	32	
Pavel Y Golovachev	31	
Maj Sultan Akhmet-Khan	30	9th Gu IAP
Fedor F Archipenko	30	
Lt Col Vladimir I Bobrov	30 (+ 13 in Spain)	9th Gu IAP
Maj Boris B Glinka	30	45th IAP, 16th Gu IAP

TOP-SCORING RUMANIAN FIGHTER PILOTS, 1941–44

Capt Prince Constantine Cantacuzene	60
Capt Alexandre Serbanescu*	50
Lt Florian Budu	40
Lt Jon Milu	18

TOP-SCORING FIGHTER PILOTS OF THE SLOVAKIAN AIR FORCE, 1941–44

2/Lt Jan Reznak	32	13 (Slovak)/JG 52
Staff Sgt Isidor Kovarik	29	13 (Slovak)/JG 82

TOP SCORING CROAT FIGHTER PILOTS, 1941–44

(All members of the Kroaten-Staffeln/JG 52)

Lt Cvitan Galic*	36
Oblt Mato Dubovak	34
Oblt Jan Gerthofer	33
Oblt Mato Culinovic*	18
Lt Dragutin Ivanic	18
Oblt Benectic	16
Oblt Jergowitsch	16
Lt Boskic	13
Oberst Fanjo Djal	13 (hanged at end of war)
Hpt Stipic*	12 (shot as POW)

TOP-SCORING SPANISH VOLUNTEER FIGHTER PILOTS IN RUSSIA, 1941–43

Cap Gonzala Hevia Alvarez-Quinones	12
Cdt Mariano Cuadra Medina	10
Ten Fernando Sanchez-Arjona Courtoy*	9
Cap Jose Ramon Gavilan Ponce de Leon	9
Cdt Angel Salas Larrazabal (+ 17 in Civil War)	7
Ten Vincente Aldecoa Lecanda*	7
Ten Damasco Arango Lopez	7

Ivan D Likhobabiyi	30	
Petr Y Likholetov	30	
Valentin N Makharov	30	
Maj Petr M Pokryshev	30 (8 shared)	29th Gu IAP, 159th IAP
Aleksei S Ehlobystov	30	

(It is not known which Russian aces were killed in combat or flying accidents. Approximately 53 more pilots claimed 25–29 victories, and 100 claimed 20–24.)

TOP-SCORING FRENCH FIGHTER PILOTS OF THE NORMANDIE-NIEMEN REGIMENT- 1943–45

Capt Marcel Albert	22 (+ 1 and 1 probable, France 1940)
Capt Roland de la Poype	17 (including 2 probables; + 1 probable with RAF)
Sous Lt Jacques Andre	16
Sous Lt Roger Sauvage	14 (+ 2 in France, 1940)
Capt Leon Cuffaut	13
Sous Lt Roger Marchi	13
Sous Lt Marcel Perrin	13
Sous Lt Albert Durand*	11
Sous Lt Georges Lemare	11 (+ 2 British aircraft at Dakar, 1940)

*indicates killed in action or flying accident during World War II.

Western Europe, 1944–45

Above: Capt Don Gentile (left, 21.84 victories), leading ace of the US 4th Fighter Group is congratulated on his success by his Group Commander, Col Don Blakeslee (14.5 victories). Both were previously members of the RAF's 133 'Eagle' Squadron.
Right: Gentile (right) with his wingman 1st Lt John Godfrey (16.3 victories) in England.

The year 1944 opened with a massive intensification of the air war over Western Europe. The introduction of the P-51B version of the North American Mustang to action as an escort fighter, and the availability of jettisonable fuel tanks at last allowed the fighters of the US Eighth Air Force to accompany the heavy bombers to all their targets, even as far afield as Berlin. The spring was to see a devastating battle for aerial supremacy between the American escort fighters and the Reich defenders – a battle which the latter were to lose steadily with fearful losses. Shortage of fuel, caused by the loss of captured oilfield facilities in the Caucasus, and subsequently by the Allied bombing campaign on the Ploesti complex in Rumania and on synthetic fuel plants throughout Europe, reduced flying training for Luftwaffe entrants, while manpower shortages kept training periods to a minimum. As a result the new men joining the Jagdgeschwadern were not a patch on their predecessors in terms of expertise – nor could they any longer equal the Allied pilots, now given the luxury of a full and comprehensive coaching at the hands of the many aces available to pass on their experience in the training schools.

Now the 56th Fighter Group found itself challenged by the Mustang units – at first particularly the 4th and 354th. Walker Mahurin retained his lead early in the year, but on 27 March he was hit by return fire from a Do 217 bomber which he shot down with three other pilots, and baled out with his score at $18\frac{3}{4}$. He

had just been overtaken by Bob Johnson who had claimed four on 15 March to reach 19, but now one of the 4th Fighter Group pilots shot into the lead. After two victories with an RAF 'Eagle' Squadron, Capt Don Gentile added $19\frac{5}{6}$ more, the last three on 8 April 1944; his score also included seven more aircraft destroyed on the ground, which at this stage the Eighth Air Force were recognizing as full victories to encourage its pilots to destroy the Luftwaffe on its airfields as well as in the air. Gentile then crashed his Mustang during a low level pass for news cameras, and was at once grounded. John Godfrey, who frequently flew as his wingman, would raise his own score to 14.33 plus three and six shared on the ground, by the beginning of May; both were then sent home on a War Bond tour.

On 8 May however, Bob Johnson reached 27 and was also sent home, the first pilot in Europe to pass Rickenbacker's World War I score; a probable was later confirmed, raising his total to 28 – equal at the time with Dick Bong of the Fifth Air Force as USAAF No 1. No other USAAF pilot in Europe was to better Johnson's score, though it would be equalled on 5 July by Maj Francis 'Gabby' Gabreski of the same group, who had gained his 20th by the end of May. Other distinguished Eighth Air Force pilots at this time included the 4th Fighter Group's leader, a pilot of a stature matching that of the 56th's 'Hub' Zemke – Col Don Blakeslee. After three victories with the 'Eagle' squadrons, Blackeslee claimed

two with the P-47, then one in December 1943 while introducing the 354th Fighter Group to action with the first P-51Bs. Obtaining these aircraft for his own unit, he added 8.5 further victories by the end of his tour at the start of July. Zemke meanwhile had raised his own total to 15.25 plus eight on the ground by the end of June. In August he took command of the new 479th Fighter Group with which he gained 2½ more victories – the last a half share in one of the new Me 262 jet fighters which began appearing in late 1944.

Lt Col James H Howard of the 354th Fighter Group had earlier claimed 6½ with the AVG in Burma. He added six more with the Mustang, including three and three probables on 11 January 1944 when he single-handedly fought off a force of interceptors attacking a bomber formation. For this he became the only fighter pilot in the European Theater to receive the Congressional Medal of Honor. Among the other 'first wave' pilots, David Schilling, one of the 56th Fighter Group's earliest aces, had increased his total to 14½ by August, when he became commander of the unit after Zemke's departure. Three more on 21 September were followed by five on 23 December over the Ardennes to raise his total to 22.5 and 10.5 on the ground; he was top-scoring ace still on operations with the Eighth at this time.

Lt Ralph K Hofer of the 4th had claimed 16½ and 14 on the ground by the end of May, but on 2 July 1944 during a shuttle mission to Fifteenth Air Force bases in Italy, he was lost during an attack on a target in Hungary, believed shot down by Hungarian Bf 109s of the

101 'Puma' Regiment. He was the highest scoring Eighth Air Force ace to be shot down in combat with opposing fighters, but ground fire had proved a much more deadly foe. Walter Beckham of the 353rd and Duane Beeson of the 4th had both gone down to become prisoners to this cause. Late in July 'Gabby' Gabreski hit the ground while strafing and followed them into prison camp with 28 air and one ground victories. In August the 4th's John Godfrey, on his second tour, also became a POW after 16.3 air and 12.66 ground victories, as did the group's James A 'Goody' Goodson (15 victories) during June. Finally on 30 October 'Hub' Zemke bailed out of an iced-up P-38 during his last sortie before going home.

New aces appeared fast, though the greater number of escort units and reduced level of opposition prevented so many pilots building up big scores so fast. Previously a P-47 unit, the 352nd Fighter Group did particularly well during 1944, producing several leading aces. Lt Col John C Meyer, the unit commander, claimed 24 in the air between November 1943 and 1 January

Above left: Col James H Howard, who claimed 7.33 with the American Volunteer Group in Burma, and then 6 in Europe with the 354th 'Pioneer Mustang' Fighter Group, was the only fighter pilot in the European Theater of Operations to be awarded a Congressional Medal of Honor.

Above: Four of the most successful pilots of the 56th Fighter Group during early summer 1944. Left to right: Col Hubert A Zemke (17.75 victories); Col David C Schilling (22.5); Col Francis S Gabreski (28); Capt Frederick J Christiansen Jr (21.5).

Above right: With 24 victories in the air and 13 on the ground, Col John C Meyer, commander of the 352nd Fighter Group, was one of the USAAF's top scorers of the war. He

subsequently added two MiGs in Korea.

Right: One of the first aces of the 4th Fighter Group, Duane W Beeson claimed 19.33 victories before he was shot down by German Flak and became a POW. This native of Boise, Idaho, is seen with his P-47D Thunderbolt late in 1943, before the unit converted to P-51s.

1945, adding 13 more on the ground. Maj George Preddy, after service in Australia, claimed 25.83 and five on the ground during the same period. On 6 August 1944 he shot down six Bf 109s in a day, and on 25 December was seen to shoot down two more, but was then himself shot down and killed by US anti-aircraft fire as he chased a third German fighter.

All the leading P-51 aces mentioned had obtained some of their early victories on other types – Spitfires or P-47s – and the actual top scorer with the Mustang was Capt Ray Wetmore of the 357th Fighter Group, who claimed 22.59. He claimed $4\frac{1}{2}$ on 14 January 1945, while his last victory on 15 March was over an Me 163 rocket fighter. The last great ace of the 56th was Capt Fred Christiansen who had claimed $15\frac{1}{2}$ prior to 7 July 1944; on this latter date he caught a formation of Ju 52/3m trimotor transports and shot down six of them.

The 354th – the 'Pioneer Mustang Group' – was in fact a part of the US Ninth Air Force, a tactical formation, and later resumed a close-support and front-line role. Here there were less

Aces of the Eighth – Johnson and Gabreski

When the 56th Fighter Group arrived in England as one of the US Eighth Air Force's first P-47 Thunderbolt units, it was already a highly trained unit, having been the first to be equipped with the big 'Jug.' In the group's 61st Squadron, one of the flight commanders was Francis S Gabreski (below), and in his flight was tough athlete and boxer, Robert S Johnson (above). Both pilots were involved in the early operations of 8th Fighter Command over Europe. Johnson claimed his first victory on 13 June 1943 and Gabreski his on 24 August – both against Fw 190 fighters.

The aggressive Johnson showed an early tendency to break away to chase any opponents, for which he was frequently in trouble with his superiors. However soon after his first victory his aircraft was badly shot-up by Fw 190s (flown, it is believed, by two of the Luftwaffe's leading 'Experten' in the West) and he only just got back; this experience sobered him somewhat. Nonetheless, he continued to achieve victories, and when on 10 October he claimed a Bf 110 and an Fw 190, he became one of the group's first aces. Gabreski followed suit on 26 November, two Bf 110s bringing his total to five. By the end of the year Johnson's score had reached 10 and Gabreski's eight.

Then came the great battles with the Luftwaffe in the spring 1944, as the Eighth Air Force – the range of its fighters greatly extended by the use of drop tanks – began to wrest control of the skies from the Germans. On 15 March, his best day, Johnson claimed three Fw 190s and a Bf 109 to raise his total to 22, passing the previous record of Walker Mahurin to become top Eighth Air Force ace. After his 24th and 25th victories on 13 April, he was posted as a flight commander to the 62nd Squadron. He saw no further combat until 8 May, when he shot down two more fighters to reach 27 – but just after the Fifth Air Force's Dick Bong had achieved the same score. Sent home and promoted major, a claim for a 'damaged' was upgraded to destroyed after his arrival in the States to take his score to 28.

Gabreski meanwhile, now commander of the 61st Squadron, continued to claim, though more slowly than Johnson. A victory on 8 May 1944, when Johnson got his last two, raised his total to 19, while on the 22nd he claimed three Fw 190s on his best day – he claimed two in a day on seven occasions. Five more victories in June, following the Allied invasion of Normandy, were followed by a Bf 109 on 5 July to equal Johnson's total. On 20 July however, having added one German aircraft destroyed on the ground, he hit the ground with his propeller during a very low-level attack on an airfield near Coblenz, and crash-landed, becoming a prisoner of war.

After a period as a test pilot in 1945, he left the USAAF in 1946, but returned the following year, and in 1951 was posted to command the 4th Fighter-Interceptor Wing in Korea, flying the F-86 Sabre. Here he was to become an ace again, claiming six and one shared MiG 15s between July 1951 and April 1952. In 1956 he commanded another old ETO unit, the 354th, now flying F-100 Super Sabres.

'Pritzl' Bär – First Great Jet Ace

The Luftwaffe had few more colorful pilots than Heinz 'Pritzl' Bär. An unteroffizier (Corporal) in 1939 with JG 51, he had become top scoring NCO pilot by August 1940. Although shot down into the channel by Spitfires in September, he already had 13 victories when the Battle of Britain drew to an end. The early days of the fighting in Russia allowed him to score rapidly, and by the end of 1941 – now commissioned – his total had increased to 91. Some 22 more victories in the early summer of 1942 were followed by a posting to I/JG 77 as Gruppenkommandeur with the rank of Hauptmann, and already with the Knights' Cross with Swords and Oak Leaves.

Now the scene changed with a move to Sicily for action over Malta, and from there late in the year to North Africa. Retreating with the Afrika Korps, he was to see action throughout the late stages of the Libyan fighting and the campaign in Tunisia. When the gruppe withdrew at the start of May 1943 he was the unit's top scorer in Africa, having claimed some 61 victories here, plus four over Malta. Bär now returned to Germany, but his health was no longer good. Flying Fw 190s now, with II/JG 1 on Reich defense, he next claimed in December 1943. By the end of April 1944 he had claimed 24 US Eighth Air Force planes shot down, his score then having reached 202. Posted as Kommodore JG 3, he led that unit in the costly Operation 'Bödenplatte' on 1 January 1945, during which he destroyed two British aircraft, but he then took over III/EJG 2, an operational-training unit with the Messerschmitt Me 262 jet fighter. With this radical new aircraft he was to claim 16 Allied aircraft during March and April 1945, the highest score achieved with this aircraft, to raise his final score to 220. Sadly this great ace was killed after the war in a light-aircraft crash.

'Johnny' Johnson – British top-scorer

James Edgar Johnson trained with the RAF Volunteer Reserve, was called up in August 1939 and joined 616 Squadron during 1940. He missed the late stages of the Battle of Britain due to a period of hospitalization, but saw action from Tangmere in Summer 1941, often flying in Wg Cdr Douglas Bader's section. He was rapidly promoted flight commander and awarded a DFC, having claimed five Bf 109s shot down by early 1942. Promoted to command 610 Squadron, he claimed two shared victories over Dieppe on 19 August 1942, but gained no further confirmed successes until early 1943, when he was again promoted to lead the Kenley Wing. This was made up entirely of RCAF squadrons at the time, all flying the excellent Spitfire IX. Between April and September he claimed 18 victories, five of which were shared. One of the latter was a twin-engined Bf 110, shared with three others – the only victory he was ever to achieve against any other type than single-engined fighters.

A period of staff work with 83 Group, 2nd Tactical Air Force, was followed by a return to operations as leader of the new 144 (Canadian) Wing of the TAF. Three victories before the Normandy invasion of June 1944, and then 10 more by late September, raised his total to 38, making him official RAF top scorer of the war. Promoted Group Captain early in 1945, he took over command of 125 (Spitfire XIV) Wing for the rest of the war. Remaining in the RAF, he enjoyed a distinguished and successful career, achieving Air rank. During all his operational tours his aircraft was only once hit – by a single shell from an opposing aircraft.

opportunities for combat, but the group – not surprisingly – was the Ninth's top scorer. The unit's most successful pilot was Lt Glenn T Eagleston, who claimed 18½ plus five on the ground between December 1943 and April 1945. The Ninth also produced several aces among its tactical reconnaissance pilots, most notably Lt Clyde B East of the 67th and 10th Tactical Reconnaissance Groups. Flying an F-6D reconnaissance version of the Mustang, he claimed two victories during 1944, and then 10 more in 1945, 3½ of them on 8 April.

For the RAF, the shorter range of their Spitfires and Typhoons denied them much involvement with the Luftwaffe's fighters until the invasion of Normandy took place in June 1944. Then, flying from airstrips in France, they were soon deeply involved as the Luftwaffe withdrew its units from every other front – including Reich defense – to throw into this fight. Canadian, Polish, Norwegian, Czech, French and Belgian pilots all played a major part in this period, flying with the British 2nd Tactical Air Force. The Canadians particularly did well, and top scorers of 2nd TAF were Sqn Ldr Don Laubman of 412 Squadron and Sqn Ldr Bill Klersy of 401 Squadron; Laubman claimed 14½ between 2 July and 28 October 1944 – including four in a day on 27 September – to raise his total to 15, while in two tours Klersy claimed 13½ between 7 June 1944 and 3 May 1945, including three on 1 March and 3½ on 20 April, to raise his total to 14½. Leading the Candian 144 Wing, Englishman 'Johnny' Johnson added 10 to his earlier total of 28, and by the end of September 1944 was official RAF top scorer with 38, although seven of these were shared victories. In his wing, Sqn Ldr Wally McLeod added eight to his Malta score of 13 to become official RCAF top scorer (though not top scoring Canadian), but was lost in combat with Fw 190s over Nijmegen on 27 September. During this period Flt Lt Otto Smik of the Czech Squadron claimed 2½ aircraft to raise his total to eight, and also brought down three V-1s.

The start of the V-1 offensive led to the withdrawal from 2nd TAF immediately after the invasion of many of the RAF's most effective new fighters – Tempests and Spitfire XIVs – to combat this menace. Following the conclusion of the battle in France in August, and the advance into Holland and Belgium the following month, there was a lull until the German Ardennes offensive was launched in December. Thereafter there was frequent heavy fighting – particularly for the fighters of 2nd TAF's 83 Group – until the end of the war at the start of May 1945. On 29 December 1944 over the Ardennes a very experienced RCAF pilot, Flt Lt RJ Audet on his first tour after a long period as an instructor, became the first and only Spitfire pilot to claim five victories in a single sortie when he shot down three Fw 190s and two Bf 109s; this 411 Squadron flight commander added 5½ more during the next month, including

Above: Maj George E Preddy was the highest-scoring American ace in Europe to lose his life in action – shot down by 'friendly' anti-aircraft fire immediately after his last victory. The 25.83 victory ace is seen (left) with another successful pilot of the 352nd Fighter Group, Capt Bill Whisner. Whisner claimed 15.5 during World War II, plus a further 5.5 in Korea.
Left: Top-scoring Mustang pilot was Capt Ray Wetmore (22.6 victories) of the 359th Fighter Group.
Right: Last great ace of the 56th Fighter Group was Maj Fred Christiansen whose score of 21.5 victories included 6 in one sortie – all Junkers Ju 52/3m transports.
Inset: Top scorer of 2nd Tactical Air Force was Canadian Sqn Ldr Don Laubman, with 15 victories.

Mustangs – Three P-51Ds and a P-51C – of the 375 Squadron, 361st Fighter Group, 8th US Air Force fly a closed-up finger four formation en route to escort bombers over Germany, Summer 1944.

Left: Tempest ace Sqn Ldr DC 'Foob' Fairbanks (right) was another American citizen with the RAF. He claimed 12½ victories before becoming a POW in February 1945.
Below: Tempest flown by Wg Cdr ED Mackie (21½ victories) as leader of 122 Wing late in the war. The aircraft carries Mackie's initials — a Wing Leader's privilege — his Wing Commander pennant and three rows of victory crosses.

an Me 262 jet, but was shot down and killed by flak on 3 March. One of the biggest operations occurred on 1 January 1945 when the Luftwaffe launched its last desperate offensive against the Allied airfields in Holland and Belgium – Operation *Bödenplatte*. While destroying many Allied aircraft on the ground, it resulted in an even heavier loss of German machines together with many pilots, including numbers of the remaining experienced formation leaders.

By now the Tempests and Spitfire XIVs were back in Holland with 2nd TAF and these types were pre-eminent in the closing weeks. American Sqn Ldr DC 'Foob' Fairbanks, who had gained one victory as a Spitfire pilot during the invasion, claimed 11½ (including an Me 262 jet) plus two on the ground from December 1944 to February 1945 while flying Tempests with 3 and 274 Squadrons; he was lost in combat on 28 February. Evan Mackie, who had done so well in the Mediterranean, also flew Tempests with 80 and 274 Squadrons, then leading the Tempest Wing – 122. He added 5½ in the air and three and two shared on the ground to raise his total of victories to 21½ by the close of hostilities. In the same wing fellow New Zealander Wg Cdr WE 'Smokey' Schrader claimed 8½ to reach a total of 12.

In the highly successful Norwegian wing, Capt Helmer Grundt-Spang of 331 Squadron, a veteran of the 1942/3 fighting, claimed four more victories – three on 29 December – to reach 10⅓, while Lt Col Werner Christie, after five and two shared victories on Spitfires in 1942–4, added four more at the head of an RAF Mustang Wing, escorting Bomber Command 'heavies' on daylight raids over Germany during the last months of the war.

This final 15 months of war had bled the Luftwaffe dry. During the spring 1944 battles the Reich defense suffered staggering losses to the US escort fighters, and during the summer, when a very high proportion of the force was pushed into France, the 'Jagdwaffe' was virtually wiped out by the combined Anglo-American fighter force. Rebuilt during the autumn of 1944, with basically good aircraft – including growing numbers of the excellent new Messerschmitt Me 262 jet fighters – but with a pilot strength made up mainly of raw and only partially-trained recruits, leavened with the remains of the old guard of Experten, the new fighter force was a shadow of its old self. In late 1944 the losses, particularly on Reich defense, and during the ill-fated Ardennes offensive, were nothing short of catastrophic, frequently exceeding 100 in a day. The disaster of *Bödenplatte* set the seal on the demise of the German fighters, but many kept fighting against impossible odds until the end. Early in 1945, following the losses of the past year, Hitler ordered a substantial number of units to the East again, where they had a rather better chance of achieving something, but even

Left: Capt John T Godfrey, 4th Fighter Group ace with 16.3 air and 12.66 ground victories.
Below left: Ace of World War II and Korea John Meyer (26 victories) as a USAF Lt Gen later in life.
Center: American top-scorer in Europe; Lt Col Francis Gabreski (28 victories) of the 56R Fighter Group.
Right: Mustang Leader; Col Don Blakeslee (14.5 victories) who flew with the RAF and USAAF.

here the inexperienced majority were to be overwhelmed by the now better trained Russians.

Among the 50 or so leading Experten killed during the first nine months of 1944 were Oblt Egon Meyer, Kommodore of JG 2, in March; he was Western Front top scorer at the time with 102, and also top scorer against the four-engined bombers with 25 of these in his total. Before the month was out the new leader against the big bombers, Lt Hugo Frey of II/JG 11, was dead, having claimed 26 of these victories among his total of 32. The great Oberst Wolf-Dietrich Wilcke, Kommodore of JG 3, was also killed in March after 162, 25 in the West, while his successor, Maj Friedrich-Karl 'Tutti' Müller, was killed in May after 140 victories, 40 of them against the Western Allies. Meyer's successor in JG 2, Maj Kurt Ubben (110 victories, 20 in the West) was killed during April, while May also saw the demise of Oberst Walter Oesau of JG 1 after 123 victories (71 West, 10 of them four-engined). The five months to June saw the loss of nearly 1850 fighters in combat. In February two of the leading Zerstörerflieger were lost; Maj Eduard Tratt who had claimed 38 victories flying Bf 110s and Me 410s, 25 of them in the West, where he led II/ZG 26 and III/ZG 76's Hpt Johannes Kiel, who had been one of the top scorers against the four-engined bombers, with 21 of these to his credit.

Losses in the weeks following the invasion in June included Hpt Joseph Wurmheller of III/JG 2 after 102 victories, all but nine in the West, as well as many other leading pilots. III/JG 54 was the most successful Gruppe at this time, Oblt Eugen-Ludwig Zweigart (69 victories) claiming 15 here before his death on 8 June, while Hpt Emil 'Bully' Lang, who had gained 148 in Russia (including the record 18 in one day) claimed 25 before being shot down and killed on 3 September. Lt August Mors of I/JG 5 was killed on 6 August after claiming 11 in a few days to add to his 56 in the East, while Hpt Theodor Weissenberger of I/JG 5 claimed 25 in six weeks and survived.

The formation of the first jet fighter commando in late 1944 led to the loss of another great ace. Maj Walter Nowotny, first to 250 victories in the East, had been rested after 255. Now he led the new Kommando Nowotny, adding three victories to his score but he was killed just after takeoff in a combat with P-51s on 8 November 1944. Shot down with him was Oblt Franz Schall, who survived and was subsequently to achieve 14 of his 137 victories with the jet. Weissenberger was also later to fly the jet as Kommandeur of the new I/JG 7, gaining his final eight victories on this type. Most successful of all jet pilots however was Heinz Bär, who gained 16 victories with the type to raise his total for the war to 220. Indeed it is estimated that over 25 pilots gained five or more while flying Me 262s, seven of them getting at least 10.

When the war drew to a close the Luftwaffe

126

Jagdgeschwader
Kommodore of units in the
West at a conference late in
the war. Left to right: Gustav
Rödel (98 victories) JG 27;
unknown; Heinz Bär (220)
JG 3; Kurt Bühligen (112)
JG 2.
Below left: Norway's third
highest-scoring ace, Capt
Helmer Grundt-Spang of
331 Squadron, seen during
his training days. He ended
the war with 10⅓ victories.

had been totally defeated. However its Experten had proved to be the most successful fighter pilots in the world. Their toughest fronts had been in the West and over Malta – among their toughest opponents the heavily armed, high-flying four-engined B-17s and B-24s of the US Eighth and Fifteenth Air Force. Most successful against these behemoths had been Lt Herbert Rollwage of II/JG 53 – one of the most successful over Malta as well – whose total of 102 included 91 against the Western Allies, 44 of them four-engined. He was followed by Oberst Walter Dahl whose 128 included 51 in the West – mainly Reich defense – 36 of them four-engined.

TOP-SCORING FIGHTER PILOTS OF THE LUFTWAFFE IN WESTERN EUROPE, 1939–45

| | Against | | |
	Western Allies	Total in war	Units
Gen Lt Adolf Galland	104	104	JG 27, 26
Obstlt Egon Mayer*	102	102	JG 2
Oberst Josef Priller	101	101	JG 26
Hpt Siegfried Lemke	95	96	JG 2
Hpt Joseph Würmheller*	93	102	JG 2
Hpt Siegfried Schnell*	87	93	JG 2
Maj Anton Hackl	73	192	JG 77, 11, 76, 26, 300
Obstlt Kurt Bühligen	72	112	JG 2
Oblt Adolf Glunz	71	71	JG 26, 7
Oberst Walter Oesau*	71	123	JG 51, 3, 2, 1
Maj Georg-Peter Eder	68	78	JG 2, 1, 26, 7
Maj Hans Hahn	68	108	JG 54, 2
Oberst Werner Mölders*	68	115	JG 53, 51
Obstlt Heinz Bär	59	220	JG 51, 1, 3, EJG 2
Maj Joachim Müncheberg*	58	135	JG 26
Maj Rolf Hermichen	56	64	ZG 1, JG 26, 11, 104
Maj Helmut Wick*	56	56	JG 2
Maj Wilhelm-Ferdinand Galland*	55	55	JG 26
Lt Herbert Rollwage	55	102	JG 53
Oblt Rudi Pflanz*	52	52	JG 2
Oberst Walter Dahl	51	128	JG 3, 300
Oberst Herbert Ihlefeld	55	130	JG 77, 25, 11, 1
Oblt Konrad Bauer	50	68	JG 3, 300
Maj Hermann Staiger	50	63	JG 51, 26, 1

TOP-SCORING LUFTWAFFE FIGHTER PILOTS AGAINST ALLIED FOUR-ENGINED BOMBERS, 1941–45

	Four-engined bombers	Total Score	Units
Lt Herbert Rollwage	44	102	JG 53
Oberst Walter Dahl	36	128	JG 3, 300
Maj Georg-Peter Eder	36	78	JG 2, 1, 26, 7
Oblt Konrad Bauer	32	68	JG 3, 300
Maj Anton Hackl	32	192	JG 11, 76, 26, 300
Lt Hugo Frey*	26	32	JG 11
Maj Rolf Hermichen	26	64	JG 26, 11, 104
Maj Werner Schroer	26	114	JG 27
Maj Hermann Staiger	26	63	JG 26, 1
Hpt Werner Gerth*	25	30	JG 53, 3, 300
Obstlt Egon Mayer*	25	102	JG 2
Oblt Ernst Börngen	24	45	JG 27
Obstlt Kurt Bühligen	24	112	JG 2
Obfw Walter Loos	22	38	JG 3, 300, 301
Oblt Hans Weik	22	36	JG 3
Obstlt Heinz Bär	21	220	JG 1, 3, EJG 2
Hpt Fritz Karch	21	47	JG 2
Hpt Rüdiger von Kirchmayr	21	46	JG 1, 11, JV 44
Hpt Siegfried Lemke	21	96	JG 2 =

[*39 more pilots were credited with between 11 and 20 bombers*]

TOP-SCORING FIGHTER PILOTS OF THE RAF AND COMMONWEALTH AIR FORCE IN WESTERN EUROPE, 1939–45

		Score in W Europe	Total	Comments	Previously Quoted Score
Gp Capt JE Johnson	British	38	38	Incl 7 shared	38
Wg Cdr B Finucane*	Irish	35	35	Incl 6 shared	32
Gp Captain AG Malan	South African	33	33	Incl 7 shared	32
Wg Cdr RRS Tuck	British	29	29	Incl 4 shared	29
Sqn Ldr HM Stephen	British	28	28	Incl 11 shared	$22\frac{1}{2}$
Sqn Ldr JH Lacey	British	27	28	1 against Japan	28
Wg Cdr DRS Bader	British	26	26	Incl al 4 shared	23
Flt Lt ES Lock*	British	26	26	Incl 1 shared	26
Flt Lt G Allard*	British	25	25	Incl al 2 shared	23
Wg Cdr DE Kingaby	British	24	24	Incl 2 shared	$22\frac{1}{2}$
Sqn Ldr MN Crossley	British	23	23	Incl 2 shared	22
Wg Cdr AC Deere	New Zealander	23	23	Incl 2 shared	22
Wg Cdr WV Crawford-Compton	New Zealander	22	22	Incl 1 shared	$21\frac{1}{2}$
Wg Cdr RH Harries	British	22	22	Incl 3 shared	$20\frac{1}{4}$
Sqn Ldr AA McKellar*	British	22	22	Incl 2 shared	21
Gp Capt WD David	British	21	21	Incl al 2 shared	20
Wg Cdr JEF Demozay	French	21	21	+ 1 on ground	22
Wg Cdr DAP McMullen	British	21	21	Incl 4 shared	$19\frac{5}{6}$
Wg Cdr JE Rankin	British	21	21	Incl 3 shared	21
Wg Cdr RG Cutton	British	20	20	Incl 3 shared	$19\frac{1}{3}$
Wg Cdr HJL Hallowes	British	20	20	Incl 2 shared	21

TOP-SCORING FIGHTER PILOTS OF THE USAAF IN WESTERN EUROPE, 1942–45

	Air	Ground	+ Victories Elsewhere
Col Francis S Gabreski	28	1	+ 6.5 in Korea
Maj Robert S Johnson	28	—	
Maj George E Preddy*	25.83	5	
Col John C Meyer	24	13	+ 2 in Korea
Maj Raymond S Wetmore	22.6	2	
Col David C Schilling	22.5	10.5	
Capt Don S Gentile	21.84	7	(Includes 2 with RAF)
Maj Frederick J Christensen Jr.	21.5	—	
Lt Col Glen E Duncan	19.5	—	
Lt Col Duane W Beeson	19.3	7	
Maj Walker M Mahurin	18.75	—	+ 1 SWP, 3.5 Korea
Maj Leonard K Carson	18.5	3.5	
Lt Col Glenn T Eagleston	18.5	5	+ 2 in Korea
Maj Walter C Beckham	18	—	
Col Hubert A Zemke	17.75	8.5	
Maj John B England	17.5	1	
Capt John F Thornwell	17.25	2	
Capt Henry W Brown	17.2 (14.2)	14.5	
Maj Robert W Foy	17 (15)	3	
Lt Col Gerald W Johnson	17	—	
Capt Clarence E Anderson Jr.	16.5	1	
Lt Ralph K Hofer*	16.5	14	
Capt John T Godfrey	16.3	12.66	

Pacific War

The Japanese attack on Pearl Harbor, Malaya and the Philippines on 7/8 December 1941 brought a whole new dimension to the war as well as bringing the United States into the fight. Initially, a relatively small force of highly trained, highly experienced Japanese fighter pilots – many with experience of combat in China or Mongolia – equipped with superior aircraft, swept all opposition before them. Backed by relatively short lines of communication and supply, and by a dedicated and single-minded command structure, they wiped out the American, British, Dutch and Australian air forces facing them in Malaya and the East Indies, in Burma and in the Philippines, while their carrier-borne compatriots played havoc throughout the Southwest Pacific, over Ceylon and the Indian Ocean, and off New Guinea.

Early successes were gained by a number of pilots of the Imperial Japanese Naval and Army Air Forces. Lt Cdr Iyozo Fujita for example, pilot of a Mitsubishi A6M-2 Zero-Sen fighter aboard the carrier *Soryu*, claimed a Curtiss P-36 over Hawaii on the first day of the war, and during the Midway battle was credited with a B-26 and shares in two others, a TBD Devastator torpedo-bomber and shares in three more, and an F4F Wildcat fighter and shares in two more of these, all over the Japanese carriers on 5 June 1942. He later flew in the Solomons, Philippines, at Iwo Jima and on home defense. One of the Navy's land-based Zero pilots, Lt (jg) Shigeo Sugio (20 victories) of the 3rd Kokutai with his wingman claimed four Philippino P-26 fighters shot down over Luzon on 12 December 1941. while on 3 February 1942 with two others he claimed nine victories over Dutch and American fighters over Surabaya, Java. An army pilot who flew Nakajima Ki 43 'Hayabusa' fighters ('Oscars') with the 59th Sentai during the early campaign, was Capt Akira Onozaki (14 victories). As an NCO pilot he shot down an RAF Brewster Buffalo over Malaya during his first combat on 21 December 1941, adding eight Hurricanes, a Blenheim and a trainer to become the unit's top-scorer by mid-1942.

Probably the most successful pilot of the early month was another land-based Zero pilot of the navy's Tainan Ku. Lt Saburo Sakai, then an NCO pilot, had already served in China, gaining one victory there. On 8 December 1941 he was to claim the first Japanese success over the Philippines, shooting down a P-40, and subsequently operated throughout the East Indies, raising his score to 13 by the end of February 1942. This total included both American and Dutch aircraft. He had been engaged in some of the first fights with US B-17 bombers; on 8 February he was credited with participation in shooting down two B-17s and claimed two more probable. After a period of illness, he rejoined his unit which was now at Lae, in New Guinea, and here during the April–August 1942 period he was to claim many victories, including numbers of P-39s and P-40s, and some B-25s and B-26s. By 8 August his score was reputed to be 58, and he had become the leading Japanese ace, but on that day he was engaged in a long-range mission to Guadalcanal. Although credited with several victories there, he was badly wounded and only just managed to get back, semiconscious and partially blinded. After medical treatment, he

returned to home defense in 1944, having lost the use of his right eye. Over Iwo Jima with the Yokosuka Ku he claimed an F6F Hellcat shot down, while on 13 August 1945 he and another pilot claimed a B-29. Reputed to be the top-scoring surviving Japanese pilot of the war, his score has been quoted as 64. It must however be borne in mind that Japanese scores were not officially confirmed, and those quoted frequently included shares, probables and sometimes ground victories; Japanese researchers consider Sakai's score to be nearer 32.

Another navy pilot active early in the war was Ensign Kenji Okabe, who flew from the decks of *Shokaku*, claiming two victories over British fighters above Ceylon during his first combat on 9 April 1942. On 8 May he was credited with eight victories (including three probables) against F4Fs, TBDs and SBD Dauntless dive-bombers of the US Navy during the Coral Sea battle. He later served in the Solomons and Philippines, and on home defense, his final score being about 15.

Against a background of disaster and ill-preparedness, there was little to bring cheer to the Allies in the air. Among the hard-pressed units fighting on the various fronts a few fighter pilots built up respectable scores, but the records of most were never to become well-known in the general collapse. At Pearl Harbor Lt George S Welsh, later to become a leading ace with the US Fifth Air Force in New Guinea, gained the first four victories of an eventual total of 16, while over the Philippines Capt Boyd D 'Buzz' Wagner was the defenders' 'star'; flying P-40s with the 17th Pursuit Squadron, he claimed four Nakajima Ki 27 fighters ('Nates') shot down on 13 December and one more on the 16th. On 30 April 1942 he retained his position of USAAF top-scorer in the area by claiming three Zeros shot down while flying a P-39 Airacobra attached to the 8th Fighter Group in New Guinea.

Over Malaya, Singapore, Sumatra and Java several pilots of the RAF did well, including Sgt RL Dovel (6 victories), Sgt JAS 'Sandy' Allan (7 victories) and Plt Off JA 'Red' Campbell, an American citizen (6 victories) – all while flying Hurricanes. In Singapore Sgt GB Fisken, a New Zealander, gained six victories while flying Buffalos – he would later become British Commonwealth top-scorer against the Japanese, and will be mentioned again later. The outnumbered Dutch pilots fought well over Java and Sumatra, but none of them was credited with more than three victories. In Java too the USAAF appeared again, a 'scratch' unit of P-40 Warhawks – the 17th (Provisional) Squadron – putting up a good performance at some cost. The unit's most famous pilot was Capt Andrew J Reynolds, who claimed four victories during February 1942. Later in the year, flying with the 49th Fighter Group in defense of Australia, he became the new US Fifth Air Force's first No 1 ace, adding six more victories between 31 March and 30 July

to raise his total to 10.

Undoubtedly the most outstanding Allied fighter achievement of this period occurred on 20 February 1942 when Lt Edward H O'Hare (11 victories) of the US Navy's VF-3 fighter squadron aboard the carrier USS *Lexington*, intercepted a formation of Mitsubishi G3M 'Betty' bombers attempting to attack the vessel as it sought to launch an air strike in the Indies. By the time help arrived, he had been credited with shooting down five planes single-handed. The navy's first ace of the war, he was also the first fighter pilot in this conflict to receive the Congressional Medal of Honor.

In Burma meanwhile the RAF and American Volunteer Group – Chennault's famous 'Flying Tigers' – were gaining the greatest level of success against the Japanese, though by May 1942 they had been driven back into India and China, defeated not so much in the air, as on the ground. Leading pilots here were from the AVG; Robert H Neale, an ex-US Navy dive-bomber pilot, was credited with 16 victories over China and Burma between December 1941 and June 1942, 14 of them by the end of February. Neale was not to transfer to the USAAF – many of the 'Tigers' did not, as they considered the terms poor. Other high-scorers of the group who saw no further service were George T Burgard ($10\frac{3}{4}$) and Kenneth A Jernstedt ($10\frac{1}{2}$). Three other pilots credited with $10\frac{1}{2}$ each did not return; John Van Kuren Newkirk was shot down and killed by anti-aircraft fire on 24 March, as was Robert L Little on 22 May. William D McGarry was brought down by ground fire on 24 March, being interned in French Indo-China.

The greater part of the Japanese territorial gains had been achieved by June 1942, when the Battle of Midway brought a sudden and unexpected rebuff which was to have a damaging effect on much of their further conduct of the war. Even in this battle, the Japanese carrier fighter pilots remained supreme, the Americans certainly coming off second best in terms of aerial combat. However, in terms of carriers sunk, the advantage now began to tilt the other way.

The war now settled down into four main zones, where most fighting was to be concentrated for the next two years or so. On New Guinea both Japanese Army and Navy air units fought the USAAF's Fifth Air Force and the RAAF; in the Solomon Island chain the JNAF fought a combined force of the US Marine Corps, Navy, USAAF Thirteenth Air Force and RNZAF units. On the Burma/India frontier JAAF units faced the RAF and a growing American element that would become the Tenth Air Force. In China the JAAF engaged General Chennault's new US Fourteenth Air Force – and later the reborn Chinese Nationalist Air Force.

While initially Japanese pilots – notably those of the Lae Wing (Tainan Ku) – took a heavy toll of the US and Australian fighters over the Port Moresby area of New Guinea, the Fifth Air Force

America's top pair – Bong and McGuire

Born of a Swedish father and Scots mother – similar parentage to that of the Canadian ace George Beurling – Richard Ira Bong (left) joined the US Air Corps in May 1941. After a period as an instructor on completion of training, he was posted to Australia to join the 49th Fighter Group of the Fifth Air Force, arriving in September 1942 with the first P-38 Lightning fighters for that unit. Flying with the group's 9th Squadron, he made his first two claims over Dobodura, New Guinea, on 27 December, shooting down an Aichi D3A 'Val' dive-bomber and a Zero fighter. This initial combat, which introduced the P-38 to the South-west Pacific fighting, preceded a period of greatly increased success in combat for the American fighters. By the end of March 1943, Bong's own score had risen to nine, six of which were identified as 'Oscars' – Army Ki 43 fighters. He was only to add two more before late July, but on the 26th he claimed four fighters – two 'Oscars' and two Kawasaki Ki 61 'Tonys' – followed by another on the 28th. This brought his score to 16 – equal to the previous Fifth Air Force top scorers.

Out of combat for a couple of months awaiting a new aircraft – for P-38s were still in critically short supply at this time – he returned to action in October, adding five more victories by early November, when he departed to the US on leave. Meanwhile Thomas B McGuire, who had qualified as a pilot in early 1942, reached the war zone in March 1943 after service in Alaska. After initial service with the 49th Group, he was posted to the new 475th. formed in 1943 in the war zone. With this all-P-38 unit he made his first claims over Dagua, New Guinea, on 18 August of two 'Oscars' and a 'Tony.' Four more fighters were claimed in two combats by the end of the month, and then a further nine by the end of the year to raise his total to 16; this included three Zeros on 17 October and three 'Vals' on 26 December.

Bong returned from the US in February 1944 and was attached to fifth Fighter Command Headquarters as a freelance, with authority to fly where and with whom he liked, a role in which he was joined by Neel Kearby and Tommy Lynch. Both were killed during March however, but Bong went on from strength to strength, bringing his score to 27 by mid-April to become official US top scorer and first USAAF pilot to pass Rickenbacker's World War I score. Sent home again on a Bond-raising tour, he learned while in the US that one of his 'probables' had been confirmed, raising his total to 28 – equal with the Eighth Air Force's Bob Johnson, who was also home at this time. He then undertook a gunnery course to improve his shooting, returning to New Guinea in September 1944. Here he was officially intended to be an advanced gunnery instructor, only meant to shoot in self-defense – a fiction that was to be maintained until the end of the war. He did of course fly combat, but now found that McGuire had gained five further victories against the increasingly scarce opposition encountered, but here Bong was to secure his position swiftly, claiming five more victories during the month, while McGuire was able to claim three – all on the 14th. Each pilot added three more in November, and then both made two claims on 7 December. McGuire got a Mitsubishi J2M 'Jack' fighter on the 13th – the third of these interceptors he was to claim — but Bong then claimed two 'Oscars,' one on the 15th and one on the 17th to take his score to 40. Already presented with the Congressional Medal of Honor by General Douglas MacArthur in November, he was now taken out of combat and sent home again.

As he left, McGuire achieved considerable success, claiming three Zeros on 25 December and four more next day to bring his total to 38 – only two behind Bong. At this point General Kenney, Fifth Air Force commander, grounded him so that Bong might reach the US number one. When allowed to fly again on 7 January 1945, he led off a section of four P-38s to Los Negros Island, but here they became engaged with two JAAF fighters which shot down the number three, Capt Rittmayer, and threatened the two inexperienced wingmen. McGuire pulled round sharply to go to their aid, still with his underwing tanks in place; the added drag from these caused his P-38 to stall and spin, and he was too low to recover –

he crashed to his death. He received a posthumous award of the Congressional Medal of Honor. In the US Bong became a test pilot on the new Lockheed P-80 Shooting Star jet fighter, but taking off in one of these on 6 August 1945, just before the end of the war, he suffered an engine flame-out, crashed and was killed.

132

Pacific War Top Scorer

Lt Hiroyoshi Nishizawa first saw action with the 4th Kokutai at Rabaul, claiming one victory here over an Australian Hudson bomber on 3 February 1942, flying an old A5M fighter. Posted to the Tainan Ku at Lae in New Guinea, he was soon one of the unit's most successful pilots, and by 15 May already had 20 victories in little more than a month. On 2 August, with five other pilots, he attacked five B-17s, all of which were claimed shot down. That month the unit became involved in the fighting over Guadalcanal, where he claimed five F4F Wildcats. His score reached 30 confirmed victories by November 1942. Returning to Japan at that time, he was posted back to Rabaul in May 1943 to the 251st Ku, although in September he transferred to the 253rd. Again he returned to Japan in October, remaining here until October 1944 when he was sent to Luzon, in the Philippines, with the 203rd Ku. On the 25th he took part in escorting the first official Kamikaze attack, during which he claimed his last two victories. Next day he was a passenger in a transport aircraft evacuating pilots, but this was intercepted and shot down by F6F Hellcats. Nishizawa – tall and lanky by Japanese standards – is reported to have got at least 87 victories, though some sources give his score as anything from 102 to over 150. However, 87 is considered the most likely in terms of confirmed successes.

US Navy Number One

A career officer, David S McCampbell saw service as a naval aviator from 1934, but had no opportunity to fly in combat until mid-1943, by which time he was Air Group Commander of Air Group 15 aboard the carrier USS *Essex*. The group included his old squadron, VF-15, and flying F6F Hellcats with pilots of this unit, he claimed his first victory over a Mitsubishi A6M 'Zeke' on 11 June 1944 over the Marianas. On 19 June he shot down five 'Judy' dive-bombers in one sortie in the morning, and then two more 'Zekes' in the evening. Over the Philippines in September October, during the Battle of Leyte Gulf, he claimed seven more in two days. On 24 October, during the Battle of Leyte Gulf, he and Lt Roy Rushing followed a large formation of 'Zekes,' and shot down 15 between them; nine of these were credited to McCampbell for a new US record. Further victories followed, and when he returned to the US early in 1945 to receive the Congressional Medal of Honor, his score stood at 34.

Burma Top-scorer – Satoshi Anabuki

Top-scoring fighter pilot of the Imperial Japanese Army Air Force by a considerable margin during World War II was Sgt Satoshi Anabuki. He joined the 50th Sentai late in 1941 as a corporal to fly the Nakajima Ki 27 fighter. He first saw action over the Philippines during the opening weeks of the war, and claiming three US fighters shot down. Subsequently his unit was re-equipped with the newer Ki 43 fighter and dispatched to Burma, where between June 1942 and October 1943 he was to claim 28 British and 13 US aircraft shot down. This score included the first B-24 four-engined bomber to be claimed in this region, on 26 January 1943; previously the aircraft had been considered invincible. On two occasions he claimed three in a day, and then on 8 October 1943 over the Rangoon area he claimed three B-24s and two P-38s in a single combat, ramming the tail of the third bomber and then crash-landing. He was awarded an unprecedented individual citation for this, but in February 1944 returned to Japan. He later claimed six F6F Hellcats during ferrying sorties to deliver Nakajima Ki 84 ('Frank') fighters to the Philippines, and in June 1945 – now flying a Kawasaki Ki 100 – shot down a B-29 for his 51st victory.

steadily gained the upper hand – beginning with successes by P-40 pilots defending the base areas around Port Darwin in Australia's Northern Territories, against Japanese air attacks. The introduction of the P-38 Lightning – soon the pre-eminent USAAF fighter in the East – and the P-47 steadily gave the Americans the edge, and the fighting in the area was to produce several of their top-scorers of the war – including the top two.

Among the JNAF pilots who were successful in New Guinea during the mid-months of 1942, the Tainan Ku at Lae produced the outstanding leaders. Apart from Saburo Sakai, the unit boasted many other top aces, who flew under the leadership of Lt Junichi Sasai. Sasai himself was said to have 27 (11 individual and 48 shared victories – many with large numbers of other pilots), plus three and 16 shared probables, by the time of his death over Guadalcanal on 26 August. One of Sasai's most striking pilots was Lt Hiroyoshi Nishizawa, who had 30 victories by November 1942 when the unit returned to Japan. He would later fly in the Solomons and Philippines, his final score being quoted at anything from 87 to 150 by his death on 26 October 1944. One of the original Tainan pilots was Lt Toshio Ohta, claiming 23 and 32 shared destroyed, five and eight shared probables before he too was lost over Guadalcanal on 21 October

1942. Wt Off Takeo Okumura was a later arrival, claiming 14 in September and October to add to four earlier in China. Later over the Solomons he would increase his total to between 30 and 54 before being killed on 22 September 1943.

With the withdrawal of JNAF units from New Guinea to the Solomons, the former area became specifically the province of the JAAF for the rest of the war. Against the prowess of the Navy Zero pilots the Americans and Australians with their P-39s and P-40s had experienced a difficult time in combat, and scores had only risen slowly. As has been seen, Reynolds and Wagner added to their totals, as did some RAAF veterans of the North African war. A young P-39 pilot with the US 35th Fighter Group, Thomas J Lynch, gained his first three victories during May 1942, but it was later in the year when the arrival of the P-38 coincided with the departure of the JNAF units that the American pilots experienced a more sustained success rate.

In the Solomons meanwhile, scores had risen somewhat faster. Fighting here began in earnest in August 1942 when US forces invaded the southern island of Guadalcanal, where the Japanese were building an airfield. Scene of the most desperate fighting throughout the rest of 1942 and into 1943, Guadalcanal was to be principally the responsibility of the US Marines. Tainan Ku Zeros from New Guinea flew long-

Left: A winning team! Joe Foss's flight with an F4F-3 of their squadron, VMF 121. Left to right: Lt Roger A Haberman (7); Lt Cecil J Doyle (5); Capt Foss (26); Lt William P Marontate (13); Lt Roy M Ruddell (4).

Above: Marines of VMF 223 with one of their Wildcats on Guadalcanal. On the left is Lt Col John L Smith (19 victories) who was US top scorer at the end of 1942 when this photograph was taken. On the right is the first Marine Corps ace, Maj Marion E Carl (18.5).

range sorties over the island, while reinforcements were rushed to Rabaul in New Britain, and to other islands in the Solomons. In defense US Marine Corps units with F4F Wildcat fighters reached Guadalcanal and were soon involved in an epic defense of the island. Major Marion E Carl, who had gained his first two victories over Midway on 4 June 1942, was one of the first on the island with squadron VMF 223, becoming the Marines' first ace on 24 August when he shot down three bombers and a Zero. By early October his score had risen to 16½; he had claimed three in a day on 30 August, and

had been shot down during September, but survived. He returned to the Solomons late in 1943 after the unit had been re-equipped with F4U Corsairs, and added two further victories to his total by the end of the year.

Even before Carl ended his first tour on Guadalcanal, his score had been overtaken by his commanding officer, Lt Col John L Smith, an older career officer of considerable experience. Claiming his first Zero on 21 August 1942, he had brought his score to 19 when he brought down an A6M 'Rufe' floatplane fighter on 10 October, less than two months later. This score included four Zeros on 29 August, and two in a day on four other occasions. When he left the island on 13 October he was the top-scoring ace of all US services, and was subsequently awarded the Congressional Medal of Honor.

Just as Smith departed, another Marine, Major Joseph J Foss claimed his first victory over the island with VMF-121. Foss had experienced difficulty in getting assigned to combat duty, as he had been considered too old at 27, and had been retained in America as an instructor. A superb marksman, he was able to get the very best out of the slow but rugged Wildcat, and although brought down sometimes himself, he was soon scoring in multiples, claiming three on 18 October and four on the 23rd. Two days later he claimed five Zeros in a day, following this with three floatplanes on 7 November and two bombers and a Zero on 12th. With his score at 23, having taken over the lead from Smith, he then suffered a severe bout of malaria, and was sent to Australia to recuperate. On return he claimed three Zeros on 15 January 1943 to bring his score to 26 – the first American to equal Eddie Rickenbacker's World War I score. Returned home, he was awarded the Congressional Medal of Honor, but like Smith and other recipients of this award, was not allowed to return to combat.

While the Marines bore much of the early weight of aerial combat over the Solomons, US carriers fought several fierce battles around the islands with their Japanese opposite numbers. During the Battle of Santa Cruz on 26 October 1942, Squadron VF-10 aboard USS *Enterprise* was heavily involved, and one pilot particularly shone. Lt Stanley W 'Swede' Vejtasa had been an SBD Dauntless dive-bomber pilot, and had claimed three Zeros shot down in one of these during the Coral Sea Battle on 8 May. Now a fighter pilot flying F4Fs, he claimed seven aircraft shot down during attacks on the carrier – all in one sortie; these were two Aichi D3A 'Val' dive-bombers and five Nakajima B5N 'Kate' torpedo-bombers. Later in the battle, on 13 November, he shot down a four-engined flying boat to raise his score to 11.

Gradually the Marines got the edge, and on the ground Guadalcanal was secured. Other islands up the chain were then invaded, providing airfields which allowed regular raids on Rabaul to be launched. As more Marine, USAAF, Navy and RNZAF units reached the area, and more modern fighters became available, Japanese reinforcements were fed down to Rabaul in increasing numbers – including the 'crack' air groups from several of the surviving carriers. While many Japanese pilots did well here, so too did the Americans, and by the end of February 1944 the IJNAF air units had been forced to abandon New Britain to its fate.

The arrival of the excellent Vought F4U Corsair fighter during this offensive phase provided the Marines with an effective antidote to the Zero. The first great Corsair ace was Capt

Left: US Navy top scorer of 1942–43 was Lt Stanley 'Swede' Vejtasa who flew F4Fs with VF 10 on the carrier USS 'Enterprise'. He is seen here after claiming eight aircraft during the Battle of Santa Cruz — seven of them in one day.
Below left: Listed as the US Marine Corps' top scorer, although six of his 28 victories were in fact claimed with the AVG in Burma earlier in the war, Maj Gregory 'Pappy' Boyington of VMF 214 'Black Sheep' is seen here in his F4U Corsair.
Right: Lt Robert M Hanson claimed more victories flying the Corsair than any other pilot – 25. 20 of these were claimed in just 17 days before his death in action.

Kenneth A Walsh, who had served with VMF-221 on Guadalcanal with Wildcats, claiming two Zeros and a 'Val' dive-bomber on 1 April 1943 when his flight commander, 'Zeke' Swett, was credited with shooting down seven 'Vals' in a single sortie. Posted to VMF-124 the following month to fly some of the first Corsairs in the Solomons, he claimed three Zeros on 13 May, one and two 'Vals' on 15 August, and four Zeros on 30 August, which with other single and double victories brought his total to 20 – 17 with the new aircraft. He later gained one more victory in June 1945 when commanding VMF-223 on Okinawa.

In September VMF-214 entered action, led by 31 year old Maj Gregory 'Pappy' Boyington, who had already flown one uneventful tour over the islands with VMF-121 on Wildcats. Earlier Boyington had served in Burma with the AVG, where he was credited with six victories (although it is believed that some of these were shared). Now with the Corsair, he claimed five Zero fighters on his first combat on 16 September, twice claiming three in a day during October 1943. On 23 December he claimed another four, while one on the 27th brought his score to 25 – only one behind Foss's record. During a sweep on 3 January 1944 he and his wingman were shot down, and he was believed killed, being awarded a posthumous Medal of Honor. In fact he had been picked up from the sea by a Japanese submarine and made prisoner. He returned after the war, reporting that in his final combat he had brought down three more Zeros to raise his total to 28, making him the Marines' top ace -- although only 22 of his voctories were claimed with their units.

Even more meteoric was the rise of 1st Lt Robert M Hanson. 'Butcher Bob' first served with VMF-214, gaining his first two victories during August 1943. Transferring to VMF-215, he shot down two Zeros and a 'Kate' over Bougainville on 1 November, but was shot down himself, returning safely four days later. During the unit's next tour he was to claim 20 victories between 14 and 30 January 1944. On his first sortie over Rabaul on 14 January he claimed five Zeros, claiming one more fighter on the 19th, three on the 22nd, four on the 25th, three on the 26th and four on the 30th. On 3 February, exactly a month after Boyington's loss, his Corsair was hit by flak. His wingtip caught the water as he attempted to ditch and the aircraft cartwheeled and crashing. He too was awarded a posthumous Medal of Honor.

While many other Marines became aces over the Solomons, the last high scorer was Capt Donald N Aldrich, also of VMF-215. Aldrich claimed five Zeros during August and September 1943, and then 12 more during January 1944, four of them in one day on 28th. He added two more on 6 February and an Army fighter on the 9th to raise his score to 20. The Marines were joined by a Navy Corsair squadron, VF-17, which had in fact been the first unit to equip with the aircraft. Flying over the Solomons between November 1943 and February 1944, the squadron claimed 154 Japanese aircraft shot down in 79 days, producing no less than 13 aces. Most successful was Lt Ira C Kepford; 'Ike' claimed three 'Vals' and a 'Kate' on his first combat on 11 November, and added eight fighters during January 1944, four of them on the 29th. Four more victories in February, including three on the 19th, brought his total to 16, making him the USN's top-scorer at the time.

USAAF units in the Solomons finally got P-38s, and a fair number of pilots of the two fighter groups serving with the Thirteenth Air Force here became aces, flying alongside the Marines. Their top-scorer was Lt Col Robert B Westbrook of the 18th Fighter Group's 44th Squadron. Initially flying P-40 Warhawks, Bob Westbrook claimed seven victories between January and July 1943, adding a further eight in the period October 1943 to January 1944, after conversion to P-38s. He later flew over the Philippines during late 1944, claiming five Nakajima Ki 43 'Oscars,' three of them on 23 October, to raise his score to 20. He was shot down and killed by ground fire on 22 November 1944.

RNZAF Warhawk units flying in the Solomons added 99 victories to the Allied totals. While several aces from Europe added further victories here, two pilots became aces in the Solomons. The leader was Flg Off GB Fisken of 15 Squadron, who had already claimed six over Singapore, as mentioned earlier. Now he claimed two Zeros on 12 June 1943, plus two more and a Mitsubishi G4M 'Betty' bomber on 4 July to raise his total to 11 – the highest score against

137

Main picture: Early in 1944 a new Navy No 1 appeared; this was Lt Ira 'Ike' Kepford of VF 17 'Jolly Rogers', a unit which flew land-based in the Solomons. Kepford is seen here in his F4U-1A Corsair just before his 17th and final victory.

Inset: Flg Off GB Fisken of 15 Squadron, RNZAF, with his P-40 Warhawk, 'Wairairapa Wildcat'. With six victories over Singapore flying the obsolescent Buffalo, and then five in the Solomons, Fisken was Commonwealth top scorer against the Japanese.

Above left: First Thunder-bolt ace in the Pacific, and quickly one of the Fifth Air Force's top scorers with 22 victories before his death in combat on 5 March 1944, was Col Neel Kearby, commander of the 348th Fighter Group.

Above: Texan Maj Jay T Robbins (22 victories) of the 8th Fighter Group, Fifth Air Force, with his P-38 Lightning.

the Japanese claimed by any pilot of the British Commonwealth air forces.

Apart from those Japanese pilots already mentioned, among the most successful over the Solomons were: Warrant Officer Kazuo Sugino (32 victories) of the 253rd Ku, who also served on *Shokaku*, and over the Philippines and Formosa; Wt Off Shizuo Ishii (29) of the 204th Ku, who claimed at last 24 (five shared) here, 17 of them in two weeks in October 1943, but was killed over Rabaul on 24 October; and Ensign Nobuo Ogiya, who gained 24 in eight weeks, including five on 20 January 1944, but was lost on 13 February.

Meanwhile over New Guinea the picture had changed completely. The first P-38s had come into action late in 1942, both Tommy Lynch and Lt Richard I Bong of the 49th Fighter Group claiming two victories with these aircraft on 27 December. Thereafter scores rose swiftly, and by the end of July Bong's score stood at 16, George Welsh equalling this total at the start of September, and Lynch by mid-September. General George Kenney, commander of the US Fifth Air Force, gave his fighter pilots every encouragement to score, and something of a race developed. Welsh returned to the States with his score at 16; Bong added five more victories during the latter part of 1943, while three in early 1944 raised his score to 24. Lynch too gained further success during the early weeks of 1944, raising his score to 20 by 5 March. Four days later he and Bong were out together, both now being attached to 5th Fighter Command Headquarters, but while straffing a small ship, Lynch's P-38 was hit by return fire and exploded as he attempted to bale out.

Only five days earlier another leading ace, who had suddenly joined the leaders, had also been killed. Col Neel E Kearby arrived in New Guinea at the head of the 348th Fighter Group

in June 1943, equipped with the first P-47 Thunderbolts to see action in the Pacific Theater. Kenney considered the P-47 of little use, but Kearby was soon to prove him wrong, for the 348th was to be a very successful unit, and its commander the greatest exponent. His first two victories came on 4 September, while on 11 October he shot down six fighters in a single combat during an attack on 33 bombers and 12 escorting fighters. For this he was awarded the USAAF's first fighter pilot Congressional Medal of Honor. By mid-October Kearby's score stood at 12, and he too was attached to Fifth Fighter Command. He added three more on 3 December, and by 9 January 1944 had raised his total to 20. On 5 March he headed for Wewak with his section, attacking 15 fighters here and shooting down two. However a third got on his tail, and he went to his death in flames.

Following the deaths of Lynch and Kearby, Bong claimed four more victories during April 1944 to bring his score to 27, making him first to pass Rickenbacker and Foss (officially), and he was sent home. While away a probable was confirmed, raising his total to 28 — which had by then been equalled by the Eighth Air Force's Bob Johnson, who was also back in the States. In Bong's absence new stars had continued to rise, the leading one being Maj Jay T Robbins of the 8th Fighter Group. Arriving early in 1943, Robbins soon proved to be a prolific scorer, claiming three Zeros during his first combat on 21 July, and four more on 4 September. Another four followed on 24 October, and when he claimed two on 16 June 1944 his score had risen to 20. On this same date another P-38 pilot, Maj Thomas B McGuire, who was flying with the new 475th Fighter Group, also claimed two, and also brought his score to 20. He gained one more in July 1944, while Robbins added one in August, but then during October McGuire

Above: A group of outstanding American fighter pilots celebrate the 500th victory of the 49th Fighter Group over the Philippines on 2 November 1944. Left to right: Lt Col George Walker, Group Commander; Col Bob Morrisey; Lt Col Gerald Johnson (24 victories); 1/Lt Milton Mathre (5) – he claimed the 500th victory; Maj Wally Jordan (6); Maj Dick Bong (40); Maj Tommy McGuire (38); Capt Robert DeHaven (14). Above right: USAAF No 3 ace in the Pacific was Col Charles H MacDonald, commander of the 475th Fighter Group, with 27 victories.

claimed three more on 14th over the Philippines, adding another five during the first 12 days of November. Robbins' 22nd and last claim was made here on 14 November 1944; he then returned to the US, his tour expired.

By now Bong was back, and he too was active over the Philippines, October and early November having brought his score to 36 – eight ahead of McGuire. Both pilots added two more victories on 7 December, while Bong claimed two more by the 17th to raise his total to 40. McGuire continued to be successful, adding three more Zeros to his total on Christmas Day and four on 26 December to raise his score to 38. Kenney then grounded him so that Bong could reach the States, where he had now been sent again, as No 1. Allowed to fly again on 7 January 1945, McGuire spun and crashed to his death during a dogfight on this date.

Two other Fifth Air Force P-38 pilots were also notable. Col Charles H MacDonald, commander of the 475th Fighter Group was active throughout, claiming his first two victories on 15 October 1943, and his 27th on 13 February 1945. He claimed two in a day on six occasions, and twice got three. In the same period Lt Col Gerald R Johnson of the 49th Fighter Group claimed 22, his first two on 26 July 1943 and his last on 2 April 1945. He claimed three on 15 October 1943, but his best day was 7 December 1944, when he was credited with four.

In the conditions prevailing over New Guinea from 1943 onward, the pilots of the JAAF enjoyed less opportunities for success than did their Naval counterparts over the Solomons. They did however have their successes, and several stood out. Lt Shogo Takeuchi flew over Malaya and Burma with the 64th Sentai, claiming three over Singapore on 31 January 1942, but then returned to Japan at the start of April. In December 1942 he joined the 68th Sentai in New

Guinea, flying Kawasaki Ki 61 'Tony' fighters, gaining the first B-24 to be credited to aircraft of this type on 20 July 1943. When he was killed in a flying accident on 21 December 1943 he had been credited with 16 victories in 90 sorties with the 68th Sentai, to bring his score to at least 19.

Wt Off Kazuo Shimizu flew Ki 43s ('Oscars') with the 59th Sentai. On 14 February 1944 he claimed three B-25s by aerial bombing, claiming two P-47s by the same method next day. He later flew on home defense and over Okinawa, his score being 18. Wt Off Mitsuo Ogura had flown over the Philippines and China with the 24th Sentai before this unit moved to New Guinea in May 1943. Here he claimed two in a day on at least two occasions, gaining most of his 16 victories by November 1943 when the Sentai withdrew. He later flew over Biak, the Philippines and Okinawa. Capt Shigeo Nango, brother of a Navy fighter ace, Mochifumi Nango, led a flight of the 59th Sentai in the Southwest Pacific and New Guinea from March 1942 until killed in action over Wewak on 23 January 1944; he was credited with 15 victories.

While Japanese Army pilots were not to have the opportunities during the Pacific War to build up scores of the magnitude of those of the Navy, it was over Burma and China that they achieved most success. Army top-scorer by a wide margin was Sgt Satoshi Anabuki (51 victories), who flew Ki 43s over Burma with the 50th Sentai; from June 1942 to October 1943 he claimed 41 victories, later serving on home defense. In the same unit with him, Sgt Isamu Sasaki claimed 32 victories, later adding six B-29s over the homeland. Wt Off Yojiro Ohbusa was credited with 19 victories between January 1943 and the end of the war, including five P-51s, four Hurricanes, two P-47s and a Spitfire; he force-landed himself four times. Master Sgt Yukio Shimokawa claimed 16 victories, and

Master Sgt Kisaku Igarashi 15, the latter claiming 12 fighters plus four probables, and three C-47s shot down, but was killed over Imphal on 17 January 1944.

Another very successful fighter Sentai in Burma was the 64th. The top-scoring pilot of this unit was Lt Goichi Sumino, who claimed 27 before he was shot down and killed by a P-38 on 6 June 1944. Some 25 of these had been claimed between March 1943 and February 1944, when he celebrated his 21st birthday. Commander of the Sentai for part of its time in Burma was Maj Yasuhiko Kuroe. He had claimed two victories in Mongolia in 1939, then flown over Malaya at the start of the war at the head of an experimental flight of Nakajima Ki 44 ('Tojo') fighters, claiming three more. Serving with the 64th from April 1942 until January 1944, he claimed over 20 victories with the unit, including two P-51As, a B-24 and two Mosquitos during November and December 1943. Returning to Japan he served as a test pilot, flying an experimental Kawasaki Ki 102A ('Randy') twin-engined fighter against the B-29s late in the war. He claimed one of these bombers on 25 March 1945 and two more in May, ending the war with a score of 30. Lt Saburo Nakamura of the 64th Sentai was killed on 6 October 1944 by return fire from a formation of B-25s, one of which he had just shot down. He had claimed 20 air and ground victories over Burma since May 1942.

Allied pilots had relatively few chances to build up big scores in Burma due to the fairly small numbers of Japanese aircraft encountered, and to initial poor equipment. The area was largely – though by no means entirely – an RAF preserve. During the initial fighting of 1942 the most successful pilots were Wg Cdr FR Carey, Flg Off WJ Storey, an Australian of 135 Squadron, and Sgt JF 'Tex' Barrick, an American with 17 Squadron, each of whom claimed five victories while flying Hurricanes. Bill Storey later became a flight commander, claiming three more victories – all Ki 43s – on 5 March 1943. Frank Carey had flown in France and the Battle of Britain during 1940, where he had been credited with 18 victories, four or five of which were shared. He arrived in Burma as commander of 135 Squadron, but was promoted to lead all the RAF fighters, and on 26 February 1942 claimed three Ki 43s in one day. It is believed that he obtained a few more victories in 1943, but his total against the Japanese is uncertain.

Later in the campaign a few other aces appeared, the most successful of whom served with 136 Squadron, the RAF's top-scoring unit against the Japanese. They flew Hurricanes until late 1943, and then Spitfires. Flt Sgt RWG Cross became the RAF's top-scorer against the Japanese with nine victories, while Flt Lt AC Conway claimed seven and two probables. An unusual case was that of Wg Cdr PE Meagher, commander of 211 Squadron flying Beaufighters during 1944. Previously a fighter pilot, he had gained

four victories flying from England. In Burma between February and May 1944, he claimed six victories in the air – including three Ki 43s on 28 April, two of which collided in a dogfight with him – and also claimed two more destroyed on the ground.

The most successful USAAF pilots over Burma were Capt Walter F Duke of the P-38-equipped 459th Squadron, who claimed 10 air and 8½ ground victories between December 1943 and May 1944, and Maj James J England who flew P-51As with the 311th Fighter-Bomber Group, claiming eight victories in four missions from November 1943 to May 1944. Duke was killed in combat on 6 June 1944 when going to the aid of his wingman, while England later added two more victories to his score in China, where the unit moved late in the year.

Over China the leading American unit was the 23rd Fighter Group, its first great ace being Col Robert L Scott, who had claimed 13 victories by the end of 1942. He was overtaken by Capt John F Hampshire, who twice claimed three victories in one day during the period October 1942 to April 1943. His last two victories on 2 May raised his score to 14, but during that combat he was shot down and later died of his wounds. Top-scorer of the group was Col John C 'Pappy' Herbst, who had earlier been a pilot with the RCAF, claiming one victory against the Germans. Aged 35 when he arrived in China, he first claimed on 17 June 1944, raising his score to 18 with the unit by the end of January 1945. Most of his successes were gained flying a P-51.

Two successful members of the AVG who had stayed with the USAAF, both ended the war with scores of over 18. Col David L 'Tex' Hill was the second-highest-scoring 'Flying Tiger,' with 12¼, adding four more during the second half of 1942 with the 23rd Fighter Group. He returned in late 1943 to lead the unit, making two further claims. Lt Col Charles H Older had claimed 10½ with the AVG, and he also returned to China later in the war, flying with the 23rd from mid-1944 until late in the war, gaining eight further victories. His first two claims over Burma both fell on 23 December 1941, while on Christmas Day he claimed four. His final successes occurred on 17 January 1945, when he was credited with three.

By 1944 Chinese-American Composite Wings had been formed with P-40s and later P-51s. Numerous US-trained Chinese pilots flew with these units. At least three pilots became aces with these units; Maj Kuan Tan claimed eight flying P-40s with the 32nd Provisional Squadron, Lt Col Wang Kuang-Fu claimed 6½ on P-40s and two with the P-51 in the 7th Squadron of the 3rd Fighter Group, while Capt Tsang SL, in that group's 8th Squadron claimed five, all in P-51s. A Col John Wong is reputed to have claimed 13, but little is known of him and it is suspected that this was in fact Lt Col Wang.

Most successful Japanese pilot in China was

Top: Col John 'Pappy' Herbst with his 23rd Fighter Group P-51B Mustang in China in 1944. He ended the war with 17 victories against the Japanese and 1 against the Germans.
Above left: RAF top scorer against the Japanese was Flt Sgt Bob Cross who flew Hurricanes and then Spitfires with 136 Squadron in Burma, claiming 9 victories.
Above center: The US Navy's second most successful fighter pilot of the

war, Lt Cdr Cecil E Harris who gained 24 victories in 2 tours, 1 land-based and 1 aboard a carrier.
Above right: Lt Goichi Sumino, top scorer of the 64th Sentai, who flew in Burma, claiming 27 victories here before being shot down and killed on 6 June 1944.
Top right: One of the two American top scorers in China was ex-'Flying Tiger' Col David 'Tex' Hill (18.25 victories) seen here with his 'shark-toothed' P-51 when commanding the 23rd Fighter Group in 1944.

Lt Moritsugu Kanai, who had already claimed seven over Nomonhan in 1939. Joining the 25th Sentai in China early in January 1944, he claimed 19 victories by the end of the year, his score including two B-29s, to P-51s, two P-38s and at least six P-40s. He was posted to Korea in 1945, but saw little further action. Prior to Kanai's arrival, Capt Nakakazu Ozaki had also claimed 19 victories with the 25th, including six B-24s, but he had been killed on 27 December 1943 when he rammed a US aircraft over Suichwan to save his wingman. Wt Off Eiji Seino claimed 15 victories with the same unit, as did Master Sgt Kyushiro Ohtake.

Maj Yokiyoshi Wakamatsu flew with the 85th Sentai, flying Ki 44 'Tojos' and later, Ki 84 'Franks.' A very precise long-distance shot, he achieved much success, estimated at 18 victories – all fighters – before he was shot down and killed over Hankow on 18 December 1944. Maj Toshio Sakagawa flew in Capt Kuroe's Ki 44 test unit in 1941–42, then taking command of the 25th Sentai in China. Here he shot down a lead B-24 over Hankow on 11 August 1943, and on 6 May 1944 claimed three P-51s in a single sortie. Posted home with his score at 15, he was later sent to the Philippines but was killed on the night of 19 December 1944 when the transport aircraft carrying him crashed on Los Negros Island.

It was not until late 1943 that the US Navy was really able to make its mark in air combat. Then the availability of new *Essex* Class fleet carriers and the excellent Grumman F6F Hellcat fighter allowed a number of major strikes to be made on Japanese bases on Pacific islands, either for neutralization purposes, or prior to seaborne landings. With the best of the opposition already worn down in the Solomons and New Guinea, the highly trained Navy pilots in their

splendid new aircraft gained an extraordinary level of ascendency over the Japanese. This culminated in the Marianas battles, prior to the landings on Saipan in June 1944, and the Battle of Leyte Gulf in October as the main Philippines invasion was launched. Here the re-formed units of the Japanese Navy were met in force and resoundingly beaten in some of the biggest air battles of the war. In the Marianas some 300 victories were claimed in a single day on 19 June, all for the loss of 14 Hellcats, while during October in several actions more than 700 Japanese aircraft were lost.

Ltd Cdr Alexander Vraciu flew with VF-6 on *Intrepid*, claiming nine victories during strikes in late 1943 and early 1944. Transferring to VF-16 on *Lexington*, he brought his score to 19, including six in a day over the Marianas on 19 June; he also claimed 21 destroyed on the ground. Shot down by ground fire over the Philippines in December, he led a guerrilla band on Luzon until the island was liberated. Lt Cdr Cecil Harris, who had earlier gained two victories over Rabaul, claimed 22 more with VF-18 on *Intrepid* during September and October 1944; he got four in a day on three occasions. Another ex-land-based Solomons F4F pilot, Lt Charles R Stimpson, had claimed seven in this area – including four D3A 'Val' dive bombers on 16 June 1943. With VF-11 on *Hornet* he claimed 10 more in just three days of combat in October to November 1944; this included five A6M Zeros on 14 October.

Ensign Cornelius Nooy flew with VF-31 on *Cabot*, claiming five Zeros in one sortie on 21 September – all while carrying a 500lb bomb beneath his Hellcat! He had 16 victories by the end of the year, returning for a second tour in July 1945, when he raised his total to 19. Ens Douglas Baker of *Enterprise*'s VF-20 gained 16 swift victories, most during October, but was reported missing on 14 December 1944, the only top Navy ace to be killed in action. The most outstanding by far was the highly experienced Air Group Commander of Air Group 15 on the *Essex*. Commander David McCampbell claimed seven in a day over the Marianas, and then on 24 October over the Phillipines set a new US record when he and Lt Roy Rushing (13 victories) shot down 15 Zeros between them, nine of them credited to McCampbell. By the end of the year his score stood at 34 plus 21 on the ground, for which he received the Medal of Honor.

Late in 1944 Patrick D Fleming began his first tour with VF-80 on *Ticonderoga*, later transferring to *Hancock* when the former carrier was damaged by one of the Kamikaze suicide aircraft which had begun appearing in number in October 1944. He claimed five Zeros on 16 February 1945, his final score being 19. Commander Eugene Valencia had claimed seven victories during his first tour with VF-9 on *Essex* in late 1943 and early 1944. For the unit's second tour on *Yorktown* and *Lexington*, he developed his own 'mowing-machine' tactics for his section of four, achieving great success during strikes on the Japanese home islands and

Okinawa during 1945. The tactics proved highly effective, and by 11 May Valencia had added 16 more to his score to become the navy's No 3 ace. All the other three members of his section had become aces.

From January 1945 the British Pacific Fleet moved to join the US Navy in the Pacific, making two large-scale strikes on Sumatran oilfields en route. Although not achieving the level of success of the Americans, the British-flown Corsairs, Hellcats and Seafires gained some considerable successes. One pilot, Canadian Lt DJ Sheppard of 1836 (Corsair) Squadron on HMS *Victorious*, became an ace, claiming four individual and two shared victories between 4 January and 4 May 1945.

By now Japan was under sustained attack not only by carrier aircraft, but also by B-29 Superfortress bombers, which proved extremely difficult to intercept and shoot down. Initially these flew from China, but later from bases in the Marianas and other Pacific islands. A new breed of home defense pilots now appeared, who fought here, and over Okinawa, Iwo Jima and the Philippines. One of the crack JAAF units was the 244th Sentai, led by the youngest Sentai commander, ex-bomber pilot Maj Teruhiko Kobayashi. Between December 1944 and mid-April 1945 he claimed 14 victories, 12 of them B-29s. His score had risen to over 20 by the war's end. One of his pilots, 1/Lt Chuichi Ichikawa, also claimed nine B-29s and six more damaged, plus a Hellcat. Both these Ki 61 'Tony' pilots brought down one of the big bombers by ramming. Flying the big twin-engined Kawasaki Ki 45 'Nick' fighters, Capt Isamu Kashiide of the 4th Sentai included about seven B-29s among his nine victories, which included several gained during the Nomonhan fighting of 1939. Capt Totaro Ito of the 5th Sentai, who also flew Ki 45s, claimed 13 victories, four of them B-24s over Ambon, Dutch East Indies, and nine B-29s over Japan.

Over Okinawa Sgt Maj Katsuaki Kira of the 103rd Sentai, a veteran of Nomonhan, New Guinea and the Philippines, raised his score to 21. Wt Off Bun-ichi Yamaguchi of the 204th Sentai, who had flown in Burma and the Philippines, was the only member of his unit to survive all campaigns; his score of 19 included six multi-engined types.

Among outstanding Navy pilots who flew late in the war, Ensign Shoichi Sugita served in the Solomons, at Buin, the Carolines and Marianas, and then on home defense, where he flew the new Kawanichi N1K1 'George' fighter, claiming four F6Fs and three probables in one of them on 19 March 1945. He was shot down by a Corsair and killed while taking off on 15 April, his total being estimated at around 70. Lt (jg) Kaneyoshi Muto, veteran of China and Rabaul, fought over Iwo Jima and Okinawa, and claimed four Hellcats in one sortie during February 1945. His score of 28 is believed to include four B-29s; he was shot down and killed by a P-51 over Bungo Strait on 24 July 1945. Another long-serving China veteran was Lt (jg) Sadaaki Akamatsu, who had over 6000 hours flying time on fighters over 14 years. Known as something of a swashbuckling hell-raiser, he was often in trouble with the authorities, but was a great dogfighter. His score is conservatively estimated at 27, some gained flying Mitsubishi J2M Raiden ('Jack') fighters over the Tokyo area with the 302nd Ku. Cdr Naoshi Kanno led the 343rd Ku during the later months of the war, having seen much combat over Yap against US Seventh Air Force B-24s. With a score estimated at 25, he was killed over Yakushima on 1 August 1945. Floatplane fighters – A6M-2Ns, developed from the Zero – were used throughout the war by the Japanese. The most successful pilot of these aircraft was NAP3/C Hidenori Matsunaga of the 934th Ku. He took part in nine combats when 17 and four probables were claimed over the New Guinea area – many of them RAAF Beaufighters. His total of 26 undoubtedly included many shares and probables.

After the fall of Iwo Jima, B-29 raids were escorted by P-51s flying from this island. It was one of these pilots who became the last ace of the war. Capt Abner M Aust Jr of the 506th Fighter Group claimed three Ki 84 'Franks' on 16 July and then on 10 August added two Zeros. However his camera gun failed, and the second of these was not confirmed until 15 years later, when eyewitness evidence to corroborate his claim was discovered in Japan by a relative!

TOP-SCORING PILOTS OF THE USAAF IN THE PACIFIC THEATER, 1941–45

Maj Richard I Bong*	40	35th, 49th FG	Fifth AF SW Pacific
Maj Thomas B McGuire*	38	475th FG	Fifth AF SW Pacific
Col Charles H MacDonald	27	475th FG	Fifth AF SW Pacific
Lt Col Gerald R Johnson*	22	49th FG	Fifth AF SW Pacific
Col Neel E Kearby*	22	348th FG	Fifth AF SW Pacific
Maj Jay T Robbins	22	8th FG	Fifth AF SW Pacific
Lt Col Thomas J Lynch*	20	35th FG	Fifth AF SW Pacific
Lt Col Robert B Westbrook*	20	44th, 347th FG	Thirteenth AF S Pacific
Lt Col Charles H Older	18.5	23rd FG (10.5 AVG)	Fourteenth AF CBI
Col David L Hill	18.25	23rd FG (12.25 AVG)	Fourteenth AF CBI
Maj William N Reed*	17.5	3 CACW (10.5 AVG)	Fourteenth AF CBI
Lt Col John C Herbst	17	23rd FG (+ 1 Europe)	Fourteenth AF CBI

Lt Col Bill Harris	16	339th, 18th FG	Thirteenth AF S Pacific
Sqn Ldr Robert H Neale	16	AVG	CBI
Maj George S Welch	16	8th FG (incl 4 at Pearl Harbor)	Fifth AF SW Pacific
Maj William Dunham	16	348th FG	Fifth AF SW Pacific
Maj Edward Cragg*	15	8th FG	Fifth AF SW Pacific
Maj Cyril F Homer	15	8th FG	Fifth AF SW Pacific

TOP-SCORING PILOTS OF THE BRITISH COMMONWEALTH AIR FORCES IN THE PACIFIC THEATER, 1941–45

Flg Off GB Fisken (New Zealander)	11	243 Sqn RAF, 15 Sqn RNZAF	Singapore and S Pacific
Flt Sgt RWG Cross	9	136 Sqn RAF	Burma
Gp Capt CR Caldwell (Australian)	8	1 Wg, 80 Wg RAAF	SW Pacific
Sqn Ldr WJ Storey (Australian)	8	135 Sqn RAF	Burma
Sqn Ldr AC Conway	7	136 Sqn RAF	Burma

TOP-SCORING PILOTS OF THE IMPERIAL JAPANESE ARMY AIR FORCE IN WORLD WAR II, 1941–45

M Sgt Satoshi Anabuki	51	50th Sentai
Wt Off Isamu Sasaki	38	50th Sentai
Maj Yasuhiko Kuroe	28	(+ 2 in Mongolia) 47th Chutai, 64th Sentai
Lt Goichi Sumino*	27	64th Sentai
Maj Teruhiko Kobayashi	20+	244th Sentai
Lt Saburo Nakamura*	20	(destroyed and damaged) 64th 64th Sentai
Lt Moritsugu Kanai	19	(+ 7 in Mongolia) 25th Sentai
Wt Off Yojiro Ohbusa	19	50th Sentai
Lt Col Nakakazu Ozaki*	19	33rd, 25th Sentai
Lt Shogo Takeuchi*	19+	64th, 85th Sentai
Wt Off Bun-ichi Yamaguchi	19	204th Sentai
Wt Off Kazuo Shimizu	18	59th Sentai
Lt Col Yokiyoshi Wakamatsu*	18	al 64th, 85th Sentai
Capt Keiji Takamiya*	17	78th Sentai
Lt Tameyosghi Kuroki	16	33rd Sentai
Wt Off Mitsuo Ogura	16	24th Sentai
M Sgt Yukio Shimokawa	16	50th Sentai
M Sgt Kisaku Igarashi*	15	50th Sentai
Capt Shigeo Nango*	15	33rd, 59th Sentai
M Sgt Kyushiro Ohtake	15	10th Chutai, 25th Sentai
Maj Toshio Sakagawa*	15	(possibly some in Mongolia) 25th, 200th, 22nd Sentai
Wt Off Eiji Seino	15	10th Chutai, 25th Sentai

TOP-SCORING PILOTS OF THE US NAVY IN THE PACIFIC THEATER, 1941–45

Cdr David S McCampbell	34	VF-15
Lt Cdr Cecil E Harris	24	VF-18, 27
Lt Cdr Eugene A Valencia	23	VF-9
Lt Cdr Patrick D Fleming	19	VF-80
Lt Cdr Alexander Vraciu	19	VF-6, 16, 20
Lt Cornelius N Nooy	18	VF-31
Lt Ira C Kepford	17	VF-17
Lt Charles R Stimpson	17	VF-11
Lt Douglas Baker*	16	VF-20

TOP-SCORING PILOTS OF THE US MARINE CORPS IN THE PACIFIC THEATER, 1941–45

Lt Col Gregory Boyington	28	VMF-214 (incl 6 with AVG)
Maj Joseph J Foss	26	VMF-121
Lt Robert M Hanson*	25	VMF-214, 215
Capt Kenneth A Walsh	21	VMF-124, 223
Capt Donald N Aldrich	20	VMF-215
Lt Col John L Smith	19	VMF-223
Maj Marion E Carl	18.5	VMF-221, 223
Capt Wilbur J Thomas	18.5	VMF-213
Maj James E Swett	16.5	VMF-221
Capt Harold L Spears*	15	VMF-2.5

TOP-SCORING CHINESE PILOTS OF 1944–45 PERIOD

(all members of Chinese-American Wings)
Lt Col Wang Kuang-Fu	8.5
Maj Kuan Tan	8
Capt Tsang S-L	5

TOP-SCORING PILOTS OF THE IMPERIAL JAPANESE NAVY AIR FORCE IN WORLD WAR II, 1941–45

Wt Off Hiroyoshi Nishizawa*	87	4th, Tainan, 251st, 253rd, 203rd Ku
Lt (jg) Tatsuzo Iwamoto	80	(+ 14 in China) Zuikaku, 281st, 204th, 253rd, 252nd, 203rd Ku
Pty Off 1 Shoichi Sugita*	70	6th, 263rd, 201st, 343rd Ku
Lt (jg) Saburo Sakai	62	(+ 2 in China) Tainan, Yokosuka Ku
Pty Off 1 Takeo Okumura*	50	(+ 4 in China) Ryujo, Tainan, 201st Ku
Pty Off 1 Toshio Ohta*	34	Tainan Ku
Wt Off Kazuo Sugino	32	611th, Shokaku, 253rd, 634th Ku

Lt·(jg) Junichi Sasai*	27	Tainan Ku
Pty Off 1 Shizuo Ishii*	26	(+ 3 in China) Tainan, *Junyo*, 204th Ku
Lt Naoshi Kanno*	25	343rd, 201st Ku
Wt Off Nobuo Ogiya*	24	281st, 204th, 253rd Ku
Ens Kaneyoshi Muto*	23	(+ 5 in China) 3rd, Genzan, 252nd, Yokosuka, 343rd, Ku
Lt (jg) Shigeo Sugio	20+	3rd, Kuiko, Kaminoike, 201st Ku
Wt Off Tetsuo Kikuchi	20+	*Akagi, Shokaku, Ryuho, Hiyo, Junyo,*, 652nd Ku
Wt Off Kiichi Nagano*	19	2nd, 203rd Ku
Wt Off Hiroshi Okano	19	1st, Tainan, 201st, 331st, 202nd, 343rd Ku
NAP 2/C Kazushi Uto*	19	Tainan Ku
NAP 1/C Masajiro Kawato	18	253rd Ku
Wt Off Sadamu Komachi	18	*Shokaku*, 204th, 253rd Ku
Ens Saburo Saito	18	*Zuikaku*, 252nd Ku (included 6 shared and probables)
Wt Off Takeo Tanimizu	18	6th, Kasugamaru, *Shokaku*, 203rd Ku
Ens Minoru Handa	17	Kanoya, 253rd, 221st, 343rd Ku
Wt Off Kiyoshi Ito	17	3rd, 202nd Ku
Wt Off Masao Masuyama	17	3rd Ku
Lt (jg) Akio Matsuba	17	(+ 1 in China) 301st, 341st, 343rd Ku

[*indicates killed in action or in a flying accident during the war years]
Many Japanese scores quoted are approximate only, or may include shared
or probable victories.

The Night Fighters

World War I had seen an initial attempt at night fighting — mainly by the British forces. These early attempts were rudimentary, but had been fairly highly developed by the end of 1918, although the reliance on the aid of searchlights or moonlight was total. By 1939 there had been few developments generally, although the introduction of radar had advanced the art considerably by providing positive information on the approach of raiders, to which the patrolling fighter could be directed by radio telephone. The defense-conscious British were thus better prepared for night bombing attacks on their territory than were the Germans — or for that matter, the French. For some years a number of squadrons had been earmarked for night fighting, and these were presently equipped with fighter conversions of the Blenheim I light bomber. The Germans had given much less thought to defense, relying mainly on their flak artillery, and apart from a few experimental 'twilight' Staffeln, there was no night-fighter defense available.

The science of night fighting was a very different one to that of fighter combat generally. It was very much an individual adventure — one fighter against one bomber. The tactics were those of the deerstalker rather than the dogfighter. Coolness and patience were the ideal characteristics of the pilot; speed, endurance and firepower those of his aircraft, these features having priority over maneuverability.

At first, as neither side did more than drop leaflets on each other, there was little call for the interception of night intruders. However once the German invasions of Norway in April and of France and the Low Countries in May 1940

took place, bombing started in earnest. Already aware that its bombers could not live over Germany by day without fighter escort, the RAF dispatched its aircraft by night from the start. Meanwhile the Germans had also begun night attacks over the British Isles, and as 1940 wore on, these increased in frequency and intensity. Already the British were struggling to develop airborne radar, but the initial interceptions were made by the Blenheims — slow and underarmed — and by day fighters flown by night. In these conditions New Zealander Flg Off MJ Herrick of 25 Squadron was first to shine, claiming two bombers in a single night (4/5 September) and adding another nine nights later. A few Blenheims carried experimental radar sets, which proved very temperamental initially, but the first really effective night fighter began to appear in small numbers late in 1940. Fitted to carry radar from the start, the Bristol Beaufighter was fast and had a powerful armament; it was to prove more than a match for all the standard

Three leading RAF night fighters; left to right: Sqn Ldr WP Green (14 aircraft and 12 V-1s shot down); Wg Cdr John Cunningham (20 victories); Sqn Ldr ED Crew (15 aircraft and 31½ V-1s).

Helmut Lent – first to 100 at night

Helmut Lent saw action during the Polish Campaign in September 1939 as a pilot of a Messerschmitt Bf 110 Zerstörer, claiming one PZL fighter shot down here on the second day of the war. In December of that year he shot down two RAF Wellington bombers over the Heligoland Bight, and then in April 1940 took part in the invasion of Norway, where he was to claim victories over three Gladiator fighters – one Norwegian and two RAF. In January 1941 his unit, I/ZA 76, formed part of the basis of the new night-fighter unit, II/NJG 1, and he commanded 6 Staffel therein. At first success eluded him, but after 35 sorties he finally managed to shoot down two Wellingtons during the night of 11/12 May 1941. Successes now followed fast, and by the end of the year he had claimed 18 more bombers, including his first two four-engined types – Stirlings on the night of 29/30 June; he had also been awarded the Knights' Cross at the end of August. The year 1942 brought 29 more victories – mainly Wellingtons, Hampdens and Whitleys, but also two Manchesters and a Ventura. Later in the year he scored his first four Halifaxes and a Lancaster. The first success of 1943, a Halifax on 18 January, brought his score at night to 50 – the first pilot to reach this total. Meanwhile he had become Kommandeur of the newly formed II/NJG 2 late in 1941, this unit being redesignated IV/NJG 1 in October 1942. June 1942 had brought an additional honor in the form of the Oak Leaves to his Knights' Cross.

By the end of July 1943 his total had risen to 65, and now included his first Mosquito. Early in August he was to be awarded the Swords to his decoration, and promoted to Kommodore of NJG 3. His total reached 100 during the night of 15/16 June 1944 when he shot down three Lancasters, and by the end of July had reached 100 purely at night – the first night fighter to achieve such a score. Now an Oberstleutnant, he was awarded the Diamonds – the first night fighter to be so honored. His final score was to reach 110 – eight by day and 102 by night. However, on 5 October 1944 while landing in daylight at Paderborn, he suffered an engine failure, his aircraft touched a high-tension cable, and he crashed. Critically injured, he died two days later; his crew of three all died in the crash.

No 1 Night Fighter of the World

Heinz Schnaufer joined II/NJG 1 in early 1942 at the age of 20. His first victory came on 2 June of that year, and by August 1943 when he was promoted to command 9 Staffel of IV/BJG 1, his score had reached 22. In the next four months he claimed 14 more victories with this unit, all but one of them four-engined types, and then on 16 December in conditions of low cloud and generally bad weather, shot down four Lancasters in a single night. A further pair on the 29th brought his total to 42, and he was awarded the Knights' Cross. During early 1944 he added nine more Lancasters, twice claiming three in a night, to join the elite ranks of those with over 50 victories at night. This was followed by a run of success in the finer spring weather, with nine more Lancasters during April – four on the night of the 27th – and then nine Lancasters and four Halifaxes in May, including three Halifaxes on the 13th and five Lancasters during the night of the 24/25th. Now Kommandeur of IV/NJG 1, he received the Oak Leaves when his score had reached 84, followed very shortly afterward by the Swords. On 9 October 1944 came his 100th victory – only the second pilot to achieve this total at night – and he was awarded the then supreme award – the Diamonds. By the end of the year his total had reached 106, passing Lent to make him the number one night fighter; further promotion had made him Kommodore of NJG 4 in November.

Yet his greatest night was yet to come. In the early hours of 21 February 1945 he brought down two Lancasters, while some hours later in the evening of that same day he claimed seven more in just 17 minutes! When the war ended his score had reached 121. Subsequently his Bf 110 was put on display in Hyde Park, London, and to this day one rudder, marked with the dates of all his victories, is in the collection of the Imperial War Museum. Schnaufer himself did not long survive the war; he was killed in a motoring accident in France in 1950.

Luftwaffe bombers facing it. One of the first went to 604 'County of Middlesex' Squadron of the Auxiliary Air Force, where it was flown by Sqn Ldr John Cunningham, who claimed his first victory in one of these during the night of 19 November 1940 over a Ju 88. By the end of the year he had claimed three bombers, and as the Blitz reached its height over London during the spring of 1941, he achieved great success. He claimed six Heinkel He 111 bombers destroyed and one probable during April, and four more in May; three of these were claimed in one night, 15 April. Radar, the Beaufighter, and an excellent radar operator with whom he developed co-operation to the full, were Cunningham's main aids. However he became a national hero during the Blitz, his success being attributed in the press to his phenomenal eyesight – radar was still secret!

While the Beaufighter was clearly the answer to the bombers, initially it was only available in small quantities, and while the Blenheims soldiered on until sufficient Beaufighters could be built to replace them, several day-fighter units converted permanently to the night role. First were the unsuccessful Defiant squadrons, their two-seater configuration giving them some chance of success. Indeed in 264 Squadron Plt Off FD Hughes and his gunner claimed three victories at night between October 1940 and April 1941, to add to two earlier day successes. Hurricanes were also pressed into service temporarily – without much success in the defensive role – but some Hurricane units converted to the American-built Douglas Havoc attack bomber. This fast aircraft could carry radar and a good gun armament, and while the USAAF was subsequently to have no real success with its own conversion, the P-70, the RAF was more fortunate. In 85 Squadron particularly, the Canadian commanding officer, Wg Cdr GL Raphael, an ex-bomber pilot, claimed four of his seven victories with this aircraft during 1941.

While most early night fighting was of necessity defensive, there developed a second, totally different form – intruding. This required fighters to infiltrate the area of the enemy's air-fields, hunting his bombers and other aircraft as they took off and landed. At first radar-equipped aircraft could not be spared for this work. Havocs without radar and Hurricanes – particularly the latter – being employed. During 1941 one pilot particularly came to the fore in this role, Flt Lt RP Stevens. He was already in his thirties when war broke out, a very experienced commercial pilot with 400 hours night-flying experience on the London–Paris route. Reportedly his wife and children had been killed in one of the early attacks on Manchester, and certainly he flew with total abandon as he hunted the bombers both in the anti-aircraft bursts over England, and over the Continent. He began with two victories – a Do 17 and an He 111 during the night of 15/16 January 1941 – adding two more He 111s

on 8 April, an He 111 and a Ju 88 on 10 April and another He 111 on 19 April. By late 1941 his score stood at 14, only one less than Cunningham, but on 15 December, having been posted from 151 Squadron to 253 Squadron, he failed to return from an intruder sortie.

By early 1942, when he was rested, Cunningham's score stood at 16, although one of these had been brought down by day, during conditions of 10/10ths cloud, rather than by night. While several other pilots were doing well, only Stevens had approached his total. However one pilot, JRD 'Bob' Braham of 29 Squadron, was gradually closing the gap. After one Blenheim victory in August 1940, Braham had claimed six more with the Beaufighter during 1941. Rested early in 1942, he shot down one Do 217 while on an instructing sortie with 51 Night Fighter OTU, and then returned to 29 Squadron as a flight commander. He claimed four further victories by the end of October 1942 although, like Cunningham, one of these successes was gained by day in conditions of bad weather.

While the first night-fighter version of the Mosquito began to come into service during 1942, the level of Luftwaffe attack was generally much reduced due to the call of other theaters of action. The intruders still found some prey, the Hurricanes of 1 Squadron gaining particular success at this time. The commanding officer, a one-armed veteran of Malta, Sqn Ldr JAF MacLachlan, who already had eight victories to his credit over the island, two of them by night, was to claim five German bombers shot down in three nights during the Spring of 1942, while one of his pilots – a Czech, Flg Off Karel Kuttelwascher – claimed 15 and four probables between 1 April and 2 July, including three He 111s on 14 May and two in a night on four occasions.

However by now radar-equipped Beaufighters had reached the Middle East, serving first in Egypt and then on the beleagured island of Malta. No 89 Squadron was the first to arrive, Canadian Flg Off RC 'Moose' Fumerton claiming three over the Suez area early in the year, and then six during June and July while on a detachment to Malta. He subsequently claimed two more in Egypt, and destroyed one bomber on the ground during an intruding attack, to raise his total – including one in England in 1941 – to 12 in the air, equal at that stage to Braham. With the same unit, Flg Off NE Reeves also claimed seven during the summer 1942, five of them over Malta.

While the German bomber offensive had been shrinking, that mounted by Bomber Command against Germany had been growing rapidly. First attempts at night fighting were made by Bf 110 Zerstörer pilots of ZG 1 based in Denmark during May 1940 and the first success was achieved against a Whitley bomber during the night of 20 July by Oblt Werner Streib. By this time the first unit, I/NJG 1, had been formed from elements of ZG 1, although a few earlier victories

Above: Sqn Ldr JAF MacLachlan, one-armed veteran of the defence of Malta, gained five victories in three nights as an intruder pilot flying this Hurricane IIC with 1 Squadron, RAF.
Right: Karel Kuttelwascher was the RAF's most successful night intruder pilot, with 15 victories in three months. His total of 18 victories also made him his native Czechoslovakia's top scorer of the war.

had been claimed by the Bf 109 pilots of the original 'twilight' units. I/NJG 1 was soon followed by two further Grüppen — mainly drawn from Zerstörer units — and in September I/NJG 2 was formed with Ju 88 and Do 17 night-fighter conversions, for the Fernenachtjagd role — long-range intruding, in which the Luftwaffe saw immediate promise. Streib remained the doyen of the night fighters during the early period, and during the night of 30 September 1940 shot down two Wellingtons and a Hampden in a 40-minute period. He received the first night-fighter Knights' Cross in October, his score by the end of the year standing at nine, all but one by night.

No efforts had yet been made to develop airborne radar for the Luftwaffe, but during 1941 a complex system of night-fighter 'boxes' was developed whereby one fighter in a zone was controlled by two ground radars — one to track the bomber and one the fighter, a controller bringing the two together. With the number of bombers now appearing, all of them flying individually to their target rather than in any stream of formation, many interceptions were made, and by the end of 1941 three pilots already had 20 or more victories, Streib still being in the lead with 22.

The Fernenachtjäger of I/NJG 2 had also enjoyed good hunting over England during the year, these activities bringing forth four pilots with double-figure scores — Wilhelm Beir (14), Hans Hahn (12), Alfons Köster (11) and Hermann Sommer (10), while three more, including Paul Semrau, each had nine. By the end of the year, however, the increasing number of raids on Germany caused Adolf Hitler to order these attacks to be ceased, all night fighting to take place over the mainland where the population could see the results wrecked on the ground. In any event I/NJG 2 was sent to the Mediterranean at this point to undertake the standard night-fighter role, and here it remained until mid-1943. Here four pilots achieved results over Africa, Sicily and Italy; Heinz Rokker being credited with six, while the Gruppe's existing Experten added further to their successes — Sommer and Semrau five each, Köster four.

While 1941 had seen the appearance of the first four-engined bombers over Europe, 1942 was to see the first 1000-bomber raids, and a growing reliance on sophisticated radio and radar aids for navigation, while later in the year the development of the bomber 'stream' whereby all aircraft on a raid passed over one point in a limited period, played havoc with the Luftwaffe's carefully developed night-fighter system. Late in the year the first 'Lichenstein' airborne radar was to be introduced to some of the German units in very small quantities, but increasingly the war was becoming one of electronic measures and countermeasures, first one side gaining the advantage and then the other. Scores doubled during the year, Helmut Lent taking the lead with a total of 49 by the end of the year, two others having 40 and another four scores over 35; Streib's total now stood at 37.

A new star in the growing night-fighter force was an aristocratic young ex-bomber pilot, Heinrich Prinz zu Sayn-Wittgenstein, who achieved 25 victories in his first three months with III/NJG 2, but then departed at the end of the year for IV/NJG 5 in Russia. On 8 January 1943 Lent became the first to achieve 50 night victories, retaining his lead throughout the year to raise his total to 76 — seven other pilots having by then also topped 50. Werner Streib, having made the first operational tests of the 'Lichtenstein' radar in 1942, tested a preproduction version of the new Heinkel He 219 fighter during the night of 11/12 June 1943. He shot down five Lancasters with this in a single sortie, although he crashed on landing and wrote the aircraft off. By July his score stood at 66, and he then ceased operational flying to become Inspector of Night Fighters. After a brief but highly successful foray in Russia, zu Sayn-Wittgenstein was back in the West with NJG 3 by July, being second only to Lent with 68 victories by the end of the year. He now flew one of the growing number of Ju 88 night fighters. As experience had grown, so too had the number of multiple 'kills'; only once in 1942 had a pilot claimed five in one night, but during 1943 such successes were to be gained on 10 occasions. Hpt Wilhelm Herget of I/NJG 4 set a new record when he claimed eight during the night of 20/21 December.

The year had also seen Bomber Command losses nearly double, from 1390 in 1942 to 2255. Greatly alarmed by these losses, the British had developed a device for homing onto the German fighters' 'Lichtenstein' transmissions. This was first fitted to the Beaufighters of 141 Squadron, now commanded by Wg Cdr 'Bob' Braham. Operating over Europe in support of the bomber stream with this device — 'Serrate' — Braham shot down his first Bf 110 night fighter on 14 June 1943, and in the next three and a half months added six more, four of them Bf 110s. That these tactics were immediately successful can be judged by the identity of some of his victims; on 17 August he shot down Fw Heinz Vinke (54 victories) and Obfw Georg Kraft (15 victories), while on 29 September he brought down Hpt August Geiger (53 victories); all were members of NJG 1. The success of the early experiments with 141 Squadron led to the fitting of similar homing and other devices to Mosquitos in 1944 and a special bomber-support force — 100 Group — was set up. Growing numbers of Mosquitos hunted the German night fighters with increasing effectiveness during the last year of the war.

This run of successes gained by Braham and 141 Squadron had taken him into the lead as top British night fighter, with 19 night victories. During 1943 the Luftwaffe had resumed its attacks on England, the remaining Ju 88s and

Do 217s now joined by numbers of fast fighter-bombers — Fw 190s and Me 410s. Only the Mosquitos were effective against these, but the latter were now available in some numbers. No 85 Squadron was among those re-equipped, and was now commanded by Wg Cdr Cunningham, who claimed three Fw 190s during the summer of 1943 and an Me 410 on 2 January 1944 to equal Braham's score. Braham would later add nine more — but all by day, as a long-range intruder pilot.

In the Mediterranean too the RAF continued to do well by night. Several more Beaufighter squadrons were sent out during the Tunisian

Wg Cdr JRD 'Bob' Braham (right) with his radar operator, Flt Lt Gregory, and an intruder Mosquito in 1944. With 19 night and 10 day victories, Braham was one of the three most successful RAF night fighters, and was responsible for shooting down at least three leading Luftwaffe night fighter 'Experten'.

Campaign, 600 Squadron particularly doing well. FD Hughes, after service with 125 Squadron on Beaufighters, had joined 600 Squadron with his night score already at four and a half, but now between January and August 1943 he added 10 more, including three Ju 88s on 11 August over Sicily. During the night of 30 April, as the Germans sought to supply their forces in Tunisia by air, F/Sgt AB Downing, on his first successful engagement, claimed five Ju 52/3m transports shot down. He remained with the unit throughout the invasions of Sicily and Italy, claiming two He 177s and a Ju 88 over Anzio during the night of 26/27 January 1944 to bring

his total to 12. Several others did very well at this time, including Sqn Ldr CP Green, who claimed four in one night over Tunisia. However pride of place has to go to Sqn Ldr JW Allan, who led a detachment of 256 Squadron Mosquitos to Malta in July to cover the Sicily landings – the first radar-equipped versions of the aircraft to operate outside the United Kingdom. During July alone he claimed 13 victories in six nights, including a Cant Z.1007 and four Ju 88s on the 15th. He added a further Z.1007 a month later on 30 August. RAF night fighters – 600 Squadron particularly – remained effective throughout the Italian Campaigns and a substantial number of pilots became aces.

While the Mediterranean had not proved an area of outstanding success for the Luftwaffe, some considerable success was gained in Russia where over 1000 victories were claimed – mainly by NJG 100, which began forming during 1943, initially from IV/NJG 5. Zu Sayn-Wittgenstein, who joined the unit on formation, claimed 29 victories in 45 days on this front, where conditions were primitive, and operations much less sophisticated. His score included six during the night of 24/25 July. However top-scorers here were Lt Gustav Francsi who got over 50 of his 56 victories in the East, Hpt Alois Lechner, who claimed 45, seven of them during the night of 27/28 October, Maj Rudolf Schönert and Oblt Günther Bertram with 35 each. Oblt Joseph Pützkuhl claimed seven during the night of 5/6 July 1944 using the recently developed 'Schräge Musik' upward-firing guns, which were also employed to considerable advantage in the West. Other units were also formed for night fighting in Russia, including NJG 200 which developed from 10(NJ)/ZG 1; leading pilot of this unit was Obfw Josef Kociok. Previously a Zerstörer pilot in Russia, Kociok had 12 victories by day, plus credit for destroying many ground targets when he began night flying. He claimed 21 at night, 15 of them in 12 days, including four on 17 May 1943. He was killed on 26 September 1943 when he collided with a Russian aircraft near Kertsch.

In the West, 1944 brought the heaviest fighting yet, not only Bomber Command, but 2nd Tactical Air Force and US Ninth Air Force, together with other elements of the Allied air forces providing opponents for the Nachtjäger. During the night of 1/2 January 1944 zu Sayn-Wittgenstein, now Kommodore of NJG 2, shot down six bombers, while on 21/22nd he got five more, to raise his score to 84, but his Ju 88G was then hit, and although he ordered his crew to bale out, he crashed and was killed while trying to save the aircraft. Lent claimed three Lancasters during 15/16 June to become the first to achieve 100 night victories, but on 5 October, having added only two more, he crashed during a daylight landing, and was critically injured.

With the two leaders dead, the mantle passed to another NJG 1 pilot, who had been quietly building up his score since June 1942, and who achieved his 50th on 25 March 1944. Heinz-Wolfgang Schnauffer claimed five Lancasters in 14 minutes during the night of 24/25 May, and by the end of 1944 was in the lead with 106; he would end the war with 121. Eight other pilots claimed 40 or more victories during 1944–5, Heinz Rökker, on his return from the Mediterranean, having been second only to Schnauffer with 56 during this period to raise his total to 63. In the last months of fighting Oblt Kurt Welter did well, gaining a number of victories flying a night-fighter version of the Messerschmitt Me 262 jet fighter – many of them Mosquitos.

The greatest multiple score was achieved by Hpt Martin Becker of I/NJG 6 during the night of 14/15 March 1945, when nine victories were claimed, three by his radar operator, Lt Johannsen, manning the flexible rear guns. When the war ended the Nachtjägdflieger had claimed over 6000 victories, nearly 5000 of them over Western Europe; NJG 1 was top scorer with 2311.

During the latter months of the war Allied night fighters were active with the bombers over Germany, over Europe in defense of the Allied armies with 2nd Tactical Air Force and US Ninth Air Force, and over England – mainly against the V-1 flying bombs. Against the latter 96 Squadron was pre-eminent, Wg Cdr ED Crew being top scorer with $31\frac{1}{2}$, followed by Flt Lt FRL Mellersh with 30. Many new aces appeared at this time, and others added considerably to their scores. Outstanding was 85 Squadron's Branse Burbridge however. Although on operations since 1942, he gained no confirmed success until early 1944, when on 22 February he shot down an Me 410. By the end of April his score stood at three and two probables on home defense, but the unit then joined 100 Group. In the next seven months he claimed 17 over German territory, including three Ju 88G night fighters and a Bf 110 during the night of 4/5 November. After conclusion of his tour in March 1945, Burbridge flew one more sweep over Denmark in April with a replacement for his normal radar operator, Bill Skelton, and shot down one more Ju 88 to raise his score to 21 plus 12 probables and damaged – the RAF's top-scoring night fighter.

RAF night fighters operated over India and Burma, but saw little action here. The busiest period occurred over Calcutta during two nights in January 1943 when five Mitsubishi Ki 21 'Sally' bombers were shot down by newly arrived Beaufighters of 89 Squadron, three of them by an ex-Malta ace, F/Sgt AMO Pring to raise his score to nine.

The Americans left most night fighting to the British early in the war, but US industry developed British radar devices successfully. In the Mediterranean USAAF squadrons at first used British Beaufighters until supplies of the purpose-built Northrop P-61 Black Widow became available later in the war. Units of P-61s had reached all theaters before the conclusion of hostilities, but other than with the Ninth Air Force in Europe, action was only sporadic. US Navy and Marine Corps night fighter units were also formed, initially using F4U-2 Corsairs with radar fitted in wing-mounted pods, but these were generally replaced later by similarly equipped F6F Hellcats. To gain experience a number of USAAF pilots were also attached to RCAF night-fighter squadrons, where they flew Mosquitos.

The US Navy's top-scoring night fighters were Lt Frederick L Duncan and Ensign John W Dear Jr, both members of a night-fighter flight attached to VF-2 on USS *Hornet* in 1944. In the early hours of 4 July they shot down seven 'Rufe'

Near right: Top-scoring night fighter pilot of the USAAF was Maj Carroll C Smith who flew with the Fifth Air Force in the Pacific war zone. He is seen here in the cockpit of his 418th Squadron P-61 Black Widow.
Far right: A very successful RAF night fighter team comprised Sergeants (later Flt Lts) AJ Owen (right) and JSV McAllister (the radar operator), who served in North Africa and then with 100 Group, Bomber Command, on bomber support duties, gaining 16 victories.

floatplane fighters between them four by Duncan and three by Dear, but at least three of Dear's other victories were gained in daylight on 24 June. Flying Corsairs, Capt Robert Baird of the Marine's VMF(N)-533, shot down six Japanese aircraft by night during 1945 while based on Ie Shima, including two in one night on 22 June 1945. USAAF top-scorer was Maj Carroll C Smith of the 418th NF Squadron which served with the Fifth Air Force in the Southwest Pacific. His first two victories were gained on 13 January 1944, flying a converted P-38 Lightning, but late in the year he was able to add five with the P-61, including four in two sorties during the night of 29/30 December. His score was equalled by Lt AA Harrington who was attached to the RCAF 410 Squadron during 1944. Harrington's best night was 25 November when he claimed three Ju 88s. In Europe the 422nd

NF Squadron became the USAAF's highest scoring night-fighter unit, producing three aces, all of whom gained five victories between late 1944 and early 1945.

Finally the Japanese forces also formed a number of night-fighter units — initially to combat night-flying B-24 bombers attacking island bases, but subsequently to intercept the growing weight of night attack launched by the Marianas-based B-29s on the Home Islands. After service as a reconnaissance pilot at Rabaul, Cdr Sachio Endo commanded the night-fighter Buntai in the 302nd Ku at Omura in 1944, flying Nakajima J1N 'Irving' fighters. He was to claim eight B-29s shot down and eight damaged by early 1945, although one of each was claimed by day on 14 January when he was shot down and killed. In the same unit NAP 1/C Yoshimitsu Naka, flying a D4Y dive-bomber converted as a night fighter, was credited with five B-29s shot down and four damaged. Another 'Irving' pilot, Wt Off Juzo Kuramoto, flew with the Yokosuka Ku claiming six B-29s shot down and two damaged by night during May 1945. Five confirmed and one damaged were claimed in a single night, 25/26th, when he and Lt (jg) Shiro Kurotiri, his radar operator, found the new equipment 'quite useless.'

The army's 53rd Sentai operated Kawasaki Ki 45 twin-engined fighters fitted with upward-firing cannon like the German 'Schräge Musik.' Top-scoring pilot of this unit was Sgt Nobuji Negishi, credited with six B-29s shot down — two during the early hours of 10 March 1945 — and seven damaged. The unit claimed some 168 B-29s destroyed or damaged in total. Flying single-engined Ki 44 'Tojo' fighters with the 70th Sentai, Capt Yoshio Yoshida claimed one B-29 by day over Manchuria in September 1944, then six more by night over Japan between 10 March and 25 May 1945, three of them on 15 April.

TOP-SCORING AMERICAN NIGHT-FIGHTER PILOTS, 1942–45

Ens John W Dear Jr (USN)	7 (3 al by day)	VF-2
Lt Frederick L Duncan (USN)	7	VF-2
Lt AA Harrington (USAAF)	7	att 410 Sqn, RCAF
Maj Carroll C Smith (USAAF) SW Pacific	7	418th NF Sqn
Capt Robert Baird (USMC)	6	VMF(N)-533
Lt Eugene D Axtell (USAAF) ETO	5	422nd NF Sqn
Lt Hermann A Ernst (USAAF) ETO	5	422nd NF Sqn
Lt Paul A Smith (USAAF) ETO	5	422nd NF Sqn

TOP-SCORING JAPANESE NIGHT-FIGHTER PILOTS, 1944–45

Wt Off Juzo Kuramoto (IJNAF)	8
Cdr Sachio Endo (IJNAF)	7 (+ 1 day)
Sgt Nobuji Negichi (IJAAF)	6
Capt Yoshio Yoshida (IJAAF)	6 (+ 1 day)
NAP 1/C Yoshimitsu Naka (IJNAF)	5

TOP-SCORING NIGHT-FIGHTER PILOTS OF THE RAF, 1939–45

Wg Cdr BA Burbridge	21	(5HD; 16 BE)	85 Sqn
Gp Capt J Cunningham	19	(all HD + 1 by day)	604, 85 Sqn
Wg Cdr JRD Braham	19	(13 HD; 7 BE + 10 by day)	29, 141 Sqn
Gp Capt FD Hughes (Irish)	16½	(6½ HD; 10 ME + 2 by day)	264, 125, 600, 604 Sqn
Flt Lt AJ Owen	16	(6 ME; 10 BE)	600, 85 Sqn
Flt Lt K Kuttelwascher (Czech)	15	(all NI + 3 by day)	1, 23 Sqn
Wg Cdr JW Allan	14	(all ME)	266, 256, 151, 29 Sqn
Wg Cdr WP Green*	14	(all HD + 12 V-1s)	85, 96, 219 Sqn
Flg Off NE Reeves	14	(9 ME; 5 BE)	89, 239 Sqn, BSDU
Flt Lt RP Stevens*	14	(all NI)	151, 253 Sqn
Wg Cdr JG Topham	14	(all HD)	219, 125 Sqn
Wg Cdr ED Crew	13	(all HD + 31½ V-1s)	604, 85, 96 Sqn
Wg Cdr RC Fumerton (Canadian)	13	(2 HD; 11 ME + 1 on ground)	406, 89 Sqn
Flt Lt MC Shipard (Australian)	13	(1 HD; 12 ME)	68, 89 Sqn
Flt Lt MM Davison	12	(8 ME; 4 HD + 1 V-1)	46, 108, 264 Sqn
Flt Lt AB Downing	12	(all ME)	141, 600, 169 Sqn
Flt Lt AJ Hodgkinson	12	(9 HD; 3 MEI)	219, 264, 23 Sqn
Flt Lt HE White	12	(all BE)	141 Sqn, BSDU
Wg Cdr JG Benson	11	(5 HD; 6 BE + 1 V-1)	141, 157 Sqn
Flt Lt GE Jameson (New Zealander)	11	(all HD)	125, 488 Sqn
Flg Off WH Miller	11	(3 HD; 8 BE)	125, 169 Sqn

[nb six more pilots got 10 victories]
HD – Home Defense; BE – Bomber Escort; ME – Middle East; NI – Night Intruder;
MEI – Middle East Intruder; BSDU – Bomber Support Development Unit.

TOP-SCORING LUFTWAFFE NIGHT-FIGHTER PILOTS, 1939–45

Maj Heinz-Wolfgang Schnauffer	121		NJG 1, 4
Oberst Helmut Lent*	102	(+ 8 day)	NJG 1, 2, 3
Maj Heinrich Prinz zu Sayn-Wittgenstein*	84	(29 in Russia)	NJG 2, 5, 100, 3
Hpt Manfred Meurer*	65		NJG 1, 5
Oberst Werner Streib	65	(+ 1 day)	NJG 1
Oberst Günther Radusch	64		NJG 1, 2, 3, 5
Maj Rudolf Schönert	64	(35 in Russia)	NJG 1, 2, 5, 100
Hpt Heinz Rökker	63	(+ 1 day)	NJG 2
Maj Paul Zorner	59		NJG 2, 3, 5, 100
Hpt Gerhard Raht	58		NJG 2, 3
Hpt Martin Becker	57		NJG 3, 4, 6
Maj Wilhelm Herget	57	(+ 15 day)	NJG 3, 4
Oblt Gistav Francsi	56	(prob all Russia)	NJG 100
Hpt Josef Kraft	56	(20 in Russia)	NJG 1, 4, 5, 6
Hpt Heinz Strüning*	56		NJG 1, 2
Oblt Kurt Welter	56	(+ 5 day)	JG 300, NJG 11
Hpt Hans-Dieter Frank*	55		NJG 1
Obfw Heinz Vinke*	54		NJG 1
Hpt August Geiger*	53		NJG 1
Maj Egmont Prinz zur Lippe Weissenfeldt*	51		NJG 1, 5
Maj Werner Hoffmann	51	(+ 1 day)	NJG 3, 5
Oblt Herbert Lütje	51	(+ 2 day)	NJG 1, 6
Hpt Hermann Greiner	50		NJG 1

TOP-SCORING PILOTS OF WORLD WAR II IN ALL THEATERS

British Commonwealth

Sqn Ldr MT St J Pattle*	South African		40+	NA, G
Gp Capt JE Johnson	British		33.91 (38)	W
Wg Cdr B Finucane*	Irish		32	W
Flt Lt GF Beurling	Canadian		31.33	W, M
Gp Capt AG Malan	South African		28.66 (32)	W
Gp Capt CR Caldwell	Australian		28.5	NA, SWP
Sqn Ldr JH Lacey	British		28	W, B
Sqn Ldr NF Duke	British		27.83 (28)	W, NA, I
Wg Cdr CF Gray	New Zealander		27.7 (27½)	W, NA, I
Wg Cdr RRS Tuck	British		27 (29)	W
Flt Lt ES Lock*	British		25.5 (26)	W
Flt Lt G Allard*	British		23.83	W
Wg Cdr DRS Bader	British		23.83 (23)	W
Wg Cdr DE Kingaby	British		23 (22½)	W
Wg Cdr B Drake	British		22.5 (24½)	W, NA, WA, I
Wg Cdr MN Crossley	British		22	W
Flt Lt W Vale	British		22 (24)	G
Wg Cdr VC Woodward	Canadian		21.83	NA, G
Wg Cdr WV Crawford-Compton	New Zealander		21.5	W
Wg Cdr AC Deere	New Zealander		21.5 (22)	W
Flt Lt RB Hesselyn	New Zealander		21.5	M, W
Wg Cdr ED Mackie	New Zealander		21.5 (22)	W, NA, I
Sqn Ldr HW McLeod*	Canadian		21	M, W
Sqn Ldr MM Stephens	British		21 (22)	W, NA, M
Sqn Ldr AA McKellar*	British		20.83 (21)	W
Wg Cdr PH Hugo	South Africa		20.5 (22)	W, NA, I
Wg Cdr RH Harries	British		20.25	W
Wg Cdr JE Rankin	British	Poss.	20.28 (21)	W
Wg Cdr FR Carey	British	Poss.	20+ (28+)	W, B
Wg Cdr WD David	British		20	W

NB Scores have been assessed here on the US method of amalgamating shares. Where previously quoted scores differ they are included in brackets. W = Western Front   NA = North Africa M = Malta   I = Italy   G = Greece   B = Burma   WA = West Africa   SWP = Southwest Pacific

Germany

Maj Erich Hartmann	352	EF	Oblt Günther Josten	178	EF
Maj Gerhard Barkhorn	301	EF	Oberst Johannes Steinhoff	176	EF, W, NA, I
Maj Günther Rall	275	EF, W			
Oblt Otto Kittel*	267	EF	Hpt Ernst-Wilhelm Reinert	174	EF, M, I, W
Maj Walter Nowotny*	258	EF, W			
Maj Wilhelm Batz	237	EF	Hpt Günther Schack	174	EF
Maj Erich Rudorffer	222	EF, W, NA	Hpt Emil Lang*	173	EF, W
Obstlt Heinz Bär	220	EF, W, NA	Hpt Heinz Schmidt*	173	EF
Oberst Hermann Gräf	212	EF, W	Maj Horst Adameit*	166	EF
Maj Theodor Weissenberger	208	EF, W	Oberst Wolf-Dietrich Wilcke*	162	EF, W, NA, M
Obstlt Hans Philipp*	206	EF, W			
Oblt Walter Schuck	206	EF	Hpt Hans-Joachim Marseille*	158	W, NA
Maj Heinrich Ehrler*	204+	EF	Hpt Heinrich Sturm*	157	EF
Oblt Anton Hafner*	204	EF, NA	Oblt Gerhard Thyben	157	EF, W
Hpt Helmut Lipfert	203	EF	Oblt Hans Beisswenger*	152	EF, Y
Maj Walter Krupinski	197	EF, W	Lt Peter Düttman	152	EF
Maj Anton Hackl	192	EF, NA, W	Oberst Gordon Gollob	150	EF, N
Hpt Joachim Brendel	189	EF			
Hpt Maximilian Stotz*	189	EF, W	EF = Eastern Front W = West NA = North		
Hpt Joachim Kirschner*	188	EF, MG	Africa M = Malta I = Italy G = Greece		
Maj Werner-Kurt Brandle*	180	EF, W	Y = Yugoslavia N = Norway.		

American

Maj Richard I Bong*	40	Fifth AF, SWP
Maj Thomas B McGuire*	38	Fifth AF, SWP
Cdr David S McCampbell	34	USN
Lt Col Gregory Boyington	28	AVG, USMC
Col Francis S Gabreski	28	Eighth AF, ETO
Maj Robert S Johnson	28	Eighth AF, ETO
Col Charles H MacDonald	27	Fifth AF, SWP
Maj Joseph J Foss	26	USMC
Maj George E Preddy*	25.83	Eighth AF, ETO
Lt Robert N Hanson*	25	USMC
Wg Cdr LC Wade*	25	RAF, NA
Lt Cdr Cecil E Harris	24	USN
Lt Cdr Eugene A Valencia	23	USN
Maj Raymond S Wetmore	22.6	Eighth AF, ETO
Col David C Schilling	22.5	Eighth AF, ETO
Lt Col Gerald R Johnson	22	Fifth AF, SWP
Col Noel E Kearby*	22	Fifth AF, ETO
Maj Jay T Robbins	22	Fifth AF, ETO
Capt Don S Gentile	21.84	RAF, Eighth AF, ETO
Maj Frederick J Christiansen Jr	21.5	Eighth AF, ETO
Capt Kenneth A Walsh	21	USMC
Capt John J Voll	21	Fifteenth AF, I
Capt Donald N Aldrich	20	USMC
Maj Thomas J Lynch*	20	Fifth AF, SWP
Lt Col Robert B Westbrook*	20	Thirteenth AF, SP

USN = US Navy USMC = US Marine Corps
AVG = American Volunteer Group ETO = European
Theater of Operations SWP = Southwest Pacific
SP = South Pacific I = Italy NA = North Africa

Japanese

Lt (jg) Tetsuzo Iwamoto	94 (14 China)	Nav
Lt Hiroyoshi Nishizawa*	87	Nav
Ens Shoichi Sugita*	70	Nav
Lt Saburo Sakai	64 (2 China)	Nav
Wt Off Hiromichi Shinohara*	58 (all Mongolia)	Arm
Wt Off Takeo Okumura*	54 (4 China)	Nav
Sgt Satoshi Anabuki	51	Arm
Sgt Isamu Sasaki	38	Arm
Capt Mitsuyoshi Tarui*	38+ (28 Mongolia)	Arm
Lt Toshio Ohta*	34	Nav
Wt Off Kazuo Sugino	32	Nav
Maj Yashiko Kuroe	30 (2 Mongolia)	Arm
Wt Off Shizuo Ishii*	29 (3 China)	Nav
Lt (jg) Kaneyoshi Muto*	28 (1 China)	Nav
Sgt Maj Chiyoji Saito*	28 (21 Mongolia)	Arm
Capt Kenji Shimada*	28 (all Mongolia)	Arm
Lt (jg) Sadaaki Akamatsu	27 (11 China)	Nav
1/Lt Isamu Hosono*	27 (21 Mongolia)	Arm
Lt Cdr Junichi Sasai*	27	Nav
2/Lt Rikia Shibata*	27 (14 Mongolia)	Arm
Lt Goichi Sumino*	27	Arm
Lt Moritsugu Kanai	26 (7 Mongolia)	Arm
NAP 3/C Hidenori Matsunaga	26	Nav
(floatplane pilot — many shares and probables included)		
1/Lt Shogo Saito*	26 al (25 Mongolia)	Arm
2/Lt Goro Furugori*	25–30 al (20 Mongolia)	Arm
Wt Off Tomio Hanada*	25 (all Mongolia)	Arm
Cdr Naoshi Kanno*	25	Navy

French

Capt Marcel Albert	23	France, NN
Wg Cdr Jean EF Demozay	21	RAF
Sqn Ldr Pierre H Clostermann	19	RAF + 1 probables
Lt Pierre Le Gloan*	18	France, Syria + 2 probables
Capt Roland de la Poype	17 (15)	RAF, NN + 3 probables
Sous Lt Jacques Andre	16	France, NA, NN
Cdt Louis Delfino	16	France, NA, NN + al 2 probables
Cdt Edmond Marin la Meslee*	16	France + 4 probables

Sous Lt Roger Sauvage	16	France NN
Lt Georges Valentin	15	France, NA, Corsica
Capt Michel Dorance*	14	France + 3 probables
Capt Albert Littolf*	14	France, RAF, NN + 4 probables
Sous Lt Camille Plubeau	14	France + 4 probables

NN = Normandie-Niemen Regiment, Russia   RAF = Royal Air Force
NA = North Africa (fighting Allies)   Syria (fighting British)   Corsica (fighting Germans)

Poland

Wg Cdr (Mjr) Stanislaw F Skalski	$18\frac{1}{2}$	11/12 ($4\frac{1}{4}$ Poland 1939)
Mjr B Michal Gladych	$18\frac{1}{2}$	(10 with USAAF, 1944)
Wg Cdr (Pplk) Witold Urbanowicz	18	(1 before war, 2 with USAAF, China, 1944)
Sqn Ldr (Kpt) Eugeniusz Horbaczewski*	$16\frac{1}{2}$	
Wg Cdr (Mjr) Marian Pisarek*	$12\frac{1}{2}$	($2\frac{1}{2}$ Poland, 1939)
Sqn Ldr (Mjr) Jan EL Zumbach	$12\frac{1}{3}$	
Sqn Ldr (Kpt) Anthoni Glowacki	$11\frac{1}{3}$	
Plt Off (Ppor) Michal K Maciejowski	$10\frac{1}{2}$	
Wg Cdr (Mjr) Henryk Szczesny	$10\frac{1}{3}$	(2 Poland, 1939)
Gp Capt (Pplk) Alexander Gabszewicz	$9\frac{1}{2}$	(1 Poland, 1939; 1 France, 1940)
Flg Off (Por) Miroslaw Feric*	$9\frac{1}{3}$	($1\frac{1}{3}$ Poland, 1939)
Flt Sgt (St Sier) Aleksandr Chudek*	9	

Norway

Capt Svein Heglund	$14\frac{1}{2}$	(3 at night) nb some sources quote $16\frac{1}{3}$
Lt Col Werner Christie	11	(includes 2 shared)
Capt Helmer GE Grundt-Spang	$10\frac{1}{3}$	
Maj Martin Y Gran	$9\frac{1}{2}$	
Capt Marius Eriksen	9	

Belgians

Lt Count Rodolphe de Hemricourt de Grunne*	13	(10 in Spain, 1937–8)
Col Count Yvan Georges Du Monceau de Bergandael	8	
Flg Off Charles FJ Detal*	7	(includes 1 shared) 1 ground
Flt Lt Jean HM Offenberg*	7	(1 Belgium, 1940)
Flg Off Victor MM Ortmans	7	(includes 2 shared)
Sqn Ldr Raymond A Lallemant	6	(includes 1 shared) 1 ground
Plt Off Jaques AL Phillipart*	6	
Flt Lt Andre M Plisnier	6	(includes 3 shared)
Wg Cdr Daniel Le Roy du Vivier	6	(includes 2 shared)
Sqn Ldr Remy van Lierde	6	+ 40 V-1s + 1 ground

Czechs

Npor Karel Kuttelwascher	20	(2 in France, 1940; 18 RAF)
Ppor Josef Frantisek*	17	(all RAF)
Skpt Alois Vasatko*	17	(15 France, 1940 – 12 shared, and includes 3 probables; 1 and 1 shared RAF)
Kpt Frantisek Perina*	15	(14 France, 1940 – 12 shared, and includes 3 probables; 1 with RAF)
Por Josef Stehlik	12	(8 France, 1940 – 4 and 4 shared, includes 3 probables; 2 shared RAF; 1 and 1 shared Russia, 1944)
Npor Miroslav J Mansfeld	10	(1 shared day; 9, including 1 shared night, all RAF) + 2 V-1s
Ppor Otto Smik	9	(includes 2 shared – all RAF) + 3 V-1s

4. POSTWAR ACES
From Piston to Jet

The Cold War was brought to an abrupt halt on 25 June 1950 when Communist forces from the north crossed the 38th Parallel and invaded the Republic of South Korea. Initially, the South Koreans were overwhelmed by the armed might thrown against them, and it was feared that their country might be engulfed before United Nations help could arrive. Urgent arrangements were made to evacuate US advisers and their families from Seoul, the capital, by air. Aerial attack on the defenseless transport aircraft involved in this emergency airlift next day, brought orders for USAF fighters from airfields in nearby Japan to patrol overhead.

Sure enough, on 27 June, North Korean Yak 9 fighters attempted to strafe Seoul airfield again, but these were swiftly driven off by F-82 Twin Mustang night fighters of the 68th and 339th Fighter (All-Weather) Squadrons. The first victory fell to 1/Lt William G Hudson of the 68th, but one of the others was credited to the commanding officer of the 339th, Maj James W Little. Little had flown P-40s with the famed 23rd Fighter Group in China during the earlier conflict, being credited with five to seven victories during 1943. That same afternoon eight Ilyushin Il-10 Shturmoviks attempted to attack Kimpo airfield, but these were harshly dealt with by Lockheed F-80C Shooting Star jet fighters of the 35th Fighter-Bomber Squadron, and four were claimed shot down without loss – for the first USAF jet victories ever.

These early combats set the scene for the three years of aerial fighting which were to stand many established precepts of fighter conflict on their heads – and it was Little's early success which was to prove the epitome of these changes. The major lesson of Korea was that experience was king in jet conflict. This lesson had been amply demonstrated for the future historian during World War II but it had been rather lost on the Allies under the pressure of their overwhelming numerical superiority. No longer was the archetypal fighter ace the young and carefree 'blood' of 20 or 21; now he was the battle-hardened veteran of World War II – 30 or 35 was no longer 'over the hill'! This new war was to be fought typically by career airmen who knew exactly what they were about.

At first the opposition in the air consisted of a relative handful of elderly Russian-built piston-engined aircraft of World War II vintage. These posed little threat, and priority was given to the support of the ground forces. Until airfields became available in Korea, most early missions were undertaken from Japan. As the jet fighters initially available – the F-80s – were in relatively short supply, and were also somewhat lacking in range performance, large numbers of stored F-51 Mustangs, 'cocooned' since the end of World War II, were recommissioned, and rushed to the area on aircraft carriers. (It should be mentioned here that the old 'P-for-Pursuit' designation of USAF fighters had been superceded by 'F-for-Fighter' shortly after the end of World War II.) Backed up by A-26 Invader and B-29 Superfortress bombers of similar 1945 vintage, covered by the F-80, and joined by Vought F4U Corsairs of the Marines and Grumman F9F Panther jets of the US navy from carriers offshore, these new arrivals were quite adequate for what was demanded of them. Frequently in the hands of experienced World War II fighter-bomber pilots, these aircraft played an important part in aiding the newly arrived United Nations ground forces (mainly US at this time) to stabilize the position, and then begin driving the North Koreans back into their own territory.

Few combats occurred after the initial days of the war, and early efforts to catch the North Korean air force on the ground paid dividends. On 10 August 1950 Maj Arnold 'Moon' Mullins, commanding officer of the 67th Fighter-Bomber Squadron, destroyed three Yak fighters on the ground in his F-51D, while on 5 February 1951 he shot down another of these aircraft. Typical of the squadron and flight commanders involved at this time, Mullins had flown P-47Ds with the Ninth Air Force in Europe during 1944, being credited with two aerial victories during that conflict.

On 15 September 1950 a daring seaborne invasion in strength was made well up the west coast of Korea at Inchon, while on the same date the US Eighth Army launched an offensive to break out of the 'Pusan Pocket' in the south. Now the North Koreans' resistance started to crumble, and by November the United Nations had advanced right through North Korea, occupying nearly the whole country. It had been intended to subdue the Communists and hold free elections throughout the united Korea, but at this point the Chinese intervened, sending a massive army across the Yalu River to the aid of the North Koreans. Greatly outnumbered, the

Above: F-86E Sabre of the 4th Fighter-Interceptor Wing in flight over Korea. This aircraft is flown by the No 3 ace of the war, Capt Manuel Fernandez, 8 of whose victories are marked on the nose.
Center: Leading aces of the 4th Fighter-Interceptor Wing in celebratory mood. Left to right: Capt Lonnie R Moore (10 victories); Lt Col Vermont Garrison (10+ 7.3 in World War II); Col James K Johnson (10+ 1 in World War II); Capt Ralph S Parr Jr (10); Maj James Jabara 15+ 1.5 in World War II); the group are flanked by Col Johnson's F-86 Sabre.
Bottom: Pilots of the 4th Fighter-Interceptor Wing celebrate the Wing's score passing the 300 point (it would eventually climb to 498). Left to right: Maj Winton W 'Bones' Marshall (6.5 victories); Col Benjamin S Preston Jr (4); Maj George A Davis Jr (14+ 7 in World War II); Maj Richard D Creighton (5); Col Harrison R Thyng (5+ 5 in World War II); Capt Kenneth D Chandler (5).

UN forces were driven back across the 38th Parallel, and by January 1951 Seoul had fallen and a complete debacle appeared possible. Only the tremendous and effective level of UN air support prevented the retreat becoming a rout, and eventually allowed the ground forces to stabilize the position and bring a halt to the Chinese advance.

Now, however, a new factor entered the equation. At the start of November 1950 a fast and modern jet fighter had made its appearance over North Korea – a fighter which quickly proved superior performance over anything the UN had available in the area – the Russians swept-wing MiG 15. Operating from bases beyond the Yalu, the MiGs played havoc with the elderly fighter-bombers, with the rather dated reconnaissance aircraft then in use, and particularly with the big B-29s. The first jet-versus-jet air fight in history occurred on 8 November when MiGs attempted to attack escorted B-29s, one of these fighters being shot down by Lt Russell J Brown of the 16th Fighter-Interceptor Squadron, 51st Fighter-Interceptor Wing, in an F-80.

The appearance of this dangerous new foe sent a shudder through the UN air forces, and at once an urgent request was sent out for modern air cover. The 4th Fighter-Interceptor Wing – descendant of the Eighth Air Force's famous 4th Fighter Group – was at once dispatched from the United States. A 'crack' unit, manned by many World War II veterans, and commanded by one of the greatest American aces of that conflict, Lt Col John C Meyer, the 4th had been one of the earliest units to receive the radical new swept-wing North American F-86A Sabre, and was already thoroughly familiar with the aircraft, having flown it for over a year. At the same time straight-wing Republic F-84 Thunderjets of superior performance to the F-80Cs were also sent to Korea – but it was to be the Sabres that were to become the war's air-superiority fighters *par excellence*.

The first squadron of F-86s – the 336th – was rushed to Korea on 15 December 1950, and first met the MiGs two days later. Lt Col Bruce H Hinton shot one down in the first all-swept-wing combat of the war. After initial successes, the Sabres, with most other units, were forced out of Korea by the Chinese advance early in January 1951. However UN reinforcements allowed a counteroffensive to be launched, and during February the Communists were driven back to the 38th Parallel, allowing the USAF's units to be hastened back from Japan early in March.

Now the ground situation became stagnant, and the air war stabilized. The UN forces were able to keep the Communists in check by the use of close-support air power – both in front line strikes and particularly, by interdiction against supplies and reinforcements. The MiG 15s could not effectively combat the UN fighter-bombers from their airfields beyond the Yalu; only if they could move forward to airfields in North Korea could they seriously hope to challenge the UN's air superiority in the battle zone; the UN fighter-bombers could prevent the use of such air strips only so long as they had the adquate protection of the F-86s. To complete this scenario, the UN air forces, for political reasons, were prevented from attacking the MiGs' home bases in Manchuria and China, beyond the Yalu.

While the bulk of the UN air forces concentrated on their ground-attack duties, for the Sabres the war became a long round of sweeps to the north to tie the MiGs as closely to the Yalu as possible, and to wear them down in combat. This area of operations became known popularly as 'MiG Alley.' These duties were interspersed with escorts to fighter-bombers, reconnaissance aircraft, and occasionally to B-29s – although the latter were soon relegated to the hours of darkness. Only rarely did the Communist air forces attempt to intervene in the ground fighting, the most notable occasion occurring on 30 November 1951. On that day they attempted to move 12 Tupolev Tu 2 bombers and 16 Lavochkin La 9 fighters, all piston-engined aircraft, to Taehwa-do airfield to make an attack on UN-occupied off-shore islands. Some 31 Sabres intercepted the formation, and despite a cover of MiG 15s, were able to claim 8 Tu 2s, 3 La 9s and a MiG shot down without loss.

For the main air superiority operations it had been found that the big wing formation of World War II was quite inappropriate and unwieldy, and formations of Sabres were kept small – operating in the classic fours at maximum height, and entering the fighting zone at a high air speed. As already indicated, most early success was gained by veterans, and aces from the earlier war added to their scores here – 'Gabby' Gabreski and Glen Eagleston, who have already been mentioned in earlier chapters being but two of these.

Capt James Jabara became the first USAF jet ace on 20 May 1951, while on 13 December of that year – by which time six pilots had qualified as aces – Maj George Davis became the first to reach double figures. Throughout this period the Sabres were constantly outnumbered, but despite this they established a healthy 'kill-loss' ratio in their favor, even though the MiG 15 offered certain performance advantages over the F-86A. In October 1951 the first of the improved F-86Es arrived, and these were initially employed to replace the F-80s of the 51st Wing,

bringing a second Sabre wing into being. Throughout 1952, as peace talks made little headway, the Sabres continued to take a steady toll of the MiGs, ranging from 16 in July to 59 in September, but running at an average of 30 per month.

In experience and pilot quality the UN continued to have the main advantage, although it had become evident early in the war that not only Chinese and Korean, but also European pilots were being engaged. Soon it was obvious that batches of new pilots were appearing at regular intervals. At first these pilots – apart from those who were obviously their instructors, and became known to the Sabre pilots as 'Honchos' – would be very green, but they would gradually improve. However, as they reached the stage where they were becoming really dangerous, they would be pulled out and a new batch would appear. The Communist Bloc countries were obviously using Korea as a training ground.

The year 1953 saw an intensification of the fighting in the air as each side sought some advantage as the peace talks began to approach agreement for an armistice. The latest F-86Fs now arrived, with the improved '6–3' wing leading edge extension, and in February the 18th Fighter-Bomber Wing converted to Sabres, followed in May by the 8th. The number of pilots becoming aces increased rapidly, and a race developed for the top place between Joe McConnell, 'Pete' Fernandez and James Jabara, who had returned for a second tour. McConnell won, becoming the first 'triple ace' of the war on 18 May 1953.

The last victory of the war – an Ilyushin Il-12 transport aircraft – fell to Capt Ralph S Parr Jr at 12.30 on 27 July, just hours before the Armistice ceasefire came into force. When the fighting stopped the UN air forces had claimed 954 victories – 827 of them MiG 15s – against a loss of 139 aircraft in air combat, 78 of which were Sabres. Sabres accounted for 792 of the victories credited – a quite astounding success ratio. Their best month had been June 1953, when 71 MiGs had been claimed *without loss*! 39 pilots had become aces, while numerous World War II aces had added further to their scores, and other pilots, who were aces in neither war solely, had joint totals for the two wars which now qualified them for this coveted title.

Among the notables were:

Major James Jabara
Jabara flew initially with both the Eighth and Ninth Air Forces during World War II, gaining 1.5 victories as a Mustang pilot with the 355th Fighter Group, Eighth Air Force. He claimed his first MiG 15 on 3 April 1951 and by the end of the month had added three more. Due to return to Japan on rotation on 7 May, he was permitted to stay on as he was then the top-

McConnell and 'Pete' Fernandez had outstripped all others with scores of 16 and 14.5 respectively, but both had then finished their tours of duty. A mere one further success had come Jabara's way in this period, but on 26 May he gained two further victories, beginning a run of success which included two more doubles, and raised his total in Korea to 15 by 15 July – second only to McConnell. His final score for two wars was thus 16.5. He died in 1967.

Colonel George A Davis Jr

George Davis was one of those who was no newcomer to air combat when he arrived in Korea. Having joined the USAAF in March 1942, he was posted to the Southwest Pacific in August 1943, joining Neel Kearby's 348th Fighter Group in New Guinea to fly the big P-47D Thunderbolt. He gained two initial victories at the turn of the year, but then saw little further opportunities for combat until the unit moved to the Philippines in December 1944. Here in three combats over the course of two weeks he shot down five Japanese fighters to raise his score to 7 in 226 operational missions.

Leaving the group in March 1945, he returned to the US, and in 1947 was transitioned on his first jet fighter – the F-80 – serving with the 1st Fighter Group in California. In October 1951 came a long-awaited posting to Korea to command the 334th Squadron in the 4th FIW. Success was swift to come, for on 27 November he claimed his first two MiGs and three days later took part in the interception of the big formation of North Korean piston-engined aircraft, claiming three Tu 2s and a MiG 15 to become a jet ace in only two combats. Multiple claims continued to come his way, with two MiGs on 5 December, and no less than four on the 13th. He was now the highest scoring pilot of the war so far, and on 10 February 1952 he added further to his total while covering fighter-bombers near Kunu-ri. He had just shot down two MiGs and was throttled back to attack a third, when his Sabre was hit; it fell out of control and crashed 30 miles south of the Yalu. Davis was the only US ace to be killed in Korea, and was the only fighter pilot of that conflict to be awarded the Congressional Medal of Honor – a posthumous award. It was to be over a year before any other pilot surpassed his Korean total of 14.

Lieutenant Colonel William T Whisner Jr

Bill Whisner, a native of Shreveport, Louisiana, reached the United Kingdom late in 1943 to fly P-47s with the 452nd Fighter Group in the Eighth Air Force. He achieved his first victory over an Fw 190 on 29 January 1944, but before gaining any further successes, his group was converted to the new P-51 Mustang. As luck would have it, few opportunities to score came his way during the great battles with the Luftwaffe during the spring and summer of 1944,

scorer, and nearest to the magic fifth victory. His opportunity came on 20 May when he attacked a number of MiGs despite the fact that one of the underwing droptanks carried by his aircraft would not release, and he was successful in dispatching two to become the first jet-versus-jet ace in history.

The Kansan pilot returned to Korea for a second tour in January 1953, but initially gained no further success. By mid-May Joe

and by mid-November his total stood at a modest 3.5. His great chance came on 21 November, while escorting B-17s over Merseburg. Now a Captain, he led 11 P-51s to attack 50 Fw 190s which were attempting to get to the bombers, and in this one combat he was able to claim five and two probables – one of the probables was later confirmed. Two further victories followed on 27 November, and then on 1 January 1945 during the famous Operation *Bödenplatte* New Years' Day attack by the Luftwaffe on Allied airfields, he shot down two Bf 109s and two Fw 190s to raise his final total for the war to 15.5 in the air and 3 on the ground in 127 missions.

In August 1951 he was sent to Korea as a major to fly in the 334th Squadron of the 4th FIW, where he was able to claim two MiGs during November of that year. Posted to command the 25th Squadron in the 51st FIW when this unit converted to Sabres, he claimed 3.5 more MiGs during January and February 1952 to become an ace in this war too, and to increase his total score to 21.

Colonel Harrison R Thyng

Harry Thyng was typical of the best that the USAF had to offer in Korea. A highly experienced and much-travelled airman, he was 34 when he became an ace for the second time in Korea. Already a serving officer at the outbreak of war in December 1941, he flew P-39 Airacobras until posted to England with the 31st Fighter Group – the very first to join the new Eighth Air Force in summer 1942. Equipped now with Spitfire Vs provided by the RAF, he took part in the operations over Dieppe on 19 August 1942, claiming the probable destruction of an Fw 190 on this date. His first confirmed victory came on 8 November 1942, and was over a Vichy French Dewoitine 520 fighter as he led his unit in to land at Oran, Algeria, on the first day of the Operation Torch Anglo-American invasion of French Northwest Africa. Over Tunisia as a squadron commander he shot down four German fighters between February and May 1943. In 1945 he commanded the P-47N-equipped 413th Fighter Group in the Pacific, leading this unit to Okinawa in May 1945; he is reported to have gained one victory against the Japanese, but this does not appear on officially published records.

Late in 1951 he joined the 4th FIW in Korea, gaining his first victory over a MiG 15 on 24 October. The following month he became the wing's commanding officer, a post he filled with dynamism and innovation for nearly a year. His fifth and last MiG went down on 20 May 1952, making him the 16th ace of the Korean war.

Colonel Royal N Baker

Royal 'King' Baker had joined the 31st Fighter Group in which Harrison Thyng was serving in North Africa during early 1943. Flying Spit-

Above left: Col Royal N Baker, fourth-ranking ace in Korea, and formerly a World War II Spitfire pilot. Above: Capt Harold E Fischer (10 victories) with his F-86E 'Paper Tiger'. Note the MiG silhouette victory marks. Fischer was shot down in this aircraft over Chinese territory, remaining as a prisoner until 1955.

fires, he gained his first successes over Pantelleria and Sicily during that summer, and when his tour ended, he left as a Captain with 3 victories to his credit – all over German fighters. His second tour took him to the Ninth Air Force in France, where he commanded the P-47-equipped 493rd Squadron in the 48th Fighter Group. Mainly fighter-bomber activities gave little chance for combat, but on 5 August 1944 he was credited with one shared victory.

Joining the 4th FIW in Korea in summer 1952, he subsequently replaced Thyng as the unit's commander, gaining considerable success in the meantime. His first victory on 20 June was over a piston-engined La 9 fighter, but thereafter all his successes were over MiGs. Only on 7 December did he claim more than one in a day, when on that date he shared a second MiG with a fellow pilot immediately after obtaining his 6th Korean victory. A further shared victory on 16 December was followed by six more individual successes between 13 January and 13 March 1953, raising his score here to 13. This total was at the time second only to George Davis, and made him leading surviving ace at the time his tour ended.

Captain Harold E Fischer

By the end of 1952 some of the later generation of USAF fighter pilots who had not seen service in World War II, but who were nonetheless possessed of considerable experience, were beginning to come to the fore. Harold Fischer had just joined the US Navy as an aviation cadet in 1945 when the war ended, and he was discharged. In 1948 he joined the army, negotiating a transfer to the USAF the following year; he finally graduated as a pilot early in 1951. Posted to the 8th Fighter-Bomber Wing in Korea, he had flown 105 missions in F-80s when rested in December. His reward came in September 1952 with a posting to the 51st FIW to fly F-86Fs with the 39th Squadron, and on 26

Above: Capt Manuel J 'Pete' Fernandez, third-ranking ace in Korea with 14.5 victories.
Above right: Korean War top scorer – Capt Joseph McConnell Jr.

November he claimed his first victory. Successes followed fast, including a double on 16 February 1953, and by 21 March his score stood at 10 and he had received promotion to Captain.

On 7 April 1953 he became separated from his wingman in combat, and inadvertently crossed into Chinese territory where his shark's teeth-marked Sabre, 'Paper Tiger,' was shot down. Fischer managed to bale out, but he was held in captivity at Mukden with four others long after the end of the war. He managed to escape once during the winter of 1954/5, but was unable to get away and had to surrender because of the intensely cold weather. Finally all five were tried in Peking in May 1955 for entering Chinese airspace, and were 'deported' to Hong Kong.

Captain Manuel J Fernandez

'Pete' Fernandez had not seen service in World War II. He was a gunnery instructor at Nellis Air Force Base, Nevada, before going to Korea in late 1952, to fly in the 4th FIW's 334th Squadron. Gaining his first victory on 4 October, he became the 26th ace on 18 February 1953 – just behind Fischer, who was the 25th. Then between 9 March and 16 May he gained 8.5 further victories to raise his score to 14.5 – the first to pass Davis's score of 14. He remained top-scorer for only two days before he was overtaken by Joe McConnell.

Captain Joseph McConnell Jr

Joe McConnell differed from other World War II veterans in Korea in that his earlier service had been not as a fighter pilot, but as a navigator in a B-24 Liberator bomber with the Eighth Air Force. He sought pilot training immediately after the conclusion of the war, and was one of the first to be trained right through to the new jet P-80 Shooting Star before seeing unit service. Posted to a unit in Alaska, he made many attempts to get sent to Korea, but was not successful until

late 1952, when he joined the 16th Squadron of the 51st FIW as a flight leader. His first victory came on 14 January 1953, and his fifth on 16 February. This was two days before Fernandez obtained his fifth and sixth, but was not confirmed until after, so that he became the 27th ace, and Fernandez the 26th.

After shooting down his eighth MiG on 12 April, his Sabre was hit and he was forced to bale out into the Yellow Sea. Luckily he was successfully picked up almost at once by a helicopter of the 3rd Air Rescue Wing. He was soon back in action, adding five more victories in a month – the last on 16 May when 'Pete' Fernandez passed Davis' score. Two days later came McConnell's best day when he shot down three MiGs to raise his score to 16 and make him the No 1 for the Korean war. Posted home, he became a service test-pilot, but he was killed in a crash at Edwards Air Force Base on 25 August 1954 when testing an F-86H. Subsequently a film was made, based on his life, called *Tiger in the Sky*, which followed the original with a reasonable degree of accuracy.

Colonel Vermont Garrison

Vermont Garrison served with the 4th Fighter Group in England from 1943 onward, gaining his first victories on P-47s during December of that year and January 1944. By the time the unit had converted to P-51s, he was already considered to be a very promising pilot and a possible leading ace, but on 3 March, after obtaining a victory which raised his score to 7.33, he was shot down and became a prisoner for the duration.

His chance to prove the experts right came some nine years later, when he was posted to his old unit – now the 4th FIW – in Korea early in 1953. He at once showed that he had not lost his touch, shooting down his first MiG on 21 February. Later in the spring he took over command of the unit from Royal Baker, and became an ace again on 5 June, when he brought down two MiGs to raise his total of these to six. By 19 July he had added four more to reach a Korean total of 10, and an overall score of 17.33.

Major John Bolt

John Bolt was to be the Navy Department's only jet ace of the Korean war – though not their only ace. A member of the US Marine Corps, Bolt was another World War II veteran, having flown in the Solomons campaign as one of 'Pappy' Boyington's famous 'Black Sheep' in VMF-214. Here he had been credited with shooting down six Zekes in his F4U Corsair between 23 September 1943 and 4 January 1944, twice getting two in a day. Later in the war he served aboard the Marine carrier, USS *Block Island*, but gained no further victories. In 1953 he was attached to the USAF to gain modern jet-fighter combat experience, and in this capacity he served with the 39th Squadron of the

51st FIW. With this unit he repeated his earlier success, claiming six MiG 15s shot down over a similar time scale – 16 May to 11 July – his last combat again bringing him a double victory.

Captain Ralph S Parr Jr

Like Harold Fischer, Ralph Parr was a very experienced pilot when he joined a Sabre unit in Korea, although not a veteran of World War II. He had indeed joined the USAAF as a cadet in 1942, but saw no active service during that war. Again like Fischer, his first taste of action was as an F-80 fighter bomber pilot, in which role he put in 150 sorties before being transferred to the 4th FIW in the summer of 1953 to have the opportunity of fighting MiGs. The war had less than two months to run when he gained his first two victories on 7 June, but only 11 days later another double made him the 34th ace of the conflict. A third double on the last day of the month raised his total to eight, followed on 12 July by a ninth and last MiG. As the Armistice approached it seemed that his chance to take his total into double figures would not arise, but then on 27 July – the last day of the war – he intercepted an Ilyushin Il-12 twin-engined transport and shot this down at 12.30 for the last victory of the conflict. The Communists subsequently claimed that he had shot down a civil airliner, but the USAF was in no doubt that the red star-marked aircraft was engaged upon military purposes.

Aside from various Marine and Navy pilots who were attached to the Sabre units, a number of pilots from other UN nationals also gained experience with them – notably members of the RAF and RCAF. Two of these were already aces in World War II and like so many of their US counterparts, were able to add further to their scores:

Squadron Leader JD Lindsay, RCAF

James Lindsay flew two tours with 403 Squadron, RCAF in 1944/45 as a member of the RAF's 2nd Tactical Air Force. Between 7 May and 3 August 1944 he was credited with six and one shared victories over German fighters, while on his second tour in April 1945 he added a probable Fw 190 to this total. Remaining in the RCAF after the war, he was attached to the USAF during 1952, serving with the 39th Squadron, 51st FIW, in Korea from July to November of that year. Here he was credited with two MiG 15s shot down and three more damaged, before returning to Canada in 1953 to a staff post.

Squadron Leader J MacKay, RCAF

John MacKay was one of the rare few who had already battled jet aircraft when he arrived in Korea. After training in Canada, he joined 401 Squadron, RCAF, in France with 2nd Tactical Air Force in August 1944. On 5 October he was one of five pilots who shot down a Messerschmitt Me 262 jet fighter – the first of these to be claimed by the British Commonwealth air forces. His first individual victory – over a Bf 109 – came on Christmas Day 1944, but then on New Year's Day 1945 he shot down an Fw 190, caused another to crash into the ground, and then similarly caused a Bf 109 to crash; on this date he also shared in damaging another Me 262. His lethal aerobatic abilities were further illustrated two weeks later, when having shot down two Fw 190s, he outturned a third, causing this too to spin and crash without firing a shot. On 28 March 1945, now as flight commander, and with his score standing at 8.2, he attacked six Bf 109s while still carrying a long-range drop tank beneath his aircraft, and shot down two of these. April saw him claim damage to three Arado Ar 234 jet bombers on the ground while strafing an airfield, while a further single victory raised his score to 11.2. Sent to Korea on an exchange posting to the USAF, he joined the 51st FIW in 1953 and on 30 June of that year shot down a MiG 15.

While most aerial combat over Korea occurred by day, there was considerable Communist activity by night. While some of this was undertaken by night-fighter versions of the MiG 15, the greater part was by slow, older, piston-engined types – both combat aircraft and trainers modified to drop a few small bombs for nuisance value – 'Bedcheck Charlies,' as they became known. Jet night fighters – Air Force F-94s and Navy F3D Skyknights – were employed, but proved too fast and heavy to deal with the latter types effectively. Eventually it was the night-fighter versions of the old F4U Corsair which proved most effective, and it was in one of these that the only US Navy ace and only night-fighter ace of the war appeared.

Lieutenant Guy P Bordelon

Guy Bordelon was flying with VC-3 on the carrier USS *Princeton* when he was detached with his Corsair to the Fifth Air Force to operate around the Seoul area in an effort to keep the 'Bedcheck Charlies' in check. The first two of these – identified as Yak 18s – fell before his guns during the night of 29/30 June 1953, while two nights later he was able to claim two Lavochkin fighters – La 9s or 11s. His fifth and final victory was claimed on 16 July, a few days before the Armistice – another Yak 18.

No Korean pilots are known to have become aces, and it is not known how many of the 'Honchos' were veteran Russian fighter pilots of World War II. However among the Chinese there were several successful aces. Chao Bao-tun gained his first victory over an F-84 Thunderjet, subsequently shooting down several F-86s and B-29s to reach a score of nine. He was awarded the order of Hero of Chinese People's Volunteers,

1st Degree. His wingman, Fan Van-Chou, also shot down an F-84 for his first victory, being credited with a total of eight. Another pilot, Kim Tsi-ok is said also to have amassed a total of nine, including a number of B-29s, while Chang Chi-Wei was credited with shooting down Maj George Davis on 10 February 1952 as his fourth victory.

For many career pilots of the USAF, the Korean conflict had given a valuable 'refresher course' to their fighter expertise and knowledge, opportunities of swift promotion, and no small fillip to their future careers. Not for all, however, was the war to have such a satisfactory outcome.

Lt Col Walker M Mahurin

Walker 'Bud' Mahurin first flew in a Stinson at the age of seven, and from that moment was determined to fly as a career. Family finances prevented his attendance at university, but by working and studying part-time he was able, by great effort, to graduate. As an apprentice engineer he then joined the government's civilian pilot training corps in his spare time, before finally being accepted as a Cadet in the USAAF in September 1941.

Posted to the 56th Fighter Group, he was one of the unit's original P-47 pilots to reach England with the Eighth Air Force, but was in trouble soon after arrival when he collided with a B-24 while trying to formate too close, and had to bale out of his Thunderbolt when one of the bomber's propellers severed the tail of his aircraft! He redeemed himself a few days later on 17 August 1943 by shooting down two Fw 190s for his first victories. Thereafter he scored fast, claiming three twin-engined Bf 110s on 4 October to raise his score to six and become an ace. Three more Bf 110s on 26 November made him the first pilot in the Eighth Air Force to reach double figures, and thereafter he retained his place in the top three, alternating with Walter Beckham of the 353rd Fighter Group and Robert Johnson in his own unit. On 27 March 1944, after 18 individual and one shared victories, he joined three others in shooting down a Dornier Do 217 bomber, but was shot down himself by the rear gunner. At the time he was heralded as the first pilot in Europe to reach 20 victories.

Coming down in France, Mahurin managed to evade capture and eventually reached England via the escape and evasion route organized by the French Resistance. Returned to the US, he undertook a second tour in late 1944 and early 1945, flying P-51s with the 3rd Air Commando Group in New Guinea, the Philippines and Okinawa. He gained one victory over a Japanese aircraft on 14 January 1945, but on a later mission was forced to come down in the sea off Formosa; on this occasion he was rescued without a hitch.

Remaining in the air force after the war, this aggressive ace left no stone unturned to get to Korea, finally organizing a 90-day detachment to the 51st FIW at the end of 1951 – a detachment he was subsequently able to extend. His first MiG fell on 6 January 1952, and when on 5 March he claimed one and a shared, his score over these jets stood at 3.5, bringing his total to 23.25. On 13 May 1952, while undertaking an experimental fighter-bomber sortie, his Sabre was hit by ground fire and brought down. Mahurin became a prisoner, and was subjected to the then-unfamiliar techniques known as 'brain-washing.' These measures were employed to coerce him into signing a document alleging that he had dropped chemical bombs on North Korean targets. This Mahurin eventually did, though only when personally satisfied that the documents contained so many errors and contradictions as to be nonsensical. On release after the war however, he found the US authorities unsympathetic, as the use of these methods by the Communists was not fully understood at that time. In consequence he faced a court-martial, and although he was later exonerated, his service career seemed irretrievably damaged, and he left for a post in the aviation industry – a poor return for one of America's greatest aces!

TOP-SCORING US FIGHTER PILOTS IN KOREA, 1950–53

	Score	WW II Score	Unit
Capt Joseph McConnell Jr	16		51st FIW
Maj James Jabara	15	1.5	4th FIW
Capt Manuel J Fernandez	14.5		4th FIW
Col Royal N Baker	13	3.5	4th FIW
Maj George A Davis*	14	7	4th FIW
Maj Frederick C Blesse	10		4th FIW
Lt Harold E Fischer	10		51st FIW
Lt Col Vermont Garrison	10	7.3	4th FIW
Col James K Johnson	10	1	4th FIW
Capt Lonnie R Moore	10		4th FIW
Capt Ralph S Parr Jr	10		4th FIW

5. MODERN COMBAT
The Electronic Age

hile the war in Korea proved the most important in terms of air combat in the decade following the end of World War II, it was however by no means the only conflict, several others pre-dating it. Subsequently other conflicts followed, and right up to the present day the years in which no military aircraft have 'crossed swords' in the sky have been few to say the least. Air action against guerrillas, terrorists, freedom fighters or others has taken place over French Indo-China, Malaya, Dutch Indonesia, Algeria, Kenya, Rhodesia, Cyprus and many other countries, but without meeting reaction in the air. Over the Congo and Biafra/Nigeria, and during the attempted invasion of Castro's Cuba by counterrevolutionary forces, both sides operated air arms of a sort, but in small numbers which ensured that any clashes were extremely limited, and always on a 'one-for-one' basis. Of greater significance were the various conflagrations between the Chinese Communists and Nationalists, in the air space above Israel and her immediate Arab neighbors, above the borders between India and Pakistan, and of course, in the long-drawn war above the emergent nation of North Vietnam.

After being expelled from mainland China following the civil war in 1948, the Nationalist forces occupied the offshore islands – notably Formosa (Taiwan). The Nationalist air force was supplied with American equipment during the later years of the war with Japan, which was subsequently kept up to date in terms of equipment and training. Although it seemed likely at first that China would invade these islands, no such action transpired. Apart from an occasional exchange of artillery fire, a sullen state of truce followed which has lasted with a steadily declining likelihood of hostilities to this day. From time to time both US and Taiwanese reconnaissance aircraft have been shot down by Chinese MiGs when straying too close to the border but only once has air fighting broken out on a major scale. This occurred on 24 September 1958 when 14 F-86Fs from Taiwan, six of them armed with new Sidewinder missiles, engaged a formation of about 20 MiGs. They emerged from the fight with the balance of success much in their favor – four shot down by missiles and six by gunfire without loss!

Even as the civil war in China was drawing to its close, the first shots in a conflict which

poses a threat to world peace to this day, were fired. In May 1948 the state of Israel was created when the British mandate in Palestine was brought to a premature close. Surrounded by hostile Arab states, several of which possessed established air forces, the Israelis started with virtually nothing. A few Avia C.210s (license-built versions of the famous Messerschmitt Bf 109G, re-engined with a Junkers Jumo engine in place of the normal Daimler-Benz, constructed in Czechoslovakia) were acquired clandestinely, and were hastily made ready for the defense of Tel Aviv. On 3 June 1948 two Egyptian Douglas DC-3 Dakotas appeared over the city, converted to bombers. A C.210s, piloted by Modi Allon, who had flown with the RAF, intercepted; one Dakota was shot down at once, and the second during its attempted escape. On 18 July, Allon added an Egyptian Spitfire to his total.

Subsequently Spitfire IXs and XVIs were obtained – some from Czechoslovakia, others rebuilt from shot-down Egyptian aircraft and wrecks on old British dumps. No 101 Squadron was formed, the Spitfires supplementing, and subsequently replacing the C.210s, which were unreliable and dangerous to fly. The unit was crewed by a mixed bag of Jewish pilots who had served with the RAF or USAAF, and by Canadian volunteers. During the War of Independence, in late 1948 to early 1949, the squadron raised the Israeli score to 21 aircraft – mostly Arab, but including five RAF Spitfires and Tempests which strayed into Israeli air space on 7 January 1949, and a Mosquito. Some 50 percent of these victories were credited to just three pilots, all of whom had previous experience in World War II. Modi Allon, Israel's first air hero, served with the unit but was killed during October 1948 in a forced-landing after being hit and wounded by ground fire; as a result he never became an ace as such. The most successful pilots of the period were:

Rudolf Auergarten
Rudi Auergarten served with the US Ninth Air Force in Europe as a 2nd Lieutenant during 1944. Flying P-47s mainly on ground-support duties with the 371st Fighter Group, he had few opportunities to become involved in air combat. However, on one of the rare occasions when his unit met the Luftwaffe on 3 October, he was able to claim two victories. Emigrating to Israel after the war, he was one of the original pilots of 101 Squadron, flying first C.210s and then Spitfires.

Above: A Czech-built Avia C-210 – the first Israeli fighter type – which provided the initial equipment of 101 Squadron. Right: John McElroy, the Canadian ex-Malta ace who served with the Israeli forces in 1948, gaining further victories with 101 Squadron – including two RAF Spitfire 18s!

In the cockpit of the latter type of aircraft he was engaged in several combats with Egyptian aircraft, sharing in the destruction of a Dakota on 11 November 1948, while on 28 December he shot down a Spitfire and shared in the destruction of two Fiat G.55s. Another Spitfire shot down and several fighters damaged brought his total to at least three and two shared in this war.

J F McElroy

John McElroy was one of the Chal Ha'Avir's Canadian volunteers, and was without doubt the most experienced and successful pilot to fly with 101 Squadron in 1948. A native of Port Arthur, Ontario, he served in the army before transferring to the RCAF. After training he arrived in England early in 1942, but from May to December served with 249 Squadron on Malta. On his return from the siege island, he was a seasoned fighter pilot with a DFC and a score of some eight and two shared, plus at least a dozen more probables or damaged. Following a year off operations, he joined 421 Squadron, RCAF, in 2nd Tactical Air Force as a flight commander, adding two German fighters to his score during the invasion of Normandy in June 1944. Promoted and posted to command 416 Squadron, he added a further victory over an Fw 190 in July and shared a Bf 109 in September, by which time he had been awarded a Bar to his DFC. The following month his tour ended and a year later he was released from the air force. Joining the Israelis in 1948, he gained three victories with 101 Squadron including a Fiat G.55 on 30 December and two RAF Spitfire XVIIIs on 7 January 1949.

JJ Doyle

Joseph 'Jack' Doyle flew with 417 Squadron, RCAF, in Italy in 1944, and was credited with at least one and one probable. With 101 Squadron he claimed a Spitfire and two G.55s while flying a Spitfire himself. Flying one of the first Mustangs to reach Israel on 7 January 1949, he claimed one further victory while escorting Harvards to become the unit's top-scorer of the first War of Independence.

Several years of precarious peace followed, allowing the Israelis the opportunity to modernize their air force by buying in ex-Swedish P-51 Mustangs, Mosquitos, and the first jets – British Gloster Meteors. During the mid-1950s hostility began to increase again, and Arab incursions into Israeli airspace finally saw the first jet battle on 31 August 1955 when Meteors intercepted and shot down two Egyptian D.H. Vampires. Massive injection of Russian arms and aid to Egypt and Syria followed the rise to power of Abdul Gamil Nasser, and the nationalization of the Suez Canal paved the way for war. War broke out on 29 October 1956 with an Israeli offensive designed to break the Egyptian blockade of the Tiran Straits. Israel entered the conflict with the knowledge that the French and British would intervene in an effort to regain control of the canal. Indeed following a French and British ultimatum to both combatants to withdraw from each side of the waterway, Anglo-French air strikes from Cyprus, from carriers offshore, and from Israeli territory (French units only) destroyed the greater part of the Egyptian air force on the ground. Over the Sinai desert, action was relatively limited, but newly acquired swept-wing Dassault Mystère IV fighters took the measure of the Egyptian MiG 15s and 17s,

Main picture: Israeli
Mirage taking off.
Inset: Groundcrew of the
Israeli Defence Force/Air
Force paint victory symbols
on Mirage IIIs.

allowing Dassault Ouragons, Meteors and P-51s to concentrate on support of the ground forces. Seven victories were claimed, plus four probables, including four MiG 15s, a MiG 17, four Vampires and two Meteors. Most fell to the Mystères, a Captain Yac being the most successful pilot, credited with two of the MiGs. Israeli losses were mainly to ground fire. In the whole conflict the only Anglo-French loss in aerial combat was a reconnaissance Canberra of the RAF, shot down by a Syrian MiG 15, while the wholesale destruction of Egyptian aircraft on the ground ensured that no opposition was met in the air.

From that time onward the names of successful Israeli pilots have not been released for security reasons and as a general principle. From 1956 to the present day, air combat has remained frequent over the airspace surrounding Israel's borders, and the virtuosity of its pilots has become legend. Without doubt they are now the most combat-experienced and successful jet pilots in the world. Their progress gives a clear indication of the general level of escalation which the Middle Eastern conflicts have witnessed.

Soon after the end of the Suez war, Egypt began receiving supplies of MiG 19s – the first Russian production fighter capable of supersonic performance in level flight. To counter these, the Israelis were able to acquire from France a number of Super Mystères of similar performance. These soon gained their first success when, during a border incursion, they shot down two MiG 17s. Fighter development was proceeding fast at this time, and no sooner were the Super Mystères in service than the Arab nations took delivery of the very latest MiG 21s. Again a counter was urgently needed, and again it was to the French that the Israelis turned, buying this time the superlative Dassault Mirage delta. These were first in action on 20 August 1963 – but again the older MiG 17s were their opponents, two being claimed shot down. The first Mirage-versus-MiG 21 clash did not come until the following year, when two Mirages shot down one of these advanced Russian aircraft. One of the few pilots who has been named, a Lt Col Ran, shot down a Jordanian Hawker Hunter on 13 November 1966, and later was credited with two MiG 21s, one shot down with a missile and one with cannon fire. These latter victories may well have occurred on 7 April 1967 when six Syrian MiG 21s were claimed shot down in a single combat to bring to 13 the number of confirmed victories gained since the end of the war of 1956.

The air forces of the Arab countries were all of a much more substantial nature by 1967 as tension rose. Egyptian closures of international waterways to Israel and an obvious intention to invade led to a well-planned and massive Israeli pre-emptive strike being launched on 5 June 1967 to open what became known as the Six Day War. As Mirages, Super Mystères and Vautour jet bombers struck air bases deep in Egypt, Syria, Iraq and Jordan, an incredible degree of success was achieved. On the first day alone 240 Egyptian, 45 Syrian, 16 Jordanian and seven Iraqi aircraft were claimed destroyed for the loss of about 20 Israeli machines. Of this total 30 were claimed in air combat, the rest on the ground; only one Israeli aircraft is known to have fallen to an Arab pilot. Lt Col Ran was involved in several strikes on this first day, and may well have gained further aerial victories. One Mirage pilot claimed two MiG 21s in one mission and one more later on this date, plus another two on 7 June. In the six days of the conflict a total of 353 Arab aircraft were claimed destroyed, 60 of them in the air, for a loss of 31 – most to anti-aircraft defenses.

The utter and humiliating defeat inflicted on the Arab nations brought another long lull, as they sought to rebuild their shattered forces, but skirmishing and aerial incursions never stopped; by November 1969 34 Egyptian aircraft had been shot down since the war had ended! Following constant Egyptian Fedayeen guerrilla attacks on Israeli settlements, and other provocations, the Israeli air force began a series of deep penetration attacks into Egypt in what became known as the War of Attrition. By the end of March 1970 total claims since 1967 had risen to over 100 for the loss of 19; 85 of these were Egyptian aircraft, the balance Syrian. By now however relations with France had deteriorated, and further deliveries of Mirages had been stopped by the government of General Charles de Gaulle. Israel urgently needed

Top: The famous McDonnel-Douglas F-4 Phantom in Israeli service.
Above: Probably the best fighter in the world today, the F-15 Eagle has already gained numerous victories in Israeli hands.

a new supplier of aircraft, and was eventually to find this in the United States. From mid-1970 Israel received deliveries of McDonnell-Douglas A-4 Skyhawk fighter-bombers and the ubiquitous McDonnell-Douglas F-4 Phantom fighter. This period of fighting reached a climax on 13 September 1973 when no less than eight Syrian MiG 21s were claimed in a single combat to bring the results of six years of intermittent fighting to 135 victories for the loss of about 25.

Israel's concern for world opinion plus poor intelligence prevented it from launching a further pre-emptive strike even though the Arab nations were observed making preparations for a further attack. On 6 October 1973 therefore, it was the Arabs who struck first on the traditional holy day, Yom Kippur. Egyptian forces struck across the Suez canal to break the Israeli defences. The Israeli air force — composed now mainly of some 128 Phantoms, 55 Mirages and substantial numbers of Skyhawks — was thrown in, but the Egyptians had moved forward with them large numbers of anti-aircraft missile batteries and radar-guided automatic anti-aircraft guns, and losses were at once severe — estimated at 50 in the first three days. Indeed the Israeli aircraft casualties were so heavy that

additional F-4s and A-4s were taken from operational US Navy squadrons and rushed to Israel as reinforcements.

In the air the Israelis were faced by some 580 Egyptian aircraft, and many others of the air forces of Syria (approximately 240) and Iraq (approximately 200), reinforced by contingents from Libya, Algeria and even Pakistan. Most of these aircraft were of Russian manufacture, including MiG 17s, 19s, 21s and 23s, Sukhoi Su 7s and 9s, and Il-28 and Tu-22 bombers, plus a number of Mirages and a few other types. Air combat proved no problem to Israel, however, for her pilots were able speedily to reinstate their superiority here, and by the end of the second

week it was believed that Arab losses included 113 Egyptian, 149 Syrian and 21 Iraqi aircraft. When hostilities ceased, total Arab aircraft losses were believed to have risen to some 440, about 25 of which had fallen to Israeli Hawk ground-to-air missiles. Total confirmed credits in air combat were 277, but Israeli losses in all arms were by far the highest suffered in any conflict. Some 118 Israeli aircraft were destroyed, but 95 of these definitely fell to guns and missiles from the ground.

Frequent fighting followed the initial armistice until the end of 1973, but subsequently relations with Egypt, much improved, have led to a cessation of hostilities with that nation. Iraq's costly war with Iran has left Syria as Israel's only remaining active enemy for the time being.

Israel has been building up her own aircraft industry steadily, and by 1973 the first examples of Super Mystères and Mirages rebuilt with American-made J-57 engines, were entering service. Subsequently, following the clandestine obtaining of plans of more advanced Dassault jet fighters, Israel has developed and built her own Kfir fighter, developed from the Mirage — which she also built as the Dagger. The US has supplied the most recent air-superiority fighter, the McDonnel-Douglas F-15 Eagle, which entered service early in 1979, and subsequently the smaller, lighter General Dynamics F-16 Falcon. The F-15s were first in action in June 1979 when they shot down four Syrian MiG 21s, a fifth falling to a Kfir for that type's first victory; all were hit by missiles. However, the Israeli pilots have always put great stress on aerial gunnery, preferring the cannon to the more expensive missile. Consequently there was some elation on 27 September 1979 when the F-15s next met the MiGs and two MiGs were brought down by gunfire. By 1981 23 additional confirmed victories had been claimed since 1973 – 18 of them during the last two years.

By now it was known that a Major G had become top-scorer with 18 victories, eight of these having been claimed in two missions on a single day during the Yom Kippur War, while several others have been credited with scores of 10–12. Indeed the pilot responsible for the first F-15 victory is known to have had seven previous successes to his credit. Of the 539 confirmed aerial victories credited to Israeli fighters by the start of 1982, over 220 have been gained by two squadrons. The original 101 Squadron is still in existence and had 120 victories by this time, including the first credited to a Kfir pilot. The second fighter squadron to be formed — the first Meteor squadron of the early 1950s — gained two victories with its Meteors, then received Mirages. With these it claimed 12 victories in the Six Day War, 29 in the War of Attrition, and 55 during the Yom Kippur War. Its score stood at 101 when it became the first to receive the new F-16.

At the time of writing the Israeli air force had again just been engaged in a period of sustained combat during operations to destroy the Palestine Liberation Organization in the Lebanon. Challenged by the Syrian Air Force during May 1982, the Israelis achieved one of their most devastating successes yet, claiming 81 opposing jets – including many MiG 23s and 25s – shot down for the loss of a single A-4 Skyhawk. At the same time the use of flares dropped to draw off Syrian infrared heat-seeking missiles, and SMART bombs which homed on to the radar transmissions of Syrian SAM launching sites, virtually rendered the whole of their air-defense system powerless. It seems that the lessons of the Yom Kippur War had been well learned!

It seems unlikely that Israeli forces will not see further aerial combat. Her pilots are the top scorers of all time in jet-versus-jet combat. Will their names and details of their achievements ever be announced to add to the sum of our knowledge on this subject? All those with an interest in air combat wait in deep anticipation.

Combat over the Indian Subcontinent

In September 1965 a festering border dispute between India and Pakistan erupted into full-scale war. The Indians possessed the larger air force numerically, composed mainly of British and French types – Hawker Hunter, Folland Gnat and Dassault Mystère fighters, Dassault Ouragon fighter-bombers and English Electric Canberra bombers. The smaller, but highly trained Pakistan Air Force was equipped in large part with F-86F Sabres, plus a few F-104 Starfighters. Fighting lasted little more than two weeks, but during that time Pakistan gained a definite ascendancy in the air, while India enjoyed the edge on the ground – particularly in regard to armored operations.

It was the well-proven Sabres that emerged with honors, being credited with all but five of the 36 victories claimed. The Indians claimed 73 victories – undoubtedly a considerable overestimate – for an admitted loss of 35. Several victories were gained by the Hunters, but it was the Gnats which achieved the best results, outmaneuvering the heavier F-86s to a degree that gained them the epiphet 'Sabre-Slayer.'

Squadron Leader Mohammad Alam
Sqn Ldr Alam of the Pakistan Air Force proved by far the most successful pilot of this brief war, adding weight to the lessons of Korea with a virtuoso performance which exceeded that of even the cream of the Israeli fighter pilots. In 1965 Alam was an extremely experienced pilot, with many hundreds of hours flying time on the Sabre. In addition he was top-scorer of the PAF in air-to-air gunnery competitions, and had flown the Hunter while on attachment to the RAF, thus being well aware of the strong points and weaknesses of what was to be his principal opponent in 1965.

Aged 32 at that time, he was commanding the Sabre-equipped 11 Squadron. His first engagement with Indian Hunters occurred over the front on 6 September, and in the dogfight which transpired he was able to claim two shot down. Next day he led a scramble by four Sabres and a Starfighter following a surprise strike on Sargodha airfield by Indian Mystères. As the Pakistanis got into the air, six Hunters swept in for a

follow-up strafe. Alam at once released a GAR 8 Sidewinder missile at the last Hunter, and brought it down. He then cut across the line of flight of the others as they broke away from their strafe, shooting down four in quick succession, thus becoming the first jet 'ace-in-a-day,' and the only jet pilot known for certain to have gained five victories in a single sortie. Alam was to have a further opportunity to add to his score 10 days later on 17 September, when he again claimed two Hunters shot down. With nine victories he was the only ace of the war; his nearest rival achieved four.

International mediation brought the conflict to an early halt, but hostility between the two nations remained unchecked, and both made great efforts during the succeeding years to build up their forces from any sources available. Pakistan acquired further Sabres and F-104s, plus Mirages from the French and MiG 19s from the Chinese. India struggled to enlarge her domestic aircraft industry, building under license Gnats, and constructing a few examples of the Indian HF-24 Marut fighter. Her main source of supply now became the Soviet Union, which supplied Sukhoi Su 7 fighter-bombers and MiG 21 fighters. It was planned to assemble the MiG 21 in Indian factories.

Above: Squadron Leader Mohammad Alam, commanding officer of 11 Squadron of the Pakistani Air Force in 1965, and top scorer of the war with India in that year. He is seen here with his F-86F Sabre in which he shot down five Indian Hunters in one sortie on 7 September. Note 9 Indian flag victory symbols, plus two smaller one to denote aircraft damaged.

Left: Wing Commander Syed Sa'ad Hatmi, who claimed 2 victories in 1965 and 3 in 1971 to become Pakistan's second ace.

The fragile peace lasted for six years, but in November 1971 war again broke out. This time the classic pattern of escalation ensured that larger forces were employed, and although the fighting lasted little longer than in 1965 before mediation brought a more permanent halt than before, the scale of operations was very heavy.

Again the Pakistanis appeared to gain the advantage in the air, claiming 104 Indian aircraft destroyed, 50 of them in aerial combat, for the loss of 54. The heavy losses included a complete squadron of Sabres lost on the ground in East Pakistan (now Bangladesh), and does not indicate the unfavorable kill/loss ratio that at first appears. Indian claims totalled 94 — like the Pakistanis, ground fire and surface-to-air missiles accounting for a much higher proportion of claims than on the previous occasion. India admitted losses of 10 — although identification of shot-down Indian aircraft by serial numbers by the Pakistanis shows a substantially higher level of loss than this.

On this occasion, possibly because of the larger numbers of units and aircraft employed, no one pilot on either side emerged as a high scorer, and the types gaining victories were rather wider spread than before — although the Sabres and Gnats again played an important role for their respective air forces. Throughout both conflicts no Indian pilot emerged with a score of five or more, but the PAF did produce another pilot in this category.

Wing Commander Syed Sa'ad Hatmi

Wg Cdr Hatmi had seen action in 1965 as a Flight Lieutenant in one of the Sabre squadrons, claiming a Hunter on 6 September and a Gnat on the 13th. The year 1971 found him as commanding officer of one of the MiG 19 units and, flying one of these supersonic jets, he shot down a Hunter on 5 December and two Su 7s on 8 December to raise his total for the two wars to five.

Vietnam

During the long period of conflict which ended with the departure of the French, the Armée de l'Air and Aeronavale had flown many thousands of sorties over the area then known as French Indo-China, but had engaged only in ground attack and bombing raids on Viet Cong guerrillas. The Viet Cong at that time possessed no air force of any kind. Following the division of the country into Communist North Vietnam and non-Communist South Vietnam, the United States became increasingly drawn in to advise the South in its military operations against guerrilla actions directed from the North. This involvement escalated steadily until US units were operating in support of the Viet Minh. At first air action was limited to counterinsurgency work by older types of aircraft, the most modern being F-100 Super Sabre fighter-bombers. However in August 1964 targets in North Vietnamese territory were raided in an effort to halt, or at least reduce, the flow of supplies and men to the South.

Now began more than six years of aerial operations during which US Air Force and Navy aircraft operated against specified ground targets in the face of a growing air-defense organization, which they were rarely allowed to attack at its sources. While the greater part of the North Vietnamese effort was always concentrated upon surface-to-air missiles (SAMs) and on radar-guided automatic weapons, they were able to build up a small, but relatively effective fighter force. Here the US forces were in a somewhat odd situation. Contemporary thinking believed that the gun was no longer the appropriate weapon for a Mach 2 performance fighter aircraft, and while the older types still in service — principally the Republic F-105 Thunderchief (or 'Thud') of the USAF and the Vought F-8 Crusader of the USN — were cannon-armed, the newer two-seat McDonnell-Douglas F-4 Phantoms of both air forces carried only missile armament. While the F-4s were to bear the bulk of the aerial fighting, the experience of Vietnam was to show that, useful as the missile might be, in air superiority work where fighter-versus-fighter combat might be expected, there is still nothing to beat the gun. Before the end of the conflict, Phantoms in service were modified to carry a 20mm Gatling-type Vulcan multibarrel

175

weapon in a pod fitted to the underside of the nose. All new US fighters have since featured gun armament.

By early 1965 raids into North Vietnam were increasing in size, and on 4 April of that year the new North Vietnamese air force gained its first successes when four MiG 17s shot down two F-105s. It was to the Navy that the first countersuccesses went, when on 17 June Cdr Louis Page and Lt Jack D Batson of VF-21 shot down two MiG 17s while flying F-4B Phantoms. Three days later another MiG 17 fell – but to an old piston-engined A-1H Skyraider, flown by Lt Clint Johnson. The Air Force's first claims came on 10 July, when two more MiG 17s were credited to Capt Kenneth E Holcombe and Capt Thomas S Roberts of the 45th Tactical Fighter Squadron, both flying the F-4C version of the Phantom. On 24 July the first loss was suffered to a SAM, when an F-4C fell to one of these missiles.

Despite the early preponderance of success by the Phantoms, they were by no means to be the sole instruments of air power as Vietnamese MiG strength increased to two Companies (60–70 aircraft). Navy strikes, flown from aircraft carriers in the Gulf of Tonkin – safe from the guerrilla attacks which were to threaten the Air Force's ground bases in the South – were carried out mainly by A-1s and A-4 Skyhawks, cover being provided by both F-4Bs and F-8E and H Crusaders. Indeed when the first phase of aerial activities virtually came to an end at the start of 1968 the Crusaders with their single-seat configuration and cannon armament had gained 14 of the Navy's 29 victories only 12 were credited to F-4s, and the remaining three were credited to A-1Hs (two) and an A-4. Between then and the end of 1971, when only the Navy engaged in any combat, five of the seven victories credited went to F-8s. All but two of these successes had been gained against MiGs – 26 MiG 17s and eight MiG 21s. On 20 December 1966 two F-4Bs of VF 114 shot down a pair of AN 2 biplane transports, the only non-fighter types claimed by US pilots throughout the war.

With the USAF, a great part of the actual weapons delivery, and SAM-suppression sorties during fighter sweeps, were undertaken by the tough F-105s, while F-4Cs provided cover above. This resulted in the 'Thuds' suffering the preponderance of Air Force losses during the 1965–67 period, but it should not be thought that they were not able to make their mark in combat. Of the 86 victories credited to the USAF by the end of February 1968, 28 were claimed by F-105 pilots. The year 1967 saw the heaviest fighting of this first phase, and was marked by four particularly heavy battles. On 2 January seven MiG 21s were claimed by F-4Cs of the 6th Tactical Fighter Wing, while on 19 April F-105s of the 355th TFW claimed four MiG 17s. Another big day came on 13 May when 355th and 388th TFW F-105s accounted for five more MiG 17s,

8th TFW F-4s adding two more. Finally on 20 May a further six MiGs – four '17s and two '21s – were claimed by 8th and 366th TFW Phantom pilots.

When operations over the North were brought to a halt for the Air Force at the end of February 1968, all the 86 claims made had been against fighters – 61 MiG 17s and 25 MiG 21s – which had been appearing in growing numbers since first met in 1966. Losses had been quite staggering – 670 US aircraft by the end of 1967, of which 52 percent were suffered by the USN during 65 percent of the operations flown. Only 50 of these were known to be in air combat, the balance being believed inflicted by ground defenses. However Vietnamese fighter pilots claimed a total of 320 US aircraft downed. This resulted in the employment of growing numbers of Electronic Counter-Measures (ECM) aircraft (notably RB-66s and F-105Fs) to disrupt the enemy's radars and other devices. However, when the 50 aerial combat losses were compared with the 110 confirmed claims achieved up to that date, the kill/loss ratio was clearly far less attractive than it had been in Korea. Indeed, during the limited operations undertaken by the USN during the first five months of 1968, losses in combat were to exceed claims.

President Lyndon Johnson's cessation of bombing of the North in an attempt to reach a compromise peace resulted in a lull in operations which lasted from the start of 1968 until the end of 1971. Indeed the USAF was to claim no aerial victories for four years, from February 1968 to February 1972. During the first period of air fighting, from 1965 to 1968, few US pilots of either service were credited with more than two victories; there was however one remarkable exception:

Colonel Robin Olds

Californian-born Robin Olds was the son of Maj Gen Robert Olds, and was once again to hammer home the lessons of experience so valuable to a jet fighter pilot. He first saw action during the summer of 1944 flying a P-38 Lightning with the 479th Fighter Group of the Eighth Air Force in England. Although a latecomer to the P-38, he gained two victories in his first successful combat on 14 August, and three more on the 25th, to become an ace in two engagements. Further victories included two on 14 February 1945 which raised his total to nine, and made him the Eighth's top-scoring P-38 pilot of the war. His unit then converted to P-51D Mustangs, in one of which he claimed another double on 19 March and his 12th victory on 7 April; he was also credited with destroying 11 aircraft on the ground with strafing attacks. Remaining in the Air Force after the war, he came second in the Thompson Jet Trophy Race during the 1946 National Air Races, and married the movie star Ella Raines. Nearly 22 years later, now a Colonel, he was the very popular commander of

Right: From being the most successful exponent of the P-38 Lightning with the Eighth Air Force in World War II, Col Robin Olds distinguished himself again some 23 years later, becoming the most successful American pilot of the first phase of the war in Vietnam, where he gained four more victories to raise his personal score to 16. Here he straps on his parachute harness before a mission over Vietnam.

the F-4C equipped 8th Tactical Fighter Wing in Southeast Asia. He led his unit to their first really big success on 2 January 1967, when seven MiG 21s were shot down, being credited with one himself. A further MiG 21 was credited to him on 4 May, and on the 20th when the 8th TFW gained its second major victory, he shot down two MiG 17s of the four claimed. With four victories he was undisputedly the most successful US pilot of this period. Subsequently promoted Brigadier General, he returned to the US to an important training job.

While the many US pilots flying over North Vietnam had enjoyed only limited opportunities to engage in combat with the much smaller number of defenders, the converse was true of the defenders, who were well-placed to engage in frequent combat. During the initial period the pilots of the 1st and 2nd Companies of the NVAF enjoyed many successes — not only against the American fighters, but also against the fighter-bombers, reconnaissance aircraft and other types employed. During the whole conflict at least 15 North Vietnamese pilots are believed to have become aces, but it was during 1967 particularly that many of these gained the major parts of their scores.

Nguyen Van Bay

Bay was the first Vietnamese ace to gain the attention of the Western media. Transferred to the air force in 1964 at the age of 28, after 12 years' service with the Viet Minh, he flew some of the first MiG 17s received in the 2nd Company, being credited with seven victories. These included two F-4s in late April 1967, an F-8 Crusader and an F-105.

Nguyen Ngoc Do

Do transferred to the air force at the same time and at the same age as Bay, having served for a

Left: Robin Olds is 'chaired' by his jubilant pilots on return from a successful sortie in 1967.

similar period with the ground forces. Flying with the 1st Company, he is known to have claimed an F-105 on 30 April 1967, an F-4 at night, and two F-101 Voodoo reconnaissance aircraft among his total of six victories. By 1971 he had risen to command his unit.

Vu Ngoc Dinh

Dinh transferred to the air force early in 1967, and was posted to the 2nd Company on completion of training. His first victory was over an F-105, following which he was given command

Below left: First North Vietnamese fighter ace to become known was Nguyen Van Bay of the 2nd Company (right), who claimed 7 victories during 1967.
Below: Two of North Vietnam's top pilots discuss tactics. In the cockpit of the MiG 21 is Capt Pham Thang Ngan (8 victories) of the 1st Company; talking to him is Capt Nguyen Van Coc (9) of the 2nd Company.

of a section formed specially to combat the EB-66s, and by October 1968 his score had reached five. His last victory came on 28 January 1970; after engaging some F-4s in cloud without success, he spotted an HH-53B 'Jolly Green Giant' helicopter at low level, and shot this down, all of its six-man crew being killed. On occasions he is known to have flown a MiG 21 carrying the number 4324; this aircraft was flown by nine different pilots, who jointly gained 14 victories while using it.

Nguyen Van Coc

Captain Coc volunteered for the air force in 1965, but his training, which took place in Russia, was delayed by his lack of knowledge of the language. He joined the 2nd Company in 1967, flying MiG 21s, and is known to have shot down an 8th TFW F-4D on 23 August of that year, and a Navy F-4 soon afterward. At least two of his nine victories were gained with 'Atoll' guided missiles.

When bombing was resumed and air fighting began again early in 1972, all further victories in both the USAF and the USN were gained by F-4s. The F-105 had long been out of production and the heavy losses of the late 1960s had led to its replacement due to shortage of aircraft of the type, while the F-8 had also been replaced due to its age. The American fighters now found themselves faced by three companies of MiGs, a new 3rd Coy being formed early in 1972. The MiG 17s and 21s had now also been reinforced with numbers of MiG 19s. The Air Force was now mainly flying F-4Ds, plus some F-4Es, while the Navy had added F-4Js to its existing F-4Bs. Disappointed with the results achieved with the missiles, the USN had reintroduced gun dogfighting after 1968 and, even using aircraft equipped only with missiles, much better results were achieved. Indeed the USN was to

achieve 25 victories in 1972/3 for the loss of only two of its own aircraft shot down in combat. The USAF did not follow suit until October 1972, and in this latter period was able only to achieve a 2:1 victory/loss ratio.

The Navy continued to get the 'firsts' when it gained the first 'kill' of the new phase; this was a MiG 21 shot down on 19 January 1972 by Lt Randy Cunningham of VF 96 for his first success. It was a month later on 21 February before the 432nd TFW's Maj Robert A Lodge also brought down a MiG 21 for the air forces's return to combat. Fighting was fierce during the early months of the year, culminating on 10 May with the biggest 'game bag' of the whole war for the US fighters. On that date Air Force F-4Ds from the 432nd TFW claimed three MiG 21s, one falling to Maj Lodge for his third victory and one to Capt Richard S Ritchie for his first. However Lodge was then shot down – it is believed by the Vietnamese ace Le Thanh Dao in a MiG 19. Three VF 96 F-4Js meanwhile accounted for six MiG 17s between them, three of these going to Lt Cunningham to make him the first US ace of the conflict. Another MiG 17 was claimed by a VF 81 F-4B and a MiG 21 by a VF 92 F-4J, to raise the total claims for the day by the Americans to 11. Cunningham's third victory of the day was over Colonel Toon, the Vietnamese top scorer, who was killed.

The Air Force was to have its own ace of the war later in the year when Capt Ritchie gained his fifth victory, but these were to be the only US 'front seat' pilots to become aces during the long conflict. When Capt Paul D Howman of the 432nd Tactical Reconnaissance Wing shot down a MiG 21 on 8 January 1973 he had gained the Air Force's last victory over Vietnam; 49 had been added since the resumption of fighting the previous February (plus two by B-52 rear gunners), these included 41 MiG 21s and eight MiG 19s. The Navy gained the last victory – another MiG 21 by Lt Vic Kowaleski of VF 161 on 12 January 1973, to raise this air force's total during the last 12 months to 25 (plus one by a missile launched by a ship).

Of the USAF's 135 victories by fighters, the most successful unit was the 8th TFW with 38.5 victories, and within that unit, the 433rd Tactical Fighter Squadron with 12. Runner up was the 432nd Tactical Reconnaissance Wing with 35, this unit's 13th TF Squadron being the second most successful squadron with 11. The USN's 58 victories (excluding the three by A-1Hs and the A-4) were shared by no less than 19 different fighter squadrons. VF 96 was the most successful with nine victories, followed by the F-8-equipped VF 211 with seven and VF 51 with six. During the Vietnam war most US victories were gained by two-seater aircraft, and in consequence it became the practice to credit rear-seat weapons systems/radar operators (some of whom were qualified pilots) with victories as well as the aircraft commander in the front seat.

Below: On 27 December 1972 Capt Pham Tuan (later an astronaut in a Russian space capsule) shot down a USAF B-52 Stratofortress bomber. Here he describes to the captured American pilot of the aircraft just how he did it.

Left: The USAF's ace of the Vietnamese war, Capt Steve Ritchie (left) with him weapons operator Capt Charles D 'Chuck' DeBellvue with their F-4D of the 432nd Tactical Fighter Wing. Note the housing for the 20mm Vulcan cannon mounted under the nose.

Above right: Bomb-carrying USAF F-4C of the 8th Tactical Fighter Wing.

Below right: First American ace over Vietnam was the US Navy's Lt Randolph 'Duke' Cunningham of squadron VF-96, seen here in his F-4 Phantom with his Weapons Systems Operator, Lt Bill Driscoll. Although the splitter plate of the aircraft appears to show 8 victory stars, Cunningham and Driscoll were in fact credited with 5 victories, including an aircraft believed flown by the leading North Vietnamese ace, Col Toon.

It is not felt, in the context of this work, that these are true aces, otherwise night-fighter radar operators would also have to be considered. Three US airmen – two USAF and one USN – are listed as aces, but are actually 'rear seat men,' their victory totals relating to victories which have *also* been credited to the pilot – thus Lt (jg) Willie Driscoll of VF 96 is listed as an ace with five victories, these being the five aircraft shot down by Randy Cunningham, who was the aircraft commander and pilot.

Lieutenant Randolph Cunningham

Randy 'Duke' Cunningham served with VF 96 on board the carrier CVW-9, flying F-4J Phantoms. He gained his first victory over a MiG 21 on 19 January 1972, adding a MiG 17 on 8 May. Two days later he was able to claim three MiG 17s in a single combat – the largest multiple kill of the war. The third of these, gained after a hard climbing and diving combat was known to be the top-scoring Vietnamese pilot, Col Toon. Cunningham was armed only with missiles during this fight, and was of the opinion that, had he had gun armament, he could have added up to three more to his total, so large was the number of available targets in the air on this date.

Colonel Nguyen Toon

Little is know of the top-scoring Vietnamese ace other than that he obtained all his 13 victories during the period from 1966 to 1968 while flying MiG 17s and 21s, and that he was killed in action in a MiG 17, shot down over Haiphong by Lt Cunningham of VF 96 on 10 May 1972.

Captain Richard S Ritchie

Ritchie flew F-4Ds and Es with the 555th TF Squadron in the 432nd TRW during 1972. He gained his first victory during the big battle of 10 May 1972, adding another on 31 May, two on 8 July and his fifth on 28 August. All his claims were against MiG 21s, and in all cases except on 31 May, his weapons-system operator was Capt Charles 'Chuck' B DeBellevue, who was involved in two other successful combats with other pilots.

Guen Doc

Doc was commander of the new NVAF 3rd Company, which saw much action during the period from May to October 1972. He was credited with five victories.

Le Thanh Dao

Senior Lt Dao was one of the 3rd Company's three most successful pilots, gaining six victories during the period from May to October 1972. He is believed to have shot down Maj Robert Lodge of the 432nd TRW on 10 May, after that pilot's third victory; Dao was flying a MiG 19 on this date. Two months later he shot down another F-4 with an 'Atoll' missile.

Nguyen Duc Soat

Another of the 3rd Company's top-scorers in 1972, Soat gained his first victory over an A-7 Corsair attack aircraft on 23 May, then claiming F-4s on 24 and 27 June, 26 August and 12 October; his sixth credited victory was over an unmanned reconnaissance drone.

ACES OF THE VIETNAM WAR

United States

Lt Randolph Cunningham	5	US Navy	VF 96
Capt Richard S Ritchie	5	USAF	432nd TRW

Weapons-Systems Operators classed as aces

Capt Charles B DeBellevue	6	USAF	432nd TRW
Lt (jg) William Driscoll	5	US Navy	VF 96
Capt Jeffrey S Feinstein	5	USAF	432nd TRW

Col Nguyen Toon	13	
Capt Nguyen Van Coc	9	2nd Coy
Luu Huy Chao	8	
Mai Van Cuong	8	1st Coy
Capt Pham Thanh Ngan	8	1st Coy
Nguyen Hong Nhi	8	
Nguyen Van Bay	7	2nd Coy
Sen Lt Le Thanh Dao	6	3rd Coy
Vu Ngoc Dinh	6	2nd Coy
Nguyen Ngoc Do	6	1st Coy
Dang Ngoc Ngu	6	3rd Coy
Nguyen Duc Soat	6	3rd Coy
Guen Doc	5	3rd Coy
Le Hai	5	
Kyong Mai	5	

Other Wars

Other wars in which both sides have used air power, and have actually clashed, rather than employing their hardware purely against ground targets, have been rare. However one of the most ridiculous wars of modern times did result in sufficient aerial combat for one pilot to become pre-eminent, although he did not become an ace as such. Difficulties and disagreements between the Central American states of Honduras and El Salvador led to an outbreak of war in 1969, a football match between the two nations proving the catalyst that led to the fighting. Although the match brought to a head the confrontation, rather than causing it, the fighting which followed became known as the Soccer War. Honduras had available five Vought F4U-4 and eight F4U-5 Corsair fighters of 1945 vintage, while El Salvador possessed a number of Goodyear-built FG-1 Corsairs and P-51D Mustangs, plus a few C-47 transports converted to drop bombs. There were several inconclusive engagements until 17 July, when Capt Fernando 'Sotillo' Soto, who had been flying Corsairs since 1960 with the Honduran Air Force, and two other F4U-5 pilots, became engaged with some Salvadorean P-51; Soto shot one down, blowing off the left wing. On a later sortie — his fourth of the day — he and another pilot were attacked by four FG-1s. Taking on two of the opposing Corsairs, Soto shot down both during a hectic dogfight, both pilots baling out. The brief war ended on 19 July, Soto's three victories being the only claims made by either side, and his victims the only losses suffered, as no aircraft fell to ground fire.

During the infamous Bay of Pigs episode in spring 1961, when Cuban expatriates attempted to invade the island from Florida with CIA support, Cuban pilots flying Lockheed T-33 Shooting Star jet trainers claimed 10 intruding aircraft shot down. These included at least four Douglas B-26 Invaders and an AT-11 trainer; one pilot, Capitan Rafael de Pino, claimed two of these, an AT-11 on 11 March and a B-26 on 17 April.

A most unusual situation surrounds the bloody war between Iran and Iraq which began with an Iraqi strike in September 1980. Each side possessed quite large and sophisticated air forces — although in both cases the suppliers had, for various reasons, ceased to advise or service them. At the outbreak Iran had the residue of some 210 F-4D and E Phantoms, 150 Northrop F-5E light fighters and 56 of the latest Grumman F-14 Tomcats. Iraq had well over 300 aircraft, including MiG 21s and 23s, Mirage F-1s, Sukhoi Su 20s, Hunters and a few jet bombers — Tu 22s and Il 28s. Both sides also had helicopters, transports and other types. Although each air force made heavy attacks on the other's air bases, and carried out many ground-attack and bomb-

ing sorties, no aerial combats are known to have taken place. The estimated 150 or so aircraft each side is believed to have lost appear to have fallen to ground fire or missiles.

Tomcats have however, been in action in the Middle East, two aircraft of the US Navy's VF 41 from USS *Nimitz* having shot down two Libyan Su 22 fighter-bombers. The latter attacked when the US fighters intercepted the latest of 36 intrusions over a US Sixth Fleet exercise in the Gulf of Sidra in August 1981; Cdr Henry M Kleeman and Lt Lawrence M Morzuski were named as the successful pilots.

As this book was nearing completion the British moves to secure the liberation of the Falkland Islands, which had been occupied during April 1982 by forces from the Argentine, led to the dispatch of a task force to the South Atlantic. The Falklands saw the most sustained aerial combat by British forces since World War II. Argentine aircraft attempted to attack the British ships and British forces landing to retake the islands. Air combat also took place as Argentina tried to resupply her garrison on the islands. Britain had available for operations two aircraft carriers, *Invincible* and *Hermes*, both small vessels fitted for the carriage of BAC Sea Harrier vertical-takeoff fighters and helicopters.

The normal complement of each carrier is five Sea Harriers, 800 Squadron on *Hermes* and 801 Squadron on *Invincible*. However others from the land-based 899 Squadron brought initial strength of the force up to 20, while RAF Harrier pilots were also aboard to bring the number of pilots for 24-hour operations up to strength. Training was stepped up, and on 8 May, 20 more aircraft, flew out to Ascension Island, being carried from there by ship to join the task force. The force included Sea Harriers of 899 and the newly formed 809 Squadrons, and RAF ground-attack Harrier G.R.3s from 1 Squadron and 233 OCU, hastily converted to carry Sidewinder missiles.

Facing the British was a much more substantial land-based air force, including 20 Dassault Mirage IIIs, 25 Israeli-built Daggers (Mirage copies), 64 A-4P Skyhawks and 75 Argentinian IA-58 Pucara ground-attack aircraft. The Argentinian Navy, which has one aircraft carrier, disposed 12 A-4Q Skyhawks and six newly delivered Dassault Super Etendard fighter-bombers.

The initial British air attacks on Port Stanley airfield on 1 May 1982 brought out the Argentine Air Force, and at 1700 hours Flt Lt Bertie Penfold, an RAF officer flying a Sea Harrier, intercepted two Daggers, shooting down one with a Sidewinder; the second was seen to crash, but apparently no claim was made. In the evening Canberra jet bombers attacked, one being shot

Above: 6 victory ace of the North Vietnamese 3rd Company, Lt Nguyen Duc Soat.
Below: The only USAF ace of the Vietnamese war, Capt Richard 'Steve' Ritchie in his F-4 Phantom after his fifth victory. Note the very substantial red star victory marks!

Left: McDonnell RF-101
reconnaissance-fighter
employed over Vietnam.
Below: Capt Fernando Soto
of the Honduran Air Force,
with his Vought F4U-5
Corsair. The only man to
gain any victories during
the Honduras-El Salvador
war of July 1969, Soto
claimed two FG-1 Corsairs
and a P-51D Mustang.
Right: Col James K Johnson
(10 victories), Commanding
Officer of the 4th Fighter-
Interceptor Wing in Korea,
seen here in April 1953
just after becoming 29th
ace of the war.

down by 801 Squadron, and a second claimed damaged. Thereafter few Argentine aircraft were intercepted until the major landings in San Carlos Water began on 21 May. Now the Argentinians attacked in force, pressing home their attacks with determination and gaining several hits on shipping, although their chances of surviving such attacks soon dropped to less than 50 percent. Some 19 aircraft were claimed shot down on this first day, including nine Mirage/Daggers, five Skyhawks and three Pucaras; eight of these fell to the Sea Harriers. Between 23 and 25 May at least 18 more Dassault jets and A-4s were shot down; on the 24th alone six Mirages and one Skyhawk was claimed by the fighters, plus one badly damaged. In one interception two Sea Harriers 'jumped' four Mirages and shot down three, one pilot hitting two with two Sidewinders. Sea Harriers also shot down two helicopters during this period, a Puma and a Bell 205.

The Puma was shot down with cannon fire by Flt Lt David Morgan, an RAF pilot attached to 899 Squadron on *Hermes*, who on another occasion with his wingman shot down all of four Mirages, Morgan personally accounting for two. Lt Cdr Andrew Ault, commanding officer of 800 Squadron, also engaged four Mirages, shooting down two with missiles and then attacking a third with cannon before this too fell to a missile fired by his wingman. On another occasion two Sea Harrier pilots attacked and shot down three of four Skyhawks, the fourth crashing into the sea as it attempted evasive action. It is believed that Lt Cdr Mike Blissett of 800 Squadron was engaged in this interception and was responsible for two of the victories.

Although the Argentinians, at the limit of their range, generally avoided dogfighting, the Navy pilots were on occasion able to put the Sea Harrier's adjustable thrust controls to good use in enhancing their maneuverability. On one such occasion three missile-armed Mirages attacked the Sea Harriers flown by Lt Cdr Nigel Ward, commanding officer of 801 Squadron, and his wingman, Lt Steve Thomas. The British pilots turned the tables on them, Ward shooting down one while Thomas hit both the others with his Sidewinders, one being seen to crash and the other being classified as damaged. On this same date Lt Cdr Ward also shot down a Pucara ground attack aircraft, while a few days later he brought down a Lockheed C-130 Hercules transport.

During the fighting pilots were frequently making up to four sorties a day, and all those mentioned above flew at least 50 sorties each during the campaign. When the fighting ended 72 Argentinian aircraft had been claimed, 22 of which were credited to the Harriers, including 17 fast jets of the Mirage, Dagger and Skyhawk types. Although most had been brought down with Sidewinders, at least four had fallen to the aircrafts' 30mm cannons. Nine Sea Harriers and Harriers were lost on operations, five of them to ground fire and two in a mid-air collision, but none were shot down in aerial combat. Ward, Ault and Thomas each received the award of a Distinguished Service Cross, as did the RAF's David Morgan, while another went to a second Thomas – Lt Cdr Neil Thomas, commanding officer of 899 Squadron, who also shot down one Skyhawk.

US Navy Phantoms and F-8 Crusaders (left background) prepare for a dawn mission aboard a carrier in the Gulf of Tonkin during the Vietnam War.

BIBLIOGRAPHY

A large number of books have been published either directly about fighter aces, or referring to their activities in a more general way. Some of these are excellent, some mediocre, and some of little use or value. This list is by no means definitive, but is intended as a guide to some of the titles which the reader may find the most useful to gain further knowledge on this subject.

B Robertson (Ed.) and Others
Air Aces of the 1914–18 War 1959

HJ Nowarra and KS Brown
Von Richthofen and the 'Flying Circus' 1958

W Musciano
Eagles of the Black Cross 1965

C Bowyer
Sopwith Camel – King of Combat 1978

ECR Baker
The Fighter Aces of the R.A.F., 1939–45 1962

C Shores and C Williams
Aces High; the Fighter Aces of the British and Commonwealth Air Force in World War II 1966

TJ Constable and RF Toliver
Horrido! 1965
Fighter Aces of the U.S.A 1979

G Gurney
Five Down and Glory 1958

WN Hess
The Allied Aces of World War II 1966
The American Aces of World War II and Korea 1968
Pacific Sweep 1974

EH Sims
The Fighter Pilots 1967
Greatest Fighter Missions 1962
American Aces of World War II 1958
Fighter Tactics and Strategy, 1914–1972

GB Stafford and WN Hess
Aces of the Eighth 1974

GB Stafford
Aces of the Southwest Pacific 1977

R Freeman
The Mighty Eighth

S Birdsall
Flying Buccaneers 1978

B Tillman
Hellcat 1979
Corsair 1979

E Obermaier
Ritterkreuzträger der Luftwaffe, 1939–45, Band I: Jagdflieger 1966

E Obermaier and H Ring
Legion Condor 1980

G Aders
German Night Fighter Force, 1917–1945 1978

C Shores and H Ring
Fighters over the Desert 1969

C Shores, H Ring and WN Hess
Fighters over Tunisia 1975

Anon
Medaglie d'Oro al Valor Militare 1969

K Keskinen, K Stenman, K Niska
Finnish Fighter Aces 1978
Other Tietoteos publications on Finnish and Russian fighters

K Rust
Fifth, Seventh, Eighth, Ninth, Twelfth, Thirteenth, Fourteenth, Fifteenth Air Force Stories. Various dates

Various
Aircam Airwar Series Nos 3, 6, 9, 11, 12, 13, 14, 17, 18, 20 and 24

FFK Mason
Battle over Britain 1969

Y Izawa and others
Japanese language publications on Japanese Army and Navy Aces

RF Futrell
The United States Air Force in Korea, 1950–1953 1961

L Davis
MiG Alley 1978

L Drendel
. . . and Kill MiGs 1974

F Olynyk
USMC Credits for the destruction of enemy aircraft in air-to-air combat, World War 2 1982
USAF Historical Study No 81
USAF Victory Credits Korean War
No 85
USAAF Victory Credits, World War II
No 133
USAS Victory Credits, World War I
USAF Combat Victory Credits, Southeast Asia

In addition to these works there are many biographies and autobiographies concerning fighter aces of many countries, and unit histories of fighter units which give much additional information, as do a number of monograms on specific fighter aircraft various campaign histories, and studies of single important days.

INDEX